THE
APOCALYPTIC
LITERATURE

D1379692

GENERAL EDITORS

Gene M. Tucker, *Old Testament*

Charles B. Cousar, *New Testament*

INTERPRETING
I · B · T
BIBLICAL TEXTS

THE
APOCALYPTIC
LITERATURE

Stephen L. Cook

ABINGDON PRESS
Nashville

THE APOCALYPTIC LITERATURE

Copyright © 2003 by Abingdon Press

This book is printed on recycled, acid-free, elemental-chlorine-free paper.

Library of Congress Cataloging-in-Publication Data

Cook, Stephen L., 1962-
  The apocalyptic literature / Stephen L. Cook.
    p. cm. -- (Interpreting Biblical texts)
Includes bibliographical references and index.
  ISBN 0-687-05196-7 (alk. paper)
  1. Apocalyptic literature. I. Title. II. Series.

  BS646.C659 2003
  220'.046--dc21

                                                                2003007329

Scripture quotations, except for the author's translations, or unless otherwise indicated, are from the *New Revised Standard Version of the Bible,* copyright © 1989, by the Division of Christian Education of the National Council of the Churches of Christ in the United States of America. Used by permission.

The Scripture quotation marked NASB is from the *New American Standard Bible®,* Copyright © The Lockman Foundation 1960, 1962, 1963, 1968, 1971, 1972, 1973, 1975, 1977. Used by permission.

The Scripture quotation marked NLT is from the *Holy Bible, New Living Translation,* copyright © 1996. Used by permission of Tyndale House Publishers, Inc., Wheaton, Illinois 60189. All rights reserved.

Excerpt from *The Complete Dead Sea Scrolls in English* by Geza Vermes (London, The Penguin Press, 1997). Copyright © G Vermes, 1962, 1965, 1968, 1975, 1995, 1997. Reproduced by permission of Penguin Books Ltd.

03 04 05 06 07 08 09 10 11 12 —10 9 8 7 6 5 4 3 2 1

MANUFACTURED IN THE UNITED STATES OF AMERICA

CONTENTS

FOREWORD

Biblical texts create worlds of meaning, and invite readers to enter them. When readers enter such textual worlds, which are often strange and complex, they are confronted with theological claims. With this in mind, the purpose of this series is to help serious readers in their experience of reading and interpreting, to provide guides for their journeys into textual worlds. The controlling perspective is expressed in the operative word of the title—*interpreting*. The primary focus of the series is not so much on the world *behind* the texts or out of which the texts have arisen (though these worlds are not irrelevant) as on the world *created by* the texts in their engagement with readers.

Each volume addresses two questions. First, what are the critical issues of interpretation that have emerged in the recent history of scholarship and to which serious readers of the texts need to be sensitive? Some of the concerns of scholars are interesting and significant but, frankly, peripheral to the interpretative task. Others are more central. How they are addressed influences decisions readers make in the process of interpretation. Thus the authors call attention to these basic issues and indicate their significance for interpretation.

Second, in struggling with particular passages or sections of material, how can readers be kept aware of the larger world created by the text as a whole? How can they both see the forest and examine the individual trees? How can students encountering the story of David and Bathsheba in 2 Samuel 11 read it in light of its context in the larger story, the Deuteronomistic History that includes the books of Deuteronomy through 2 Kings? How can readers of Galatians fit what they learn into the theological coherence and polarities of the larger perspective drawn from all the letters of Paul? Thus each volume provides an overview of the literature as a whole.

The aim of the series is clearly pedagogical. The authors offer their own understanding of the issues and texts, but are more concerned about guiding the reader than engaging in debates with other scholars. The series is meant to serve as a resource, alongside other resources such as commentaries and specialized studies, to aid students in the exciting and often risky venture of interpreting biblical texts.

Gene M. Tucker
General Editor, *Old Testament*

Charles B. Cousar
General Editor, *New Testament*

PREFACE

This volume aims to introduce readers to the apocalyptic literature of the Bible, both Old (First) Testament and New (Second) Testament. The goal immediately raises questions and problems. Interpreters vary wildly in defining apocalypticism, finding it hard to agree on which biblical texts to call "apocalyptic." I have been intentionally broad and inclusive in this survey, hoping to introduce readers to the complete "family" of biblical apocalyptic texts. In the case of each text treated, readers should make their own judgments about the intensity of "family resemblance" to full-blown apocalypticism, such as that found in Daniel and Revelation.

It will seem brash for a single scholar to treat both testaments in an age of specialization, but there are payoffs beyond producing a volume of broad appeal. Insights into apocalypticism in one of the Bible's two testaments frequently illuminate texts in the other. In addition, because understanding apocalyptic writings so frequently demands hearing their echoes and allusions to other Scriptures, there is a distinct advantage to tracing the interrelationships of apocalyptic texts throughout the Bible. Foregrounding Israelite texts and their theology, treating them in parallel with New Testament texts, also helps counter an annoying tendency of some New Testament scholars: the tendency to disparage Old Testament apocalypticism as somehow sub-Christian.

The apocalyptic literature is complex and varied, so almost all the standard critical methodologies prove illuminating at one point or another. I have chosen in this book to speak less of scientific tools for interpretation than of general interpretive stances. My conviction is that gaining familiarity with some broad hermeneutical insights and caveats will assist the reader in letting the apocalyptic texts speak in as plain, authentic, and theologically relevant a manner as possible. The alien and offensive traits of apocalyptic texts make them an exciting and exacting testing ground for hermeneutics. They are perhaps unique among the Scriptures in yielding their intelligibility only to a disciplined, self-reflective theological interpretation.

Part 1 (chapters 1–4) introduces biblical apocalypticism and outlines standard pitfalls and extremes to avoid in reading the literature. It provides a general framework and specific guidelines (a canonical approach) for unveiling the scriptural sense of apocalyptic texts. It also offers brief forays into the roots of the apocalyptic imagination and the social worlds behind the apocalyptic texts. The focus of the series is not the world behind the Bible, but the forays help correct a widespread misconception that apocalypticism is a coping mechanism for dealing with persecutions or deprivations.

Part 2 (chapters 5–9) tours the specific apocalyptic texts of the Bible in rough chronological order. The guided tours help readers hear the claims of each text and make sense out of them. Each pays particular attention to matters of genre and worldview, to scriptural echoes and allusions, and to the quality of theological witness that compelled successive generations of readers to preserve each text in canonical form. Chapter 7 is different, in that it focuses on the search for the historical Jesus rather than on a particular canonical writing. In each of its chapters, part 2 will be most helpful in conjunction with a careful reading of the portions of the Bible being examined. Encouraging close, informed interaction with the biblical literature is a key goal of this series.

Numerous people have provided inspiration and help as I have wrestled with apocalyptic literature over time. Dr. John A. Gettier first introduced me to the scholarly study of apocalypticism in an undergraduate seminar at Trinity College in Connecticut. His superb, rigorous teaching in that and numerous other courses effectively launched my scholarly career, and I am very grateful. I also gratefully acknowledge my training at Yale University under Robert R. Wilson and Brevard S. Childs, whose approaches and theories are evident on almost every page of this book.

My colleagues at Virginia Theological Seminary have my heartfelt gratitude for supporting my writing with warm collegiality. I especially thank my New Testament colleague John Yieh for welcoming me into his seminar on the book of Revelation in the autumn of 2001. The staff at the Bishop Payne Library met all my bibliographic needs with their legendary grace and efficiency.

Gene M. Tucker has been a particularly exceptional editor to work with on this project. I am indebted to him for his sharp critical eye, hearty support, and wonderful humor at every stage of my work. In all my teaching and writing, my deepest appreciation goes to my wife, Catherine Elizabeth Cook, M.Div., M.A., for her unfailing inspiration and encouragement.

LIST OF ABBREVIATIONS

AB	Anchor Bible
ABD	*Anchor Bible Dictionary.* Edited by D. N. Freedman. 6 vols. New York, 1992.
BAR	*Biblical Archaeology Review*
CBQ	*Catholic Biblical Quaterly*
CD	*Damascus Document*
FOTL	Forms of the Old Testament Literature
HBT	*Horizons in Biblical Theology*
HDR	Harvard Dissertations in Religion
ICC	International Critical Commentary
JSOTSup	Journal for the Study of the Old Testament: Supplement Series
JSP	*Journal for the Study of the Pseudepigrapha*
JSPSup	Journal for the Study of the Pseudepigrapha: Supplement Series
J.W.	*Jewish War* by Josephus
NICNT	New International Commentary on the New Testament
NIGTC	New International Greek Testament Commentary

LIST OF ABBREVIATIONS

OTL	Old Testament Library
OtSt	*Oudtestamentische Studiën*
StABH	Studies in American Biblical Hermeneutics
VT	*Vetus Testamentum*
WBC	Word Biblical Commentary
WMANT	Wissenschaftliche Monographien zum Alten und Neuen Testament
ZAW	*Zeitschrift für die alttestamentliche Wissenschaft*

PART ONE

ISSUES IN INTERPRETING APOCALYPTIC TEXTS

CHAPTER 1

ENCOUNTERING APOCALYPTIC WORLDS

Readers encounter wonderfully diverse worlds to explore in most parts of the Bible, but the apocalyptic parts—Revelation, for example, or Daniel—offer one that is uncommonly expansive and venturesome. Apocalyptic horizons dwarf other worlds within the Bible, encompassing the very destiny of the cosmos. Beyond its vastness, the apocalyptic world is illumining. Within its horizons, ethical lines are fully exposed. There is no difficulty identifying the allies of God or the enemies.

Entering an apocalyptic world within the Bible, the reader cannot remain neutral for long. Battle lines are drawn between the forces of good and evil. The stakes are profound, and they force a quick choosing of sides.

One's daily routines and encounters take on new meaning, framed against a supernatural battle. It is hard not to become engaged with present, earthly life when a purposeful, cosmic backdrop is revealed to lie behind it. Against such a backdrop, focused by the Bible's apocalyptic literature, individual existence brims with urgency and vibrancy.

Fantastic wonders and extreme horrors fill the apocalyptic worlds of the Bible. These worlds provoke readers' imaginations with highly metaphorical and mythological language. This colorful and elastic language is intrinsically flexible, encompassing diverse human situations and challenges and revealing heaven's cosmic perspective on them all.

The vista is breathtaking and enlivening but subject to much abuse. Too often, in fact, people read apocalyptic literature with misguided motives and interests. Eager for clairvoyant speculations or sensational entertainment, they miss the texts' real import. Apocalyptic texts aim much more to clarify the patterns and conflicts at stake in present experience than to speculate about the details of the future.

Wakefulness about God's interests and goals and their impact on present experience is the core concern of apocalyptic texts. A good example of how this works occurs in an apocalyptic hymn among the Dead Sea Scrolls, interpreted by John J. Collins, a major scholar of apocalyptic literature. Collins's discussion of the hymn illustrates the relevance of an apocalyptic world for the immediate situation of the document's author. Collins writes:

> The space in which the author of this hymn moves is the cosmic space of Sheol and the eternal height. The time in which he moves is the eschatological period of wrath against [Satan]. The pattern of future tumult and deliverance is already manifest in his own experience.[1]

The Bible's apocalyptic worlds can put off modern readers. The light of apocalyptic illumination is piercing, cutting through the many gray areas familiar from our daily experience. The tone of crisis and catastrophe of apocalypticism is jarring. It pulls the rug of normalcy out from under our feet.

Apocalyptic worlds even call into question common religious beliefs. The apocalyptic reign of God has nothing to do with many spiritual assumptions and aspirations typical of religious believers in the Western world. For example, it does not set its future hopes on an ethereal realm of heaven, populated by souls enjoying a beatific afterlife. Rather, its fervent hope centers firmly on a tangible, physical renewal of the cosmos and natural environment and of humanity and human community.

A realized, undisputed reign of God would necessarily contradict humanity's will to power, disrupting and overthrowing the powers and structures presently forging human history. It would have cataclysmic implications for earth's present systems of politics, economics, and society. In addition, since sovereignty over the whole cosmos—heaven and earth—is God's prerogative, an advent of God's ultimate reign would be cosmic in scope. Its impact would change nature, space, and time alongside human society.

Despite their strange and disconcerting traits, the Bible's apocalyptic worlds continually captivate large numbers of readers. These worlds must appeal to real, deep human needs.

As the twenty-first century begins, apocalyptic fears, hopes, and dreams are everywhere. Ongoing research into the apocalyptic imagination of the Dead Sea Scrolls enthralls scholars of religion and the educated public alike. The question of whether Jesus of Nazareth was an apocalyptic prophet currently stimulates even greater interest and debate. In popular culture, the *Left Behind* series of novels about the end of the world has now sold more than fifty million copies in twenty-one different languages. Three of the novels in the series have reached number one on the New York Times best-seller list.

Many people experienced the terrorist destruction of New York City's twin towers on September 11, 2001, as an apocalyptic specter. The baseline normalcy of things we took for granted suddenly appeared vulnerable and transitory in the wake of the disaster. What is more, our decent and acceptable world revealed a gory potential for demonic tragedy in a way hard to contest. United States culture as a whole was jarred—at least for a few months—with an existential shock usually confined to individual experience, when a person loses a parent or spouse to death and comes face-to-face with the unacceptable, the catastrophic.

The apocalyptic texts of the Bible come to terms with the very revelations about the world unveiled by the tragedy of September 11. They grapple with the unmistakable truth that components of "normal" life are fundamentally inhuman, completely unacceptable. Biblical apocalyptic worlds take for granted that space/time reality, as we know it, contains tangible signs of inherent catastrophe. They claim God has a plan of cosmic redemption to address that problem.

Despite modern suspicions and reluctance about the Bible's apocalyptic imagination, the apocalyptic dream may well be the only one worth dreaming. If our post–September 11 realism is accurate, the world suffers irredeemable wrong, and salvation is only possible with God's climactic intervention. The New Testament scholar Dale C. Allison elegantly expresses the point:

> If our wounds never heal, if the outrageous spectacle of a history filled with cataclysmic sadness is never undone, if there is nothing more for those who were slaughtered in the death camps or for six-year olds devoured by cancer, then let us eat and drink, for tomorrow we die. If in the end there is no good God to calm this sea of troubles, to raise the dead, and to give good news to the poor, then this is indeed a tale told by an idiot, signifying nothing.[2]

WHAT IS APOCALYPTICISM?

The term *apocalyptic,* given to the biblical worlds before us, comes from the Greek word *apokalyptein,* which means, "uncover, reveal." The apocalyptic worlds of the Bible peer beyond mundane political and social realities, revealing a new world coming. Profoundly realistic about humanity's limitations and shortcomings, the literature recognizes that this better world, while a fundamental human longing, will never come as a human achievement. It comes only with the advent of God's sovereign rule on earth.

"Apocalyptic," as a label, fits several different phenomena. It applies to a body of literature (a genre), to a particular type of religious imagination (a worldview), and to a specific sort of group within society (a social entity). Apocalyptic, or "millennial" groups, share an apocalyptic imagination, an apocalyptic view of the world around them. Such groups may or may not produce writings. If they do, these writings, which reflect the group's imagination, are termed apocalyptic literature.

Scholars nowadays are reluctant to speak of the essence of apocalyptic literature or to make a list of necessary characteristics. They conceive of the literature, rather, as a body of texts sharing a family resemblance. A complex set of common features and differences interconnect family members, but they are not necessary, fixed features or any ultimate essence.

One can begin exploring apocalyptic literature by sampling a particular text. The apocalypses of the Bible are examined closely below, so we can begin with an extrabiblical document, one from the Dead Sea Scroll community at Qumran.

The Qumran community was a priestly and apocalyptic ("millennial") sect within early Judaism. It is one of the best-known early Jewish apocalyptic groups. Its sectarian founders abandoned privileged posts at the Jerusalem temple to move to the Judean desert and prepare for the world's end. The Qumran scrolls date relatively late, to Greco-Roman times, so beginning with one of them has the benefit of providing a look at a well-developed example of apocalyptic literature, with full-blown apocalyptic features.

Let us briefly survey two columns of text from the *Community Rule* scroll (1QS) of the Dead Sea sect, columns III.13–IV.26. The *Community Rule* is likely a charter, a regulatory document for those choosing to live as permanent members of the Qumran community. Its original manuscript dates to around the end of the second century B.C.E. This makes it one of the community's older documents.

Our text lays amid other sections of the scroll that state the community's aims, admission procedures, organization, and rules for common life. It forms a compact statement of the community's beliefs and teaching, with particular emphasis on the nature of human existence and the spirits of truth and falsehood that govern it.[3]

In the current era, according to the text, two spiritual forces coexist in extreme tension—"the spirits of truth and of injustice" (III.18-19). The technical term for such a stark, either/or (binary) opposition of spirits is "moral dualism." It is widespread in apocalyptic literature.

Each spirit fiercely opposes the other with an "eternal enmity," which God has put "between their (two) classes" (IV.16-17). God established the forces "in equal parts until the last time," but, for the time being, evil has the upper hand. All human beings must choose sides in the ongoing struggle, which will continue until God's climactic "visitation" of earth at the end of days. Each human being belongs in one of the two camps.

The text makes clear that real people are not ideal types, purely negative or positive. In the current era, at least, people behave in both good and evil ways. This results from the dual influence on all people of both spirits of truth and injustice (cf. III.21). One of the two spirits predominates in each individual, however, so each person belongs with either the children of light or the children of darkness.

The moral dualism of the text is not absolute. Having no eternal, independent existence, the power of evil is not really on a par with God. In strong monotheistic statements, the text declares God the creator of both spirits of light and of darkness. God "created the spirits of light and of darkness, and upon them founded every deed" (III.25). Since God created the possibility of evil, God can, and will, exterminate all dark powers at the end of days.

According to the *Community Rule,* angels and other supernatural figures play key roles in the ongoing struggle of the forces of good and evil. These figures function primarily as mediators between heaven and earth. Their existence and role in apocalyptic texts highlights another type of dualism characteristic of this literature: a metaphysical dualism.

Apocalyptic literature frequently imagines heaven and earth as separate realms of existence, which parallel and mirror each other. Transcendent molds, or archetypes, in heaven often prefigure and orchestrate the course of history on earth. Supernatural entities in heaven frequently invade earth to achieve divine goals.

In our text, a figure called the "Prince of Lights" wields control over righteous human beings as they walk in the ways of light (III.20). At some points in other Dead Sea Scrolls, the Prince of Lights appears to be the archangel Michael. Michael is a highly significant individual angel in apocalyptic texts such as Dan 12:1; *1 Enoch* 9:1; and Rev 12:7. The *Community Rule* terms good angels in general "the sons of heaven" (IV.22).

An "angel of darkness," by contrast, has complete control of all humans aligned with injustice on earth. The text states: "Complete control over the sons of injustice lies in the hand of the angel of darkness, and they walk in the ways of darkness. It is through the angel of darkness that all the sons of righteousness go astray, and all their sins, their iniquities, their guilt, and their deeds of transgression are under his control" (III.20-22). Elsewhere in the Dead Sea Scrolls, this commander of the spiritual forces of wickedness is called "Belial" ("uselessness," "wickedness"; *Damascus Document* [CD] IV.12), "the angel of enmity" (CD XVI.5, 1QM XIII.11), and "the prince of the kingdom of wickedness" (1QM XVII.5b-6a).

Humans must endure the struggle of light and darkness for the present, but this will not always be the case. God has a fixed plan to create a world where truth will prevail. Apocalyptic texts frequently contain this further type of dualism between the present age of struggle and darkness and an age to come, forever purged of darkness and evil.

The *Community Rule* uses glowing language to describe the coming new era, when God will reign on earth. In the new era, the chosen that presently walk in truth will experience an Eden-like paradise—"all the glory of Adam" (IV.23). There will be "healing, abundant peace with long life, fruitfulness with every everlasting blessing, eternal joy with life forever, and a crown of glory with a garment of honor in eternal light" (IV.6-8).

Apocalyptic texts generally expect an imminent divine intervention in history to permanently expunge evil. The expectation is a type of "radical eschatology." (*Eschatology* refers to beliefs about "last things," such as the last days of history.) In our text, from beyond the veil separating earth from heaven God terminates evil and renews the world by breaking into history's last days. The text refers to this coming intervention as God's "visitation." God has already decided on an appointed time for the visitation, a "time decreed for judgment" (IV.20). The judgment that occurs at God's climactic visit involves both punishment and reward, the latter of which goes to the children of light (III.14-15).

When the visitation comes, God's intervention destroys evil, forever putting "an end to the existence of injustice" (IV.18). At that time, God will "destroy it forever" (IV.19). This, in turn, allows truth to appear in the world forever, a benefit of the undisputed reign of God. Righteous human beings get to experience eternal bliss on earth from that point forward.

God appears in complete control of history. From before creation, God worked out "everything that is and will be," specifically fixing "all their plans" (III.15). In other words, God preplanned and predetermined the course of all events on earth. This notion of predetermination of earth's events, or at least of the end of human history, is a key feature in many apocalyptic texts.

God's sovereign control and divine plan for the periods of

history are a mystery to humans, however. Any insight into the plan is necessarily secret, "deviant" wisdom. As mentioned above, apocalyptic knowledge usually seems suspicious and jarring to most readers. It calls into question the everyday world they take for granted.

Our text describes the orchestration and timing of God's end-time intervention as a matter of God's "mysterious insight and glorious wisdom" (IV.18). The "mysteries of God" are the private knowledge of the Qumran covenanters, to whom God has revealed God's secrets.

Some apocalyptic groups are open and evangelistic about apocalyptic beliefs, but the Qumran community exercised extreme secrecy. In fact, the rules of the community forbade any general, open disclosure of God's apocalyptic plans. Among the ways and behaviors of the "sons of truth," our text specifically speaks about circumspection and about "concealment of the truth of the mysteries of knowledge" (IV.6).

The Jewish historian Josephus (writing around 79 C.E.) reports that initiation into Essene communities, like that of Qumran, involved a binding oath never to reveal the group's secrets even if tortured to death (*J.W.* 2.141). All the covenanters swore never to tell strangers about their group plans, above all about their preparations for an end-time war between the sons of light and the sons of darkness. The Essenes' end-time war involved the real defeat of political adversaries. Such expectations for the downfall of contemporary world powers, if made public, would surely have provoked the hostility of the authorities.

BIBLICAL APOCALYPTIC LITERATURE

A group of scholars working under the leadership of John Collins formulated a widely accepted definition of the genre "apocalypse" in the late 1970s. Collins reports the conclusions of the group as follows: "An apocalypse is defined as: 'a genre of revelatory literature with a narrative framework, in which a revelation is mediated by an otherworldly being to a human recipient, disclosing a transcendent reality which is both temporal, insofar as it envisages eschatological salvation, and spatial insofar as it involves another, supernatural world.' "[4]

Several key characteristics stand out in this definition.

Apocalyptic visions are supernatural revelations, not public knowledge or observations of the senses. They differ in what they reveal, but all disclose a transcendent realm—a supernatural, otherworldly reality. This transcendent reality is separate from the created world in spatial terms; it parallels and mirrors earthly, physical reality. It is also separate temporally; history must wait for transcendent reality to manifest itself on earth in a decisive manner.

About fifteen Jewish apocalypses were written between 250 B.C.E. and 150 C.E. They include 4 Ezra—a deuterocanonical (i.e., apocryphal) work—as well as several works among the Pseudepigrapha, such as *1 Enoch* and *2 Baruch*. Christian apocalypses also appeared in this period, and afterwards. The *Apocalypse of Peter* (ca. 135 C.E.) and the *Apocalypse of Paul* (ca. 388 C.E.) are examples. Additional examples of apocalypses are found within Greco-Roman and Persian literature outside of the Judeo-Christian tradition.

Only two biblical works qualify as "apocalypses" in the strict sense: Dan 7–12 in the Hebrew Bible and the book of Revelation in the New Testament. The remainder of the ancient texts fitting the genre "apocalypse," narrowly defined, fall outside of canonical Scripture. A survey of these extracanonical works, though tempting, falls outside the scope of the present series—Interpreting Biblical Texts—and is not included in this volume.[5]

The visions of Dan 7–12 expect a steady increase of worldwide evil, followed by an end-time triumph of God over its forces. God is about to intervene in history, according to Daniel's visions, destroying the evil embedded within the world's empires. When that happens, God will overthrow all imperial systems of control, establish an everlasting dominion on earth, and reward those who have remained faithful.

Like Dan 7–12, the New Testament book of Revelation reveals heavenly mysteries that lie behind earth's current troubles and ambiguities. John of Patmos, its author, witnesses activities and plans of heaven that reveal a transcendent realm on the verge of invading earth. The invasion, according to John, will defeat all forces—such as the "beast" and the "great whore"—that lie about life and seduce humans away from God. Just as the downfall of the "beast" is sure, so is the cosmic victory of Christ, the slain but conquering "lamb."

Only a circumscribed set of specific Hellenistic books, including Dan 7–12 and Revelation, can be termed "apocalypses." A far greater number of texts, from a much wider period, however, share a similar worldview, a similar apocalyptic imagination.

The *Community Rule* scroll from Qumran, surveyed in the first part of this chapter, is a case in point. Strictly speaking, the Qumran community did not produce any "apocalypses." Qumran's sectarian literature generally lacks standard literary features of the genre. Several of the Dead Sea Scrolls, such as the *Community Rule*, however, reveal an imagination with obvious apocalyptic family resemblances. We may call these scrolls "apocalyptic literature," avoiding the narrow term "apocalypse."

Texts from the centuries preceding Qumran's scrolls and the contemporaneous Hellenistic apocalypses exhibit a related apocalyptic imagination, at least in incipient form. Many scholars see evidence of an apocalyptic imagination within Israel as early as prophetic texts from the exilic and postexilic periods (the sixth and fifth centuries B.C.E.). Among this literature, the most significant works are selected texts within Ezekiel, the bulk of Zechariah and Joel, selected sections of Isaiah, and the book of Malachi.

Other parts of the Hebrew Bible also display an early apocalyptic imagination, according to some scholars. Prominent among them are several texts within the first half of the book of Daniel. Daniel 2, for example, envisions the reign of God crashing into human history, crushing all earthly empires and filling the whole earth. I demonstrated in a 1992 article that some postexilic editing and new composition in the book of Psalms has an early apocalyptic character.[6]

The presence of at least an incipient apocalyptic imagination within late Israelite prophetic, wisdom, and psalm texts is hard to deny. These texts have an interest in the transcendent realm and in heavenly doings that stands out against the rest of the Hebrew Bible. They pin their hopes for salvation farther than usual beyond history and historical events. They speak of mythological entities in a radically new way, not in the language of poetic hyperbole but of literal, concrete reality.

The armies of Gog, for example, have real mythological properties in Ezek 38–39. They embody cosmic chaos and collective evil. This is a qualitative change from earlier prophetic visions, where God's enemies are historical, geopolitical realities.

Evidence from the social sciences corroborates the argument that exilic and postexilic texts such as Ezek 38–39 express a new, distinct imagination within biblical tradition. Social scientists have observed beliefs kindred to these texts among millennial groups across many cultures. Millennial groups have a distinct character, differing from other guilds, schools, and circles in society. Their members think differently from everyday prophets, sages, liturgists, and others.

The cross-cultural parallels between the Bible's postexilic apocalyptic texts and the beliefs of various millennial groups are wide-ranging. Just as Ezek 38–39 expected the supernatural defeat of Gog, the millennial Native American group known as the Smohalla cult expected the imminent annihilation of all European Americans. Just as Zechariah and his supporters looked forward to a supernatural messiah, the millennial Manseren cult in Melanesia expectantly awaited a supernatural figure known as Manseren Mangundi, who had gained great power by capturing the morning star. The egalitarian outpouring of God's spirit on all genders and classes in Joel 2:28-29 resonates strikingly with the ideals of the Taiping Rebellion, which proclaimed the equality of all men and the liberation of all women.

The burgeoning apocalypticism of the postexilic, Persian-era literature clearly represented a new worldview in Israel, but it did not emerge full-blown. The early apocalyptic imagination of this era has moved considerably beyond the historically oriented perspective of earlier Israelite prophecy and wisdom. However, it falls short of the well-developed transcendent view of salvation found in the later Jewish and Christian apocalypses of 250 B.C.E. to 250 C.E.

The apocalyptic traits of the Persian-era texts regularly show signs that they are still developing. In the vision of earth re-created as a paradise in Isa 65, people enjoy incredible longevity but not personal immortality (as in 5 Ezra). Various angels populate Zechariah's "night visions," but they do not yet have specific names and developed functions as they do in *1 Enoch*. A figure termed "the satan" appears in Zech 3, but he appears less demonic than the "Satan" of Rev 12:9, "that ancient serpent, who is called the Devil and Satan, the deceiver of the whole world."

The apocalyptic literature of the biblical world becomes increasingly radical and complex as it enters the Hellenistic era.

The metaphors and mythological motifs of the literature take on an increasingly physical reality. Understandings and speculations become detailed and systematic. Some Hellenistic apocalypses delve thoroughly into the limits of the earth and the demographics of heaven. It is at this point that scholars speak of full-blown apocalypticism.

Widespread features of the Greco-Roman world contributed to apocalypticism's development at this time. Hellenism supplied motifs such as the otherworldly journey. It encouraged speculative reflection on cosmic reality, both terrestrial and celestial.

Just as the Hebrew Bible contains a variety of apocalyptic texts beyond the book of Daniel, the New Testament contains various apocalyptic worlds beyond its primary "apocalypse," the book of Revelation.

Scholars are currently enmeshed in debate over the Jesus of history and his message, with Jesus' apocalypticism a central point of contention. Many scholars at least agree, however, that key actions of Jesus point symbolically toward some type of coming new era of renewal for Israel. Other scholars go farther, seeing several of Jesus' key symbolic actions and sayings as revealing an ardent apocalyptic perspective.

The raging debate about Jesus shows no sign of resolution, but more agreement is in place about apocalypticism elsewhere in Christianity's development. A general scholarly consensus accepts that dramatic apocalyptic expectations propelled Jesus' immediate predecessor, John the Baptizer. An apocalyptic imagination was also a driving force behind the work of Paul of Tarsus, Jesus' most influential successor.

Many of the letters of Paul preserved in the Bible express strong apocalyptic expectations. Whole sections within his Thessalonian and Corinthian correspondence can rightly be termed apocalyptic literature.

At least in his early letters, Paul expects the return to earth of the risen Jesus, the Parousia, in his lifetime. Jesus' return ushers in the resurrection of the dead, the "redemption of our bodies," and God's worldwide judgment. While waiting for Jesus' second coming, Paul advises his readers to take their present sufferings as eschatological woes that must precede the reign of God.

The Gospel writers, who organized and expanded the tradition of Jesus, expressed apocalyptic fervor at several points. Chief among these is the passage known as the "little apocalypse," found in Mark 13 and its parallels in Matt 24 and Luke 21. The "little apocalypse" of the Gospels gathers into one discourse sayings in the Jesus tradition about the birth pangs of the end times, Daniel's end-time signal of an "abomination of desolation," the second coming of Jesus, and a call to be wakeful about the advent of the reign of God on earth.

THE ROOTS OF APOCALYPTIC IMAGINATION

Since the apocalyptic worlds of the Bible are uncommonly expansive and extreme, full of fantastic symbols and deviant understandings, they have long provoked questions. What are the roots of the Bible's apocalyptic imagination? How did these images and ideas find a place within biblical tradition?

Interpreters have long viewed apocalyptic worlds as out of place within Scripture. Christian scholars, such as Gerhard von Rad, have struggled to fit the apocalyptic imagination into their models of Old Testament theology. Students of Judaica, such as G. F. Moore, have noted rabbinic Judaism's suspicions of apocalypticism's radical eschatology. Jesus researchers, such as Marcus Borg, have found an apocalyptic orientation incompatible with Jesus' role as wisdom teacher and social critic.

Unable to imagine apocalypticism as native to Israel's religious and biblical heritage, scholars frequently relegate it to the margins of biblical tradition. Commonly, they judge its inclusion in the Bible as an unfortunate mistake. A widespread scholarly view assigns apocalyptic thinking to fringe groups, alienated to the periphery of society. An equally popular (though older) view holds apocalypticism to be a foreign import, native to Persia, not Israel.

Let us first consider the common notion that apocalypticism is a religion of the oppressed or powerless. The view is commonplace, appearing as recently as 2000, in Sidnie White Crawford's entry on "Apocalyptic" in *Eerdmans Dictionary of the Bible*. Puzzling about "the reasons for the rise of this type of literature," she concludes, "There seems to be a strong connection with some crisis, bringing about a sense of social, political, or religious powerlessness."[7] Paul Hanson's entry in the *Anchor Bible Dictionary* makes the same claim. He argues that apocalypses "all reflect a situation of crisis and aim at offering assurance of salvation to those alienated from the power structures of this world and suffering for their religious convictions."[8]

It is easy to envision the apocalyptic imagination as a cry of despair in response to a crisis—a desperate means to deal with an overwhelming hopelessness. Such a view is reductionist, however. It reduces the apocalyptic texts of the Bible to a sort of opiate, a psychological compensation for persecution or other suffering. Oppressed and alienated people might cling to apocalyptic thoughts as a way of enduring the worst of times, but religion and religious worldviews are surely more than mere coping mechanisms of the psyche.

Cross-cultural study of millennial groups shows their members are not necessarily deprived or from the periphery of society. The Brethren of the Free Spirit of thirteenth-century Europe, who came largely from well-established families, form a case in point. The group appealed especially to the idle elite of urban society. The rise of Joachimism in Europe is a further example. The Franciscan Spirituals at the center of the movement came from the more privileged strata of society. Or again, the Irvingite "Catholic Apostolic Church," which formed in nineteenth-century Britain, had leaders belonging to the wealthiest social classes.

A view of apocalyptic texts as desperation literature robs them of their edge, at least for many middle-class and wealthy Western readers. Perhaps most readers of the present volume are ensconced, comfortably and securely, in a suburban lifestyle. With such a lifestyle, in the absence of real hardship, it is easy to react to a "literature of desperation" with self-congratulation. A literature of desperation may provoke our pity at best and more likely our smugness and condescension.

A reaction of pity may say rather little about the circumstances of this literature's writers, however, and more about our own inability to imagine a transcendent dimension to reality that relativizes much we take for granted. If readers allow themselves to take the apocalyptic visions of Scripture seriously, they surely inspire not pity of their authors but a re-visioning of existence.

Eugene Peterson eloquently makes these points in his theological and pastoral study of the Revelation of John. Peterson cautions us against feeling sorry for the first-century Christian readers of the book of Revelation. The stance too easily deflects Revelation's ability to help readers re-vision their lives.

> Nothing could be farther from the truth than to imagine the Christians in those seven Asian congregations as huddling wretches, holding on to the faith by their fingernails, with St. John, their pastor, reaching frantically for a desperate means (apocalypse!) to secure their endurance through the worst of times. . . . The people who gathered each Lord's Day to sing their Lord's praises and receive his life were the most robust in the Roman empire. They were immersed in splendors. They brimmed with life.[9]

A second way scholars marginalize apocalypticism, making it seem peripheral to the Bible, is taking it as a foreign transplant. Norman Cohn pursues this approach in his 1993 volume, *Cosmos, Chaos and the World to Come: The Ancient Roots of Apocalyptic Faith.* Cohn views such apocalyptic notions as supernatural evil, resurrection, and the transcendent messiah as "innovations" within biblical tradition, "clearly of foreign origin."[10] The foreign point of origin is most likely Persia.

Persian Zoroastrian religion involved significant apocalyptic beliefs, including belief in supernatural evil (Angra Mainyu), an imminent supernatural victory of good (by the supreme god, Ahura Mazda), and the world transformed into a perfect, blissful environment. Many scholars argue that these Persian, Zoroastrian beliefs, especially moral dualism, heavily influenced the development of Israelite and early Jewish apocalyptic texts.

Cohn's approach reminds us that Jewish apocalyptic writings did not emerge in a vacuum. Undeniably, these writings, along with most biblical texts, were influenced by foreign cultural traditions. Highlighting such influences is an aid to interpretation, illuminating images and backgrounds, unless scholars mistakenly imply that *foreign* and *alien* mean "suspect" and "discountable."

A value judgment equating *foreign* and *suspect* confuses meaning with origins, ignoring how biblical texts often critically and skillfully co-opt source material. The Psalms and Isaiah, for example, deftly co-opt pre-Israelite motifs and ideals of kingship, subsuming them under a stream of theology centered on Zion and David. Although the ideology of kingship is a foreign transplant in these writings, it would be hard to argue that it is peripheral to biblical theology.

Zoroastrianism doubtless did influence the Jewish apocalyptic literature of the Hellenistic period, produced in Palestine after 250 B.C.E. Far from deriving straight from Persia, however, the apocalyptic imagination has primary roots in Israelite religion of postexilic times. In the end, value judgments about the influence of foreign sources on biblical apocalypticism are largely devoid of practical significance.

Late biblical texts such as Ezek 38–39, Zechariah, and Ps 108 provide ample evidence. These postexilic writings stem from a period before Persian influence (aided by Hellenism's mediation) takes hold in Jewish apocalyptic writings. As we have seen, even at this early date a burgeoning apocalyptic imagination is apparent.

Scholars sometimes call writings such as Ezek 38–39 and Zechariah "protoapocalyptic" texts, because they anticipate the later Hellenistic apocalypses. They see history approaching a crisis, universal divine judgment on its way, and the imminent advent of Eden conditions on earth. Indeed, they contain the seeds of all of the supposedly foreign ideas that Cohn cites. For the notions of supernatural evil, resurrection, and the transcendent messiah, see, respectively, Zech 3:1-2; 5:5-11; Isa 26:19; and Zech 12:8; 13:7.

The Hellenistic apocalypses link up with more of the biblical tradition than just late prophetic texts. Upon close inspection, apocalypses such as the book of Revelation show striking continuities with a broad range of earlier biblical images, symbols, and themes. In the 404 verses of Revelation, scholars have counted 518 references to earlier scriptural texts. The biblical tradition in general informs Revelation's apocalyptic imagination.

Revelation depicts an ultimate ingathering of biblical people and biblical hopes. The people of Israel and the people of Jesus come together, represented by twenty-four elders on twenty-four thrones—the twelve tribes of Israel and the twelve apostles of Jesus (Rev 4:4). The stories, aspirations, and longings of this totality of God's people and their long history now gather and organize around God's throne. This picture, in itself, makes it hard to go along with the recurring scholarly argument that apocalypticism is discontinuous with the rest of the Bible, a foreign way of speaking about the work of God and God's people.

Protoapocalyptic texts much earlier than Revelation also construct the core of their apocalyptic imagination out of the general biblical tradition. The book of Joel, for example, uses exact phrases from elsewhere in the Bible in a half dozen places. The total number of references to other scriptural passages in the short book's three chapters may be over twenty.

Zechariah and the extrabiblical *1 Enoch* 1–36 (also called the *Book of Watchers*) bristle with references and allusions to earlier Scripture as well. This includes verbal citations, iconography, and visual symbols. In his recent study of these works, Eibert J. C. Tigchelaar concludes that these texts "expounded, commented, and expanded on older traditions. In Zechariah's sermons these older traditions are attributed to . . . 'the prophets of old.' "[11]

Consequently, a responsible approach to unearthing apocalypticism's roots must grant a central role to standard biblical images, values, and aspirations. Traditional images and symbols appear to be the basic building blocks of the apocalyptic imagination. It takes them up and rearranges them into a new, eschatologically charged vision of reality.

Social scientists are arriving at the same understanding in interpreting the rise of apocalypticism in various millennial groups around the world. Their research helpfully clarifies the nature of the apocalyptic imagination in biblical texts. Apocalyptic thinking arises cross-culturally in groups of various backgrounds as a radical, but highly coherent, re-visioning of the world. In each case, it expresses itself in notions and visual images drawn from a group's traditional "symbol storehouse."

A study of the roots of the Native American Ghost Dance tradition by Trudy Carter Thomas provides an excellent example of these ethnographic conclusions. The Ghost Dance movement and its dance rituals arose among Native Americans in 1890. Apocalyptic in character, its core beliefs included an imminent resurrection of dead ancestors (ghosts) followed by the advent of a new era of paradise.

Thomas traces the origins of the symbols of the Ghost Dance in her study, analyzing the designs preserved on decorated garments and other artifacts of the movement. She discovers the primary source of inspiration for the Ghost Dance symbol system to be traditional Native American motifs and images, such as those found on traditional native shields.

The apocalyptic imagination, Thomas concludes, is "a creatively reorganized composite of established cultural patterns."[12] In the new composite, the native symbols undergo an apocalyptic shift in orientation. In the Ghost Dance's case, the shift involved a new emphasis on select motifs and a new use of colors. Re-presented in an apocalyptic worldview, standard Native American symbols now focused on the re-creation of the world and the regeneration of its life-forms.

What Thomas calls a new emphasis on *select* motifs is key. Foremost among motifs especially influential in the Ghost Dance symbolic universe are ones drawn from mythology, especially myths about creation. A culture's traditional creation mythology frequently feeds directly into outbursts of apocalypticism that arise in its midst.

The established poetry and mythology of many cultures revolve around creation and cosmic order. One might expect an apocalyptic imagination to spring out of a cognitive recombination of this type of content. Apocalypticism's focal concerns have everything to do with the interplay of cosmic order and chaos. Central to apocalypticism as well are concerns with the structure and hierarchy of the cosmos and the transcendent archetypes and forces behind cosmic ordering.

Mythic images of creation and cosmic order were at home in ancient Israel from early monarchic times. Co-opted from the rich mythologies of Israel's ancient Near Eastern neighbors, they helped biblical traditions express the cosmic implications of God's saving actions on Israel's behalf. The apocalyptic worlds of the Bible appear far more deeply rooted in this symbolism than in postexilic feelings of powerlessness or in foreign religious systems.

Israel's native mythology, like the store of myth in many cultures, has an inherent dualistic (binary) nature. As Israel's apocalyptic imagination formed out of established mythic building blocks, mythology's binary nature provoked the strong dualism of Israelite apocalyptic literature, a family trait of apocalypticism we observed in the Qumran scrolls. This accounts for the apocalyptic dualism in the biblical literature. There is no need to explain that dualism through recourse to a social divide between the powerless and the powerful or an influx of Persian religion into early Judaism.

Across world cultures, mythological discourse typically revolves around pairs of realities that oppose and contradict each other. Binary pairs of symbols—such as night and day, good and evil, north and south, pure and impure—are extremely frequent in mythic stories. The narratives of these stories aim to account for the oppositions and logical contradictions raised by the existence of these pairs.

The social anthropologist Claude Lévi-Strauss popularized this key insight. His "structural" analysis of how myths function within the cultures of the world focused on how myths help the people of a culture make sense of fundamental contradictions in life. In answer to the question of what myths do for humans, he wrote, "The purpose of myth is to provide a logical model capable of overcoming a contradiction."[13]

Part 2 of this volume examines specific apocalyptic texts of the Hebrew Bible and reveals their mythological building blocks. For now, it may be helpful merely to take note of the poetic and mythic symbolism of a nonapocalyptic text of the Bible and point out its potential fertility for later apocalyptic thinking. A good text for this purpose is the third chapter of the book of the prophet Habakkuk, a hymn of praise to God.

The Hebrew Bible often depicts God intervening powerfully through human events to modify history. These interventions of God are generally finite and localized. Nevertheless, prophets such as Habakkuk often emphasized their supernatural quality using Israel's poetic and mythological traditions.

Habakkuk 3 expresses hope of a future supernatural event, when God will march forth in a pyrotechnic display to defeat evil. It speaks of the melting and splitting of mountains and valleys at the marching forth of the Divine Warrior (a theophany).

Several images of God's cosmic power in Hab 3 reappear in later apocalyptic texts. Just as God's presence shatters the mountains in Hab 3:6, so a late dated prayer in Isaiah for God's apocalyptic intervention petitions God to "tear open the heavens and come down, / so that the mountains would quake at your presence" (Isa 64:1; cf. also Zech 14:4-5).

Just as Hab 3:12 describes God trampling the nations in indignation and anger, a later vision in Isa 63:3 depicts God as an apocalyptic warrior, trampling evil humanity in wrath.

Just as Habakkuk trembles at his vision of God's theophany,

Daniel later turns deathly pale and loses sleep at the apocalyptic vistas revealed to him (Dan 8:27; 10:8).

Later apocalyptic texts are similar to Habakkuk in awaiting the blazing appearance of God in human life and history. They differ from him in the radical quality of their expectations, however. Whereas in prophetic texts the language of the march of the Divine Warrior is Semitic hyperbole, the writers of apocalyptic literature expected a concrete, physical undoing of earthly reality. They expected not merely the historical defeat of Israel's enemies but earth's literal, divine re-creation.

Apocalyptic eschatology is more pessimistic and radical than Habakkuk about human history and about the extent of God's coming intervention in it. In the expectation of the writers of the apocalyptic literature, the supernatural realm is on a collision course with human history, leading to a cataclysmic impact that will supernaturally transform the world in a way that no one can ignore. God's reign on earth is not yet universally apparent to believers and unbelievers alike, but it will be in time.

CHAPTER 2

THE DANGER OF DOMESTICATING THE APOCALYPTIC TEXTS

Like it or not, as the twenty-first century begins, interpreters of the Bible find themselves up against the Bible's apocalyptic texts. The apocalyptic literature is as prominent as ever, whether because of its intrinsic fascination, its relevance at a time of catastrophic terrorist acts, or its immutable inclusion in the scriptural canon. Perhaps its prominence is due to a combination of all these and other factors. The apocalyptic literature of the Bible is so strikingly fantastic, horrific, and utopian, however, that readers may balk at the challenge of interpretation, even if they are trained scholars.

Face-to-face with these texts, interpreters eagerly seek a handle on them. Mainstream scholars and preachers, in particular, faced with interpreting apocalyptic texts, search for some sane, learned, and respectable control over them.

Too often, unfortunately, the desire of interpreters to bring a level of control and comfort to their interpretive task quickly moves them to "domesticate" the apocalyptic literature. To domesticate the apocalyptic texts of the Bible means to rob them, in one way or another, of their ability to speak on their own terms. It means shifting the focus in reading away from a serious grappling with their overt theological witness about God's fantastic future work of re-creating reality.

DOMESTICATING APOCALYPTIC TEXTS THROUGH SPIRITUAL AND SYMBOLIC READINGS

Modern people are not used to direct, supernatural interventions by God in the world. They often read the accounts of God's miracles in the Bible with a sense of distance and skepticism. Perhaps they allow fantastic miracle stories to encourage their morale, as religious believers, but they take them with a grain of salt. If miracles within history are hard to accept, it is even more difficult to imagine God's ultimate supernatural work of creating or re-creating the heavens and the earth, and history itself.

The Bible's language about this sort of thing—creation and apocalypse—is hard to accept on its own terms, and readers often look for the truth of this language at some level of meaning other than its face value. Apocalyptic language must be poetry or hyperbole. At most, it must stand for some new work of God to emerge within history, probably one achieved by historical, human agents on God's behalf.

Some recent scholars have tried to downplay the radical, cosmic scope of apocalyptic expectations in the Bible. One illuminating example is N. T. Wright's interpretations of biblical apocalypticism in his popular book, *The New Testament and the People of God.*

In this work Wright argues that most Jewish and Christian apocalyptic literature does not hope that God will re-create the cosmos. Rather, the literature expects merely that God will soon act decisively in the continuing, mundane world. When first-century Jews and the early Christians described the coming New Age in apocalyptic terms, Wright believes, they were merely speaking metaphorically about a great new act that God will perform on the historical stage.[1]

Attempts of scholars, such as Wright, to downplay the radical, cosmic expectations of ancient apocalyptic groups fail to grasp the meaning of apocalyptic texts.

Specific texts among the Dead Sea Scrolls show incontrovertible evidence that some Jews in the Hellenistic and Roman periods consciously anticipated an actual, physical culmination of the course of history and of the cosmic order. The scrolls clearly come from the intertestamental period, and they clearly speak of cosmic upheaval.

The second psalm in column 11 (1QH 11, formerly col. 3) of the Qumran Thanksgiving Hymns (the *Hodayot*) is a case in point. The final sections of the hymn read as follows.

> The torrents of Satan shall reach
> to all sides of the world.
> In all their channels
> a consuming fire shall destroy
> every tree, green and barren, on their banks;
> unto the end of their courses
> it shall scourge with flames of fire,
> and shall consume the foundations of the earth
> and the expanse of dry land.
> The bases of the mountains shall blaze
> and the roots of the rocks shall turn
> to torrents of pitch;
> it shall devour as far as the great Abyss.
> The torrents of Satan shall break into Abaddon,
> and the deeps of the Abyss shall groan
> amid the roar of heaving mud.
> The land shall cry out because of the calamity
> fallen upon the world,
> and all its deeps shall howl.
> And all those upon it shall rave
> and shall perish amid the great misfortune.
> For God shall sound His mighty voice,
> and His holy abode shall thunder
> with the truth of His glory.
> The heavenly hosts shall cry out
> and the world's foundations
> shall stagger and sway.
> The war of the heavenly warriors shall scourge the earth;
> and it shall not end before the appointed destruction
> which shall be for ever and without compare.[2]

The hymnist is experiencing some present distress, which he describes as a foretaste of a coming all-out assault on earth by Satan. The magnitude of the assault is global, reaching all the world's edges and its very foundations. All humanity bears the shock, raving in the calamity. Finally, the powers of heaven also enter the fray, and again the foundations of the world stagger and sway. The heavenly warriors do not break off their attack until they accomplish an incomparable and eternal end of the earth in its present form.

Like other apocalyptic texts, this hymn from Qumran is full of archetypal and mythological language. It gropes to describe happenings beyond normal history, beyond the realm of cause and effect. According to early Jewish and Christian apocalypticism, the end time (Ger. *Endzeit*) involves a resurfacing of the chaos present before history began (Ger. *Urzeit*).

Our Qumran hymn uses the mythic poetry of chaos in describing earth's coming calamity as a roar of heaving mud that causes even the deeps of the great Abyss to groan. In the hymn, earth reverts to the aqueous sludge over which God's spirit first brooded before creation, when only darkness was over the surface of the Abyss (Gen 1:2).

This resurfacing of creation mythology is no imaginative flourish in apocalyptic writing but signals that a new creation is coming, on a par with God's original Genesis victory over mythological chaos. To claim that Israelite apocalypticism has nothing to do with the end of space and time is tantamount to claiming that Gen 1 is not really about a cosmic-scale ordering of heaven and earth. Like ancient Near Eastern creation mythology, ancient apocalypticism describes a sacred time of beginnings, when God sets straight the universe as a whole.

The texts from Qumran are not our only evidence that apocalyptic texts are radical and cosmic. Domesticated understandings of biblical apocalypticism have little connection to apocalyptic beliefs that ethnographers have observed cross-culturally among actual apocalyptic (millennial) groups.

The Native American participants in the apocalyptic Ghost Dance movement, for example, believed their ceremonies and battles with the U.S. Army were the start of something vastly larger and unprecedented. The native movement arose in 1890, when a messianic figure named Wovoka (also known as Jack Wilson) propagated its central teaching among many tribes. This teaching held that a messiah was now on earth and that a resurrection of ancestors and a golden new era were imminent.

42

The apocalyptic believers of the movement expected their dead ancestors—the ghosts of the Ghost Dance—to return to life at any moment, at which time the anticipated new era would begin. The visions induced by participating in the Dance revealed the ancestors' imminent arrival on earth, accompanied by thick game. Upon their return, the earth would renew itself, physically and concretely, so that a new creation would result.

Mythological symbols of creation from traditional Native American culture played a central role in the rise of the apocalyptic imagination ("symbolic universe") of the Ghost Dance. In the traditional, preapocalyptic mythology of the Plains tribes, creation oriented itself around a sacred tree sprouting at the center of the world. As a conduit for the supernatural powers of the universe, the tree blessed earthly creation, sheltering human and animal life, allowing it to flourish and multiply. The traditional Sun Dance ceremony of the Plains revolved around a ceremonial pole symbolizing this sacred symbol of the order of creation. The same symbolic pole, or cosmic tree, appears in various guises in the Native American Ghost Dance. In that new apocalyptic movement, it was a central implement for participating in the end times and preparing for the eschaton.

An actual tree formed the liturgical center of the Ghost Dance ritual in the practice of certain tribes. In other cases, dancers used images associated with the cosmic tree on ritual garments of the Ghost Dance and in body painting. The dancers claimed to have seen these creation-oriented mythological images in their dance trances. The archetypal symbols of their visions, they believed, were about to assume physical reality on earth.

Some versions of Ghost Dance doctrine held that the traditional, Native American image of the cosmic tree would physically sprout on earth at the end time. A coming catastrophe would rock the earth and wipe out European Americans. At the time of the catastrophe, tribal believers would have to rendezvous and strip off all dress and utensils of the current age. The cosmic tree would grow out of the rendezvous locale, and would radiate health and new life in all four cardinal directions.[3]

Take the example of the Ghost Dance among Sioux tribes. In a speech delivered on Pine Ridge reservation, October 31, 1890, a leader of the Ghost Dance named Short Bull described the cosmic tree in the following manner. "Now, there will be a tree sprout up,

43

and there all the members of our religion and the tribe must gather together. That will be the place where we will see our dead relations. . . . But before this time we must dance the balance of this moon, at the end of which time the earth will shiver very hard."[4]

Native American apocalyptic believers expected a real cosmic tree to physically sprout on earth, ushering in the new age. After the tree sprouts, the dead return and the earth convulses at the birth of the millennial era.

Short Bull identified a physical locale—Pass Creek—where the cosmic tree would sprout. His people would have to leave all earthly things behind and gather naked at the spot when the time was ripe. He states, "Now, we must gather at Pass creek where the tree is sprouting. There we will go among our dead relations. You must not take any earthly things with you. Then the men must take off all their clothing and the women must do the same."[5]

The way that the apocalyptic imagination shared by Short Bull re-visions traditional, creation-oriented images as historically real entities that invade the world in earth's last days is parallel to what we see in the apocalyptic literature of the Bible. There is little reason to doubt the writers of the biblical literature would have shorn off their earthly possessions just as readily as their Native American counterparts and met at a designated rendezvous point, if that was their plan, upon receiving the longed-for news of the glorious arrival of God's Messiah.

DOMESTICATING APOCALYPTIC TEXTS THROUGH FUTURISTIC READINGS OR THROUGH HISTORICIZED READINGS

Other ways of domesticating the apocalyptic literature of the Bible are commonplace, even among those who grant that this literature envisions a radical interruption of time and a physical transformation of the cosmos. One such means of domesticating apocalyptic texts—widespread among interpreters—is reading them as if they were coded documents. Secret documents, written in code, aim to communicate a factual, one-dimensional message to a select audience. They cloak this communication in puzzling symbols, which only the initiated find intelligible.

If the Bible's apocalyptic texts are merely coded documents, the key to their interpretation is breaking the code. It consists in identifying the individuals, nations, time lines, and calendars behind all the wild, bizarre imagery of the texts. If a beast with heads and horns appears in a text, it is a cipher for a specific kingdom, such as ancient Persia or the modern United States and its allies. When a text refers to a figure such as the "king of the North," it is thinly veiled language for an individual of history, such as the Seleucid monarch Antiochus IV Epiphanes (175–164 B.C.E.) or Saddam Hussein, the former leader of Iraq.

Once decoded, the text reveals its convictions about the details and divine interventions of the "time of the end." The reader may either accept or discount these convictions.

If this decoding approach is valid, the goal in interpreting the apocalyptic literature is clear. Understanding the apocalyptic texts of the Bible involves nothing more than mapping apocalypticism's images into straightforward history descriptions, news reports, or political agendas.

In actual practice, much of what passes for interpretations of apocalyptic literature unfortunately takes this form of decoding. Ironically, the approach is a trap for interpreters across the theological spectrum. You can see it in the work of both conservatives and liberals.

Fundamentalists and cult interpreters most often decode apocalyptic texts as predictions of current events, cloaked in biblical symbols. They imagine that the ancient texts peered far into a distant future, namely, our own time. One can term their readings and interpretations "futuristic."

Rationalist critics, alternatively, see apocalyptic texts oriented in the other direction: toward the past rather than the future. They decode apocalyptic texts as ciphers for ancient political events. What may initially appear to be a detailed prophecy about the future is actually a religious or political agenda for an ancient audience, the first readers within the original historical milieu of an apocalyptic text. Since critics who operate in this mode anchor apocalyptic texts in the events, politics, and programs of ancient history, one can term their mode of interpretation a "historicized" reading.

Modern historical critics favor a "historicist" approach, but it has ancient roots. As a mode of reading apocalyptic texts, it goes back to the third-century polemicist Porphyry, an enemy of

Christianity. Porphyry was interested specifically in the apocalyptic book of Daniel and wrote history's first critique of the traditional view that this book is supernatural prophecy from the period of Israel's exile (the sixth century B.C.E.).

Dating the book of Daniel far later than his predecessors, Porphyry's treatise dismissed its value as authentic prophecy about the future. He interpreted the book instead as religious literature of reassurance for late, Maccabean times (the persecutions and military conflicts of the Jews around 175–164 B.C.E.). Its Maccabean author creatively placed fantastic surveys of world events in the mouth of a figure named Daniel from four hundred years before his own times. This literary technique of pseudonymous authorship helped him offer his readers religious confidence.

Daniel's secret Maccabean author produced a retrospective recap of four centuries of preceding history, disguised it as prophecy, and placed it far back in time—at the time of Daniel, of Israel's exilic period. Daniel thus appears in the book to have a sure knowledge of the events of the future. The accuracy of this God-given knowledge assures readers of God's foreknowledge and control of Israel's destiny.

Beginning in the Enlightenment, many modern critics have followed Porphyry's lead in interpreting apocalyptic literature.

Both the futurist and historicist approaches to apocalyptic literature are inadequate. Imagining that they have solved the mystery of the literature by cracking its code, the proponents of these interpretive approaches domesticate the biblical texts. Let me begin a critique of both stances by summarizing the limitations of the futurists.

Futurist interpreters place far too much stake in apocalyptic texts as clairvoyant literature. David Koresh provides an extreme example. The modern messianic leader of the Branch Davidian community interpreted Daniel and Revelation as encrypted predictions of the events of the 1990s. Believing, in fact, that the texts addressed him directly and personally, he relied on them for interpreting his confrontation with the U.S. government at his settlement compound outside Waco, Texas. He clearly had no knowledge or appreciation of Porphyry's ancient arguments that the book of Daniel does a rather poor job predicting the exact details of what is yet to take place.

Whatever the weaknesses of Porphyry's critique, his early work on Daniel did convincingly demonstrate that the book is no crossword puzzle hiding precise knowledge of the future. Porphyry wrote, "Whatever [Daniel's Maccabean author] spoke of up till the time of Antiochus [i.e., the author's contemporary, Maccabean times] contained authentic history, whereas anything he may have conjectured beyond that point was false." Most modern scholars believe that Porphyry is not far wrong here. Daniel's authors lacked focused predictive ability. Their conscious knowledge of historical detail becomes murky beyond their contemporary Maccabean period.

This fact should give futurist interpreters of the apocalyptic literature great pause. If the visionaries behind the book of Daniel provide us with little exact knowledge about the immediate period after Antiochus's reign, they can probably tell us even less about the exact details of our own times. Apocalyptic literature simply does not work well as a set of cryptographic predictions about the twenty-first century.

I hasten to add that Porphyry's approach judges visionary insight in the Bible on an unfair basis. The Bible's classical prophets and apocalyptic seers often saw deeply into the character and essence of God's plans for humanity. That is, they excelled at what scholars call "ontic insight." They left behind texts full of deep insights and expansive language with relevance far beyond their own period. Their words are not moored in their times.

Porphyry is on target, however, in observing that clairvoyance about the future was not the forte of these inspired figures. They never sought such powers, being little attracted to the role of soothsayer or foreteller of events. What scholars call "noetic insight"—conscious knowledge about names and dates of the far future—was, for them, irrelevant speculation and esoterica.

The reminder that biblical prophets and visionaries made their immediate contemporaries a priority raises a second problem with the futurist mode of interpretation. Futurist interpreters excel at making the Bible alarmingly applicable to modern times, but they often forget that biblical texts had to have been meaningful and applicable for their ancient audiences too. Futurist interpreters often leave themselves with no way to account for the *ancient* relevance of apocalyptic texts.

David Koresh assumed that the whole standpoint of the book of

Revelation is modern times. He viewed it as a message in a bottle for the last days, two thousand years after its time of writing. Its ancient author closed and sealed it after he finished capturing the vision in writing. Koresh saw himself as the "lamb" of Rev 5, who opens God's sealed book of revelations.

Practically the same view appears in Tim LaHaye and Jerry Jenkins's best-selling *Left Behind* novels. Millions of people have purchased these books, in which characters discover the Bible's foreknowledge of the distant future as end-time events—such as the rapture—unfold around them. The Bible's foreknowledge of events convinces the characters that God exists and is in control of everything they are experiencing. According to the *Left Behind* series, "Bible prophecy is history written in advance."[6]

This understanding fails at any number of levels. Social scientists have studied apocalyptic groups across history and around the globe to find out who produces and treasures literature like the book of Revelation. Cross-culturally, apocalyptic groups expect the end times to occur imminently, within the lifetimes of group members. They do not record visions relevant only for unborn generations. Revelation's first audience would not be any different. They would have found the book directly relevant.

The first hearers and readers of Revelation learned immediately that it is about things that "must *soon* take place" (Rev 1:1, my emphasis). "The time is near" for the end times to begin, according to Rev 1:3 and 22:10. Three times in the final chapter of the book, Jesus promises, "I am coming soon" (Rev 22:7, 12, 20).

Given this language, Revelation's ancient Roman readers must have hoped and expected that the second coming of Jesus could occur at any time. Along with the closing benediction of the book, they would have prayed, "Amen. Come, Lord Jesus." They must have seen the references and images of Revelation as highly applicable for understanding contemporary events, and used the book to discern the spirits at work in their times.

One final piece of evidence assures us that the book of Revelation is no bottled message for the future. Revelation begins with letters addressed to seven contemporary churches in Asia Minor, addressing real people, and real situations (Rev 2–3). It is passionately concerned with the workaday struggles of actual, ancient church members in Ephesus, Smyrna, Pergamum, Thyatira, Sardis, Philadelphia, and Laodicea.

Whatever the book's relevance for understanding the twenty-first century, it was clearly applicable to the earthly struggles of Christians in the first century. Those struggles, Revelation argues, interconnect with heavenly, cosmic conflicts. When the book urges its readers to "conquer" (Rev 2:7, 17, 26), it understands their local experience to be part of God's ultimate, cosmic victory (Rev 21:7).

Now, let me switch my critique to the other brand of decoding apocalyptic texts, the historicist approach.

A liberal reader, taking a historicist approach, would find that David Koresh had completely departed from the clear, original meaning of the books of Daniel and Revelation. Daniel 11:24, for example, cannot be speaking of Saddam Hussein's Scud missile attack on Israel during the Persian Gulf War, as Koresh argued. Rather, it must be about an ancient leader from Maccabean times known to the original writers of Daniel.

Specifically, in fact, the verse refers to the tyrannous rule of Antiochus. Biographical details about the twentieth century would have no relevance for the original readers of Daniel. However, they would have had a pressing need to understand Antiochus's arrogant claims and his abuse of the people of Judea.

Jean-Pierre Prévost's popular introduction, *How to Read the Apocalypse,* offers actual examples of a historicist approach to interpreting the book of Revelation. At points, Prévost makes it sound as if apocalyptic discourse is simply ancient history coded in rich images. He writes of John of Patmos, "Even if his language is steeped in imagery, we must not forget that he is translating a perception of events which have taken place, for him, since the 60s: persecutions, wars, exile, etc. . . . The 'realistic' part of the events described by John focuses first and foremost on the period contemporary to him."[7]

Prévost understands most of the events of Revelation as ancient history. He writes:

> The "events" evoked by the Apocalypse have already taken place as far as we are concerned. . . . We have every reason to believe that the visions and revelations described in the Apocalypse relate to history contemporaneous with the author. In other words, for us

49

these events are things of the past: a break with Judaism, the persecution of Christians, emperor worship, etc.[8]

The validity of this assessment is dubious.

Historically oriented interpreters are correct that apocalyptic visions must have been comprehensible and relevant to contemporary readers, or they would never have gained currency. Books such as Daniel and Revelation betray their character as antique, historical documents by their concrete social and political references, which often require modern-day clarifications. In other words, scholars who investigate apocalyptic literature's original milieu are exploring a valid dimension of its interpretation. The undeniable historical character of apocalyptic texts, however, does not alter their determined orientation on last things, on God's plans for the end of days.

Their original authors' expectations about an immediate end proved premature, but apocalyptic texts nonetheless point forward, with rich ontic insight, to the end of days. This orientation on *last things* stands in tension with a purely historicist reading strategy. The faith communities that first preserved the apocalyptic literature of the Bible did not share modern interpreters' antiquarian preoccupation with "history contemporaneous with the author." Rather, they treasured books such as Revelation for their witness about a coming consummation of God's plans for humanity. If John's revelations are primarily about past events, and particularly, if these past events never fulfilled the apocalyptic hopes of the revelations—that is, if no visible culmination of history materialized as part of those events—the faithful would never have preserved them as canonical Scripture.

But synagogue and church have preserved the apocalyptic literature of the Bible. The earliest interpretations of these texts that we know of saw no reason to think that history had disconfirmed their message. Rather, the faithful believed that the events of the past had not exhausted their meaning, and their vision about God's plans for the cosmos awaited a fulfillment yet to be realized. Just as we do apocalyptic literature a disservice by anchoring it in the future as Koresh did, we equally domesticate it by mooring it in the past.

Historical critics are doubtless correct that the biblical apocalyptic groups—such as the Maccabean editors of Daniel and the early Christian prophetic circle of John of Patmos—hoped and expected their apocalyptic visions to be completely fulfilled in their own times. The visions' gruesome images of evil and their vibrant expectations must have resonated strongly with contemporary experiences. The Bible's apocalyptic visions are spongy, resonating with truth on multiple occasions when doomful circumstances well up in magnitude.

The Daniel group hoped God's reign would begin when Antiochus met his downfall "not by human hands" (Dan 8:25). John of Patmos ends Revelation with Jesus' words, "I am coming soon," and the prayer, "Amen. Come, Lord Jesus" (Rev 22:20). Neither of these books makes any immediate promises to its readers, however. The Bible baldly states that no one knows the day nor the hour of the apocalypse. The early biblical authors and editors hoped for a speedy fulfillment, but never claimed these hopes were part of the inspired revelations they recorded. The book of Daniel never mentions Antiochus by name. It never claims that he must be the final antimessiah to be destroyed at the apocalyptic coming of the Son of Man.

Putting ourselves in the shoes of the Daniel group, we can imagine their doubts in considering the apocalyptic vision of four beasts in Dan 7. Surely they hoped they were living at the climactic fourth stage of the vision's timetable. Equally possible, however, was the alternative that they were dealing merely with the third stage of the timetable, with the third beast in a succession of four. A close look at the chapter shows plenty of room for the latter interpretation.

Beast number three in Dan 7:6 with its four heads fits their Maccabean, international scene well. This was the period after the division of the empire of Alexander the Great. The third beast's four heads look like the four divisions of Alexander's empire: Asia Minor, Syria, Egypt, and Macedonia (cf. Dan 8:8, 21-22).

Daniel 8:27 may confirm that the Daniel group puzzled over the intelligibility and applicability of their apocalyptic visions. After witnessing the vision of chapter 8, Daniel remarks, "I, Daniel, was overcome and lay sick for some days; then I arose and went about the king's business. But I was dismayed by the vision and did not understand it" (cf. Dan 7:28). In light of this portrayal of Daniel's reaction to his visions, any certitude on the part of a reader of Daniel about God's apocalyptic timetable appears completely presumptuous.

The expansive, awesome visions of the Bible's apocalyptic literature defy a critic's attempt to reduce them to one set of historical circumstances. The history of interpretation shows the visions' rich capacity to speak to multiple situations over a long expanse of time.

Porphyry and modern historicists are wrong to characterize Daniel's visions as oriented toward past history. These visions are fundamentally prophetic and future oriented. The Daniel group saw that they partially fit their own times and hoped that they would live to see the start of God's reign on earth. When this did not happen, however, the visions continued to point to the future. The community of the faithful continued to treasure them as Scripture and to await expectantly God's greater fulfillment of them.

The fundamental weakness of approaches of futurism and historicism is their aim to reify the images and symbols of apocalyptic literature. Both interpretive stances take apocalyptic images as mere code for observable objects and events of history. But far from mere code, the image-rich landscape of apocalyptic literature is full of realistic, supernatural entities inhabiting a heavenly plane of existence.

The apocalyptic texts of the Bible use their specific, unique discourse to help readers come to terms with transcendental forces in reality, forces lurking behind human persons and groups. The rhetoric of apocalyptic texts is supposed to focus us on (not divert us from) the suprahuman forces and structures at work in our world.

A suprahuman force cannot be objectified, that is, equated with a historical reality, such as a present-day nation. Historical reality is rarely so straightforward as to embody fully the neat, dualistic archetypes of apocalypticism. Modern people seem to know this intuitively. Consternation arises around the world when a U.S. president singles out specific nations, such as North Korea and Iraq, as unqualifiedly evil, or as part of an "axis of evil" (as stated in President George W. Bush's State of the Union address, January 2002, and presupposed in his subsequent course of action).

Even the apocalyptic writers of the Qumran community realized that the force of evil could not be reified. In their *Community Rule* document, they state that spirits of both truth and injustice influence all human beings until the end of days. It is only at the last judgment—when God intervenes to inaugurate the new age—that a divine judgment assigns individuals unequivocally to the camps of darkness and light.

DOMESTICATING APOCALYPTIC TEXTS THROUGH OVERLY CREDULOUS OR OVERLY SUSPICIOUS READINGS

A third way that interpreters may domesticate the apocalyptic literature of the Bible is through overly credulous or overly suspicious readings. These habits of reading suffer from a lack of spiritual imagination. They rob the apocalyptic texts of the power to engage readers' hearts and spirits, and reform the very ways they think about life.

Interpreters are overly credulous when they read apocalyptic texts as pristine, unblemished dogma. Reduced to something unsullied and unassailable, the apocalyptic texts no longer provoke readers' religious imagination; they deaden it. Conversely, interpreters are overly suspicious when, distracted by the human limitations and imperfections in apocalyptic texts, they lose sight of their theological richness, beauty, and awe.

Without sophistication and imagination, interpreters can perpetuate language and images in apocalyptic texts that have long felt unsafe to some people and have been used to degrade others. That is not the worst of it. History attests that horror and death may come when people appropriate the language and images of apocalyptic literature without care and criticism. Particularly egregious tragedy can occur when apocalyptic images inspire human scapegoating and violence.

The prostitute and the dragon in Rev 17:3 provide one example of apocalyptic language and images that have been put to violent misuse. For centuries in Europe and North America, people used this apocalyptic material to dehumanize women accused of witchcraft. Equating accused witches with the "great whore" of Revelation, people judged them worthy of hatred. Indeed, they went further than just hating and dehumanizing accused witches. Partially because Rev 17:16 speaks of the burning of the prostitute, Babylon, with fire, people jumped to burn accused witches at the stake.[9]

Women have not been the only group to suffer from the misuse of apocalyptic literature. Take the example of King Philip's War in seventeenth-century America. The violent apocalyptic language of Mal 4:1-3 was one inspiration behind this bloody conflict, when New Englanders forcibly expanded into Native American territory between 1675 and 1676. Their conquest resulted in the loss of three thousand Native American lives. Interpreting the war as the Great Day at the end of Malachi, they saw themselves as executing apocalyptic judgment by treading down the wicked.[10]

To equate fantastic apocalyptic images with real women, Native Americans, or any other cross section of humanity is a tragic failure of human imagination. These images are transcendental realities of suprahuman proportion. As such, they are completely stereotyped and excessive by their very nature. They sum up and embody inclinations, qualities, and characteristics in a way that no historical person or group ever could. To reduce them to finite persons is pure domestication.

It is similarly tragic and arrogant for human beings to mimic God's apocalyptic warfare through human violence. When God marches forth out of heaven as the Divine Warrior, it is to accomplish something that human violence never can. God marches to battle to save humanity and creation from hostile forces that humanity finds hopeless to defeat. As the transcendent, all-seeing God, the Divine Warrior easily identifies the enemy—the totality of opposition to salvation. Such discernment is impossible for unaided, human perception.

Lack of literary sophistication and imagination clearly lead to tragic misuse of apocalyptic literature all too frequently, but the problem is not merely with interpreters of apocalyptic texts. The texts themselves must share the blame.

Recent interpreters, particularly feminist scholars, have exposed inherently disturbing traits in apocalyptic literature that play particularly dangerously to an overly credulous literalism in interpretation. Catherine Keller produced such an exposé in her 1996 volume, *Apocalypse Now and Then*. The work focuses on the New Testament book of Revelation, which she calls the Apocalypse.

Because of its disturbing features, Keller advocates midrashic playfulness in interpreting the Apocalypse rather than submissive literalism. Her book's title betrays her playful, imaginative spirit of interpretation.

Reading Keller's book, one soon empathizes with her dismay and pain at the implications of a simple, naive submission to the Apocalypse. Its author had an opposition mentality that could prove very destructive under a different set of conditions. The "hostile dualisms" of such a mentality could easily become the bread and butter of a fanatic.

The Apocalypse's author seems guilty of patriarchy too. He seems completely insensitive that future female readers would find his images of women hurtful and depersonalizing. According to Keller, an encoded "poetics of power" in the Apocalypse can seem "pitted against female flesh." Various passages truly look guilty of misogyny.[11]

The New Testament scholar Tina Pippin has also pointed out how unacceptable an overly credulous reading of Revelation can be. Pippin analyzes the inherent problems of the language and symbols of Revelation in her 1992 volume, *Death and Desire.* She demonstrates that the use of female language and symbols in the Apocalypse, such as the images of mothers and brides, is always either negative or male dominated. This state of affairs is both disempowering and dangerous to women.

Take the figure Jezebel in the letter to Thyatira (Rev 2:18-29) for example. It is completely unfortunate that the prime individual singled out for inciting apostasy is the one active, expressive woman of the Apocalypse. The book viciously attacks her and threatens her with death.[12] This happenstance does anything but help modern women feel safe in positions of church leadership.

Jezebel is just one instance of Revelation's unconscious patriarchy. Pippin is shocked that the images conveying Revelation's message are blatantly patriarchal throughout. This is true even when the tenor of the book is laudable and liberating.

The apocalyptic texts of the Bible did not come directly from God in any sort of pure form, but bear distinct marks of transmission by finite human authors and editors. As human literature, the biblical apocalyptic texts have blind spots against which an approach of submissive credulity has no defense.

Under the conditions of their world, the Bible's apocalyptic visionaries did not share our modern consciousness of such evils as gender discrimination and ecological exploitation. Responsible interpreters must thus strive to distinguish the texts' blind spots from their theological witness. They must work hard to appropriate only the latter as relevant for today. The effort will not succeed without much struggle, sophistication, and serious reflection. Scholars refer to such critical, disciplined engagement with texts as hermeneutics.

Let me now turn to a critique of overly suspicious readings of apocalyptic literature. This type of interpretation can domesticate apocalyptic texts as readily as the very different interpretations I have just examined.

Tina Pippin's and Catherine Keller's work have helped us expose overly credulous readings of the Apocalypse. Unfortunately, these same scholars provide handy examples of the drawbacks of prioritizing a hermeneutic of suspicion.

Tina Pippin's book, *Death and Desire,* clearly takes up what I am calling an approach of suspicion to the apocalyptic literature of the Bible. She labors to critique the Apocalypse's textual/sexual strategies as dangerous to women's consciousness. Because she finds the book unsafe for women, she argues that responses to it of fear and horror are just as appropriate as responses of hope.[13]

Catherine Keller's work on the book of Revelation provides another good example of a radically suspicious stance toward biblical apocalypticism. Feminist and other doubts about the biblical text prevent her from appropriating many main themes of the Apocalypse. Indeed, far from appropriating them, she works to counter the oppressive, nonliberating parts of the book.

Keller does have a positive view about "zones of liberation" within Revelation, such as the Apocalypse's solidarity with martyrs who give their lives in the cause of human liberation. Nevertheless, Keller finds the biblical text so irritating at points that she seems unable to read it as a theological message—a proposal or witness about God and God's plans for the world. She understands the apocalyptic literature instead in anthropological terms. (An anthropological approach to Scripture understands it to reflect human ideology and psychology, not divine word.)

Keller interprets Rev 21:1, for example, as the expression of the psychology of the human author of the text. The exact way she words her argument is instructive. For her, it is the author of the

Apocalypse, not God, who terminates sun, moon, and stars.[14] In doing so, the author displays a "chilling indifference" to the first creation. Apparently, Keller finds it inconceivable that John of Patmos could be communicating a divine word at this point. He must be speaking his own (warped) mind.

When she reaches chilling texts, such as Rev 21:1, Keller breaks out of the role of Bible interpreter in a strict sense. Ceasing a mode of reflecting on the intended meaning of the biblical text, she commits only to remain within the text's "force field." She focuses her work as a reader on forming contemporary, feminist "pearls" out of her irritated reactions to the text, not on illuminating what the text says.

Keller is straightforward and honest about her decision to do theology in reaction against the biblical text, not based on its exegesis. She openly distances herself from Revelation, and aims to construct a "counterapocalypse." Because she is so honest and straightforward about these decisions, I would like to focus on her work in offering my brief critique of approaches of suspicion in interpreting apocalyptic literature.

Keller's approach of "countering" biblical texts is worrisome. It bears the potential to reject the hard and painful images and themes of biblical texts out of hand. In short, it risks domestication. If readers jump too soon to the conclusion that a text bears nothing but a defective, anthropological message, they preempt the chance to appropriate its possible theological witness.

The practice of premodern interpreters offers a very different model than Keller's approach of countering the text. It inspires emulation, because of its commitment to seek truth even when the going is painful. Many readers will find this model of interpretation more rewarding, if used responsibly and critically, than Keller's alternative.

Premodern Bible scholars often pushed themselves hard to keep within what today we call the "hermeneutical circle." That is, they read and reread even offensive biblical passages until they received some illumination as to the texts' theological witness. Sometimes this involved a creative transformation on their part, a sort of conversion experience. Significantly, the truth of the text often ended up being something far different from literalism. They believed it to be the inherent, true sense, nonetheless, of the rich scriptural writing before them.

Their practice of struggling to discover the true witness of biblical texts often led premodern interpreters to a broader interpretive framework for reading hard portions of the Bible. Keeping the larger biblical context of a passage in mind helped to rule out what some texts seemed to say at first glance. Biblical cross-references of keywords, for example, helped faithful interpreters illuminate profound nuances in difficult passages that on the surface seemed to irritate and offend.

The efforts of premodern scholars to search for the true witness of each scriptural passage pushes readers today to be more critical of our underdefined use of the term *literalism*. The premodern commitment to search for the *literal sense* of Scripture through wrestling, prayer, and meditation is something quite different from most modern connotations of *literalism*. The classical interpreters understood the literal sense as the sense of the text in its full symbolic richness, scriptural context, and witness to theological reality.

A positive word here about the value of an ongoing search for the literal sense of biblical passages, as the classical interpreters understood it, is in order. Such a word is necessary, since many modern interpreters of apocalyptic literature—Tina Pippin and Catherine Keller are simply sophisticated examples—are at pains to distance themselves from what they take to be a literal sense.

The history of exegesis shows the value of the literal sense. An understanding of the Bible's theological meaning and of its relevance for life and ministry came much easier to the premodern, classical interpreters. It was with the rise of modernism in the seventeenth, eighteenth, and nineteenth centuries, and especially the discovery that the biblical narrative did not generally make for good scientific history, that theological reflection on the Bible became increasingly difficult.

Beginning in the seventeenth century, there was an eclipse of the Bible's narrative storyline, of its textual art, and of its theological vitality. Abandoning the biblical literature as a theological witness, interpreters of the modern period substituted an anthropological study of the Bible. Their interests shifted to the Bible's original authors and the quest of these authors for religious understanding and meaning in life. The Bible's apocalyptic literature, unfortunately, does not fare well when evaluated in these "anthropological" terms.

When scholars bracket its witness to a supernatural, transcendent perspective, apocalyptic literature quickly begins to look like an unthinkable wish for creation's demise. Thus, reflecting on the passing away of heaven and earth in the Apocalypse (Rev 21:1), Catherine Keller, as noted, accuses the author of Revelation of "chilling indifference" to the first creation. She is unwilling to collude with apocalypticism's notion that the present creation must revert to its primordial beginnings—to the precreation Abyss of chaos. A "return to the *nihilo*" is unacceptable to Keller, because it would spell "an*nihil*ation."[15]

Similar stances against the apocalyptic idea of re-creation appear in other recent studies of the Apocalypse, including Ronald Farmer's work on Revelation in his book *Beyond the Impasse*. Working from the perspective of a process theology, in reliance on the philosophy of A. N. Whitehead, Farmer conceives of God as inextricably related to the dynamic processes of the world itself. Confining God's activity to such normal temporal processes, Farmer argues God "works with what is" to bring about what can be.[16] Farmer's bottom line is that, despite the literal sense of the Apocalypse, the God of the Bible does not abandon the present creation, but works within the constraints of its dynamics.[17]

From a human, anthropological perspective, destroying creation is unacceptable, as Keller and Farmer rightly affirm. The apocalyptic literature of the Bible, however, claims to witness to a transcendent perspective, from which the prospect of the death and rebirth of the cosmos looks entirely different. In comparison to the heavenly, transcendent realm unveiled by the apocalyptic texts, the present world of human experience is fully incomplete and tenuous. It will do no good to treasure it as an eternal good. Making the survival of the present creation of unrestricted religious value, the apocalyptic literature claims, would be a case of idolatry.

The apocalyptic perspective on God's desire for re-creation is not at odds with modern scientific knowledge. The best guess of scientists is that—lacking some impossible, supernatural intervention—the cosmos will slowly cool over the millennia and finally perish with a whimper. The world of daily routines seems a baseline norm from a human, twenty-first-century perspective, but in the big picture of science, "normal" reality is transient and unsustainable.

Furthermore, from the transcendent perspective of our literature, it is a caricature to say that God is planning a chilling annihilation of the cosmos. Rather, the texts make the mysterious and paradoxical claim of *continuity*, as well as discontinuity, between the present world and the coming new paradisiacal one. Paul's apocalyptic discourse in 1 Cor 15, for example, drives home this claim with a brilliant agricultural metaphor. Just as organic continuity connects a seed and a mature plant, so God's apocalyptic work utterly transforms the world, but does not obliterate it.

In short, the apocalyptic literature claims God's coming, awesome transformation of the cosmos is appealing, not appalling. The coming return of primordial chaos does not "an*nihil*ate" creation and humanity, but forms a portal to positive, glorious transformation and ultimate peace. For the faithful, the apocalyptic passage through chaos to transformation is a matter of profound hope, not a death wish.

Jacques Ellul eloquently captures how revulsion at the prospect of apocalyptic transformation is a limited, anthropocentric perspective:

> Those who refuse this vision of a radical judgment, of a collapse of the world for its own redemption, for its new creation (but new creation of *this* world), for the recapitulation of history and of the work of men—those who deny the negative phase—express the absence of hope. It is not possible that the dialectical movement end without passing through the crisis provoked by the decisive negation. . . . If there is no passage through this, there is no possibility of recapitulation and summation: then no hope. It is essential therefore to take account of the fact that the movement of hope in the Apocalypse has nothing to do with good sentiments, with pity, with a spirit of moderation. . . . All that is actually the exclusion of hope to the profit of a mediocre consolation.[18]

Modern science fiction offers many illustrations that help us to imagine some of the perspectives of the apocalyptic literature of the Bible. In some of these works, the characters discover the world around them is radically other than the normal, baseline reality they perceive it to be.

In the movie *The Matrix*, for example, the protagonist discovers that his whole existence is a mere virtual reality. All people, in fact, are trapped in a digitally created experience designed to imprison humanity. At the end of the film, the protagonist over-comes the forces opposing him, and dissolves the Matrix-prison into the stream of digits that make it up. He can then live life in the real physical world, rather than in the prison house of his pre-vious, mundane experience.

It is strange that while the average audience is willing to enter-tain this imaginative, cinematic depiction of a morally positive apocalypse, skeptically oriented scholars commonly refuse to entertain the possible theological value and positive moral insight of the apocalyptic imagination of key biblical Scriptures.

CHAPTER 3

A NEW SEARCH FOR THE LITERAL SENSE OF APOCALYPTIC TEXTS

The Bible's apocalyptic literature makes modern, mainstream interpreters uneasy. The literature pronounces judgment and doom on large numbers of human beings, privileges certain chosen others, and predicts the violent upending of the world we see around us. Many readers struggle to affirm and appropriate such ideas, finding them disturbing and potentially dangerous, at least at face value. They search for helpful ways to think about them, ways that differ from the interpretations of extremists and obscurantists.

A simple dismissal of the apocalyptic texts would be cavalier, since from early on they have nourished the life and development of synagogue and church. Despite their severity and scandal, Jews and Christians have preserved these texts as Scripture in the conviction that they bear a continuing theological witness, accessible to the faithful, persistent reader. The harsh, offensive qualities of the literature call not for dismissal but for critical engagement and interpretive sophistication. Such sophisticated engagement starts with abandoning approaches of literalism and historicism, turning instead to a new search for apocalyptic literature's "literal sense."

Literalism typically means an uncritical submission to the biblical text, which may deaden the imagination and perpetuate outmoded, injurious aspects of the text's original idiom. It generally entails a flat-footed reading, which views apocalyptic literature in one-dimensional terms. A search for the Bible's literal sense is different. It sees apocalyptic texts as symbolically rich, inspired literature that invigorates the imagination, offering readers new orientation and resolve about the life of faith.

Reacting strongly against literalist interpretations, some modern scholars advocate a stance of resolute suspicion toward the apocalyptic literature. This stance avoids the drawbacks of literalism, but abandons the search for the literal sense of apocalyptic texts. Moving outside the hermeneutic circle, its advocates appear to give up on the apocalyptic writings, concluding they really are nothing but an encoded "poetics of power" or a thinly veiled political diatribe.

Doubtful of gleaning theological insight from such writings, readers of suspicion move to expose and counteract the texts. In so doing, they leave readers without instruction about other ways—except resorting to literalism—of approaching and apprehending the strange, alien world of biblical apocalyptic literature.

Searching for a literal, scriptural sense of the apocalyptic worlds of the Bible begins with recognizing their imaginative and even alien tenor. Their vibrant images and compelling visions do not encode the banal, mundane world of politics and protest. Neither do they offer an almanac about the world's end, a reference book on the name of the Antichrist and the urban plan of the New Jerusalem. Rather, they envision Scripture's most powerful symbols and paradigms finally coming to fulfillment on earth, blossoming in concrete, material form.

A respectful approach to this literature hesitates to jump to expose its blind spots, allowing it a chance, instead, to expose us—its readers. The external world of the reader, the apocalyptic literature claims, is not what it appears. The transcendent is already starting to impinge on the mundane world, the world of the here and now.

FORMULATING A CANONICAL APPROACH

Several interpretive keys prove helpful in the search for a literal, "canonical sense" of the apocalyptic literature. The first is remembering that the building blocks of apocalyptic visions are scriptural ideals and images. Echoes and allusions to earlier Scriptures form the fabric of their imagination. Recognizing these biblical references is central for grasping the literal sense of apocalyptic texts.

The rise of apocalypticism in the biblical world went hand in hand with the rise of textualization and scribalism in religious practice. That is, apocalypticism arose concurrent with new forms of devotion involving the scribal preservation and study of written Scripture. The apocalyptic visionaries of the Bible—from Ezekiel, to Paul, to John of Patmos—were learned students of Israel's sacred writings. They expressed their new, end-time revelations in the idiom of preceding sacred texts.

The allusive language and inner-biblical mode of expression of apocalyptic texts has signal implications for how to interpret the literature. Rather than viewing apocalyptic literature through a rational or historical lens, interpreters are more likely to access its literal sense by reading it in the context of the Bible's own inner world: its narrative assumptions, values, and aspirations. Close attention to inner-biblical cross-referencing gives the interpreter a vital framework for understanding apocalyptic writings.

Consider, for example, Isa 24's picture of earth's inundation by doomsday chaos, a vista seemingly devoid of any good news for humanity. It is a hopeless vista indeed, until one recognizes how it evokes images and themes from Noah's flood (e.g., vv. 5, 18). The cross-references remind readers that God's normal work is a continual sustaining of creation. Noah's flood burst forth only when God—who unrelentingly holds cosmic chaos at bay—relaxed a grip on the floodgates. Moreover, the cross-references remind readers that God acts to send such a flood only to reverse a state of utter spiritual catastrophe on earth. God acts apocalyptically only to halt the sort of downward spiral away from Eden depicted in the Noah story's larger context (Gen 1–11).

Or consider Paul's apocalyptic image in 1 Thess 4 of a "rapture," in which Christians are caught up together in the clouds. Many modern readers have difficulty understanding what Paul is envisioning. The interpretations of literalists—openly expressed in Christian music, novels, and movies—offer little help. They often seem instead to rob Christian faith of dignity. A popular bumper sticker now reads, "In case of the rapture, can I have your car?"

It helps greatly to realize that the Bible's first testament supplies the needed cross-references and context for interpreting Paul's language. First Thessalonians 4 directly echoes the Greek text of Septuagint passages such as Isa 11:12; 35:10; 40:11; 43:5; 52:12; 60:4; Jer 38:10; Ezek 11:17; and Zech 2:10. These Scriptures all speak of God's gathering of all faithful people into one great community of fellowship at the end of days. In light of Paul's biblical allusions, his message about "rapture" in 1 Thess 4 must refer primarily to God's end-time work on earth of ingathering, reunion, and comfort.

Or again, consider the glaring absence of the church in many popular Christian visions of the end times. If the *Left Behind* novels by LaHaye and Jenkins are correct, the bulk of Revelation's narratives give the church absolutely no role to play in earth's darkest hours. But it is difficult to ignore the church if one takes seriously Revelation's Hebrew Bible language and symbolism.

The church's earthly ministry in the end times is apparent from Rev 11, among other texts, if only its background in the Hebrew Scriptures is explored. Revelation 11:3-6 describes two witnesses of God ministering on earth during the end times. Upon inspection, they emerge as two symbolic olive trees from an apocalyptic vision in Zech 4. Cross-referencing Zechariah leaves no doubt that these symbolic figures are ideal leaders of God's faithful people. Revelation wants the church to know that its leaders and congregations must prepare for a ministry of perseverance, service, and witness during the coming era of apocalyptic tribulation on earth.

Especially influential in the rise of apocalypticism in Israel were traditional mythical and archetypal symbols and images, particularly creation mythology. A second interpretive key to the literal sense of apocalyptic texts is recognizing the special role of these pictures. It is crucial to resist the temptation to decode and reify.

The resurgence of mythology in Israelite apocalypticism is remarkable. Before the rise of the apocalyptic imagination, the traditions of the Bible generally struggled with mythological language and belief. Key biblical texts particularly oppose polytheistic ideas about a pantheon of deities, many of whom mingle their powers with the forces of nature and fertility. In general, the Torah and Prophets emphasize a historical, covenantal, and ethical approach to religious thinking.

Throughout Israel's history, however, biblical traditions continually drew on mythological themes and narratives. In a mode of critical appropriation, they broke myths open, "demythologizing" them and subordinating their themes and ideals in service of covenant theology, or prophetic proclamation about history, or liturgical confession about God's identity. They risked co-opting mythology for good reason: It provided motifs and language for speaking about the numinous and transcendent dimensions of salvation history.

Examples abound. Habakkuk 3 uses poetry about a theophany of God on earth to depict a coming military defeat of Babylon. Psalm 110 likewise uses mythic motifs to emphasize God's powerful deliverance of Israel, celebrating God's covenantal promises to the Davidic dynasty in the language of hyperbole, especially in the idiom of ancient Near Eastern pronouncements about sacral kingship. Again, Ps 46 uses a mythic motif—the river of paradise—to symbolize God's promises to Jerusalem of bounty and peace. Verse 4 speaks of "a river whose streams make glad the city of God, the holy habitation of the Most High."

In the apocalyptic literature, mythological images reappear as building blocks of a new worldview, a new symbolic universe or "sheltering canopy." This is the case with the three examples just cited. Thus, Isa 64:1 makes the language of Hab 3 concrete. It beseeches God to intervene on earth, but now without any thought of mediating human armies. A direct assault of heaven against earth is called for—a personal, thunderous, and incontestable break-in of God.

The hyperbole about Davidic royalty in Ps 110 likewise reappears in the apocalyptic literature, specifically in Paul's letter to the Corinthians. Paul in 1 Cor 15 reads the psalm as messianic prophecy, deducing from it that God's Messiah will visibly and decisively subdue all God's antagonists at the end of days (vv. 25, 27).

The mythic river of Ps 46 also reappears in later apocalyptic texts, particularly those offering visions of a coming paradise on earth. Both Zech 14:8 and Joel 3:18 declare that in God's coming earthly reign, a fountain will burst forth from the Jerusalem temple to irrigate surrounding lands. Revelation 22:1 speaks of the same paradisiacal river, describing its refreshing delights available to all associated with God's New Jerusalem.

In reading apocalyptic literature, do not confuse these symbols for artistic representations of the ordinary and mundane. Too often interpreters mistake the blazing, mammoth characters of apocalyptic narratives for colorful expressions of the routine and commonplace—for persons, places, or events within human experience and history. It is a limited and even egoistic view to reduce to a banal level this literature's pains toward a comprehensive grasp of how the celestial and terrestrial interact.

The apocalyptic imagination has little to do with the tried and true—the merely organic and mechanically regular. It leans on mythology's ability to envision the transcendent, the otherworldly. This is the very reality that grows physical, visible, and painfully unavoidable in apocalyptic thinking. So too, apocalypticism leans on mythology's propensity to lay bare elemental conflicts, evoke primal fears, and resonate with humanity's unconscious impulses of awe and praise in the face of the divine.

Apocalypticism is not itself mythology, however, but puts mythic archetypes to new service. In the apocalyptic imagination, these archetypes appear in new forms and in a new visionary context. In particular, they take on realistic, material existence. At the end times, they physically invade history as "mythic-realistic entities." Their existence becomes incontestable, and earth's people react with awe or despair.

A third interpretive key unlocking apocalyptic literature involves grappling with its claims about a transcendent reality, which interacts with earthly experience in multidimensional ways. A flat-footed literalism misses the relevance of apocalyptic insights into transcendence for a great variety of reader circumstances.

The focal period of apocalyptic texts is the situation at the end of the age, when a transcendent, celestial backdrop to terrestrial history becomes visible and increasingly tangible (cf. Dan 7; 1 Cor 15; Matt 24). The apocalyptic imagination details the backdrop in its full-blown, end-time contours, but claims it is always present to human experience. If this claim is true, readers in all manner of circumstances—living at the end of the age or ensconced in the midst of history—can learn from end-time texts about a hidden dimension of their own existence.

Jacques Ellul states:

> [Apocalyptic literature] tends to act upon the reader, well inserted in history; it seeks to disclose to him the "mysterious riches" of the present. . . . Last things are present, actual; it is in terms of them, from now on revealed and so discernible, that we have to read our actuality.[1]

For readers living at ordinary times, apocalyptic literature helpfully reveals an invisible dimension of reality, which remains "safely" intangible. The literature takes on a more critical relevance, however, when readers find themselves experiencing unexpectedly *tangible* forays of the transcendent into their workaday existence. The community of the faithful appears to experience such forays periodically, so apocalyptic texts illuminate multiple contexts of salvation history.

Discussion of Dan 7 in the preceding chapter revealed its original audience to be Jews in turbulent conflict with the forces of Antiochus IV. The chapter's first readers doubtless identified Antiochus with the vision's final, boastful little horn (v. 8). Doomsday never arrived in Antiochus's period, however. History backed away from an uncontrolled spiral into chaos.

Those who preserved Dan 7 as Scripture realized history would press on long beyond Maccabean times. They must have concluded that the book's apocalyptic scenario had received only preliminary, anticipatory fulfillment in the second-century B.C.E. experience of its first audience. The cosmic dikes had sprung a leak, but God had stepped in to postpone an ultimate flood of transcendent, apocalyptic chaos.

God's postponement of doomsday does not mean that Dan 7 failed its original audience. In retrospect, what the audience experienced was a microcosm of the ultimate, apocalyptic scenario—a close brush with God's termination of history. In their crisis with Antiochus, apocalyptic chaos temporarily "boiled over" into earthly experience and prefigured history's final hour.

Daniel 7 gave its original audience a mirror to understand all this, the later preservers of the text surely reasoned. It illuminated the spiritual dimensions at play in that partial apocalyptic incursion of chaos into space/time. Preserved as canonical Scripture, the vision would likewise help future readers understand repeat experiences of miniature apocalypses.

Helge S. Kvanvig has aptly described how apocalyptic texts illuminate miniature eruptions of apocalyptic chaos in ordinary time. Arguing that history in apocalyptic thought is not so simple as a straight progression toward a goal, he offers an alternative metaphor. History, in the apocalyptic imagination, is better conceived as a track winding along a cliff. At certain wild turns, the track comes perilously close to the abyss. The reign of Antiochus was surely one such point. The course of history nearly careened its travelers over the edge of the abyss.

Kvanvig writes that in the apocalyptic imagination,

> History does not only move toward the end, it also moves along the end. . . . History is then colored by the signs of chaos. History is close to the end. But God intervenes in history in ordinary ways and makes it move away from the cliff again. At one particular time, however, history will turn over the edge. Then the real end time tribulations will break loose. . . . This means that all believers who through periods of tribulations have seen the signs of the end were not mistaken. The signs of the end were present. The mistake was done if they thought that they could, through these signs, calculate the time when the real end time battle would take place.[2]

Apocalyptic texts are not just about an ultimate fulfillment of the divine plan at the end of time. The rich, archetypal symbols of the literature give it a "spongy" quality, illuminating of preliminary, anticipatory fulfillments spaced throughout history. The literature thus proves elastic and applicable to changing times, to the fall and rise of leaders and state powers and to the varying challenges and threats confronting faithful readers and the world as a whole.

The hermeneutical notion that apocalyptic texts have a polyvalent quality, so that they are capable of ongoing fulfillment over the ages, is especially significant in forming useful, relevant interpretations and expositions. Even if they are *sure* that they are living far removed from the end of history, readers of the apocalyptic literature should not assume it lacks instruction for their world. They can read apocalyptic literature as a mirror for understanding their times and comprehending their full dimensions.

THEOLOGICAL CONTRIBUTIONS OF APOCALYPTIC TEXTS

The apocalyptic literature contributes a radical vision of salvation to theological reflection, challenging competing perceptions of the nature and goal of God's redeeming work. First, this literature rejects the widespread perception that salvation is individual and spiritual, focused on the fate of individual souls after death. Countering this narrow and spiritualizing view, it insists that God's saving goals encompass global human society, worldwide ecology, and even space/time reality. Rather than thinking of ethereal pearly gates, it asks readers to imagine earth's people joined on earth, sharing in a sumptuous banquet of juicy, rich food and pure, choice wines (Isa 25:6).

Second, the apocalyptic texts counter a liberal optimism that reduces God's program of salvation to the level of social work or etiquette training. Readers of the Bible in suburban, Western contexts often have a completely tame, insipid idea of salvation because they lack a sense of catastrophic crisis in local and global existence. They may recognize serious evils facing humanity, but often view them as surmountable challenges. For them, human resolve and effort at solution will eventually prove sufficient to tackle humankind's problems.

In his theological study of the book of Revelation, Jacques Ellul writes:

> We generally attempt in modern Christian milieus to validate history and the efforts of man, to diminish the decisive character of sin, to show the positive aspect of human achievements in politics, technique, work (fulfillment of the creation); we seek to attenuate the rigor of Christian morality and the presence of the Judgment; we yield to the optimistic logic of progress, and we live with the assurance of a progressive approximation of the Kingdom in history, not an end given by God, but work accomplished by humankind.[3]

The apocalyptic imagination sees things otherwise. It perceives a deeper catastrophe besetting humanity and describes a qualitatively more radical salvation than the anthropological perspective that Ellul summarizes.

Evil will persist—even increase—until history's conclusion (e.g., Dan 12:10) according to apocalyptic texts, but the end given by God will permanently wipe it out. God's ultimate salvation will set right all the outrageous evils of experience, from plagues to death camps, and will permanently halt poverty, racism, ethnic hatred, famine, and war on earth. At God's saving end, God even removes the veil of death that presently hangs over all humanity (e.g., 1 Cor 15:54-55).

The apocalyptic vision of salvation claims to be relevant for the here and now, as well as for the end times. It gives readers a "sense of an ending" to existence and history, assuring them that the life of faith has a satisfying conclusion despite appearances to the contrary. Envisioning the journey of God's people through history as a well-written novel, readers can reframe their frustrations and tragedies as mere episodes of puzzlement and suspense in what will prove ultimately to be a fascinatingly profound story with an illuminating conclusion.

I mentioned Ellul's claim that apocalyptic texts unveil the "mysterious riches" of the present as well as the drama of the end times. This claim reveals a further relevance of apocalyptic salvation for the here and now. Its saving vision puts readers in touch with transcendent reality as a dynamic, vibrant backdrop to the events of daily routine.

Eugene Peterson captures the same thought well. The apocalyptic literature (in this case, the book of Revelation) gave its first readers, Peterson argues, a new vision about the depth of meaning and drama of incident at stake in their lives.

> We must never forget that the pictures of wildly celebrative praise in heaven and catastrophic woes wreaked on earth, the exposure of evil in its hideous blasphemies and the revelation of goodness in its glorious adorations—that all this was made out of the stuff of their daily traffic. . . . In this heaven-penetrated, hell-threatened environment they lived their daily lives.[4]

Peterson speaks not only about salvation's glorious goodness but also about evil's "hideous blasphemies." He thus suggests another theological contribution of the apocalyptic literature: deep insight into the nature and threat of evil. Of all the varying viewpoints in the Bible's many texts, the apocalyptic literature is surely the most honest and serious about this dimension of experience.

The evil at stake in apocalyptic scenarios is often a transpersonal evil that masks itself as benign but quickly turns oppressive. It emerges in human systems and institutions as an invisible network of influences or an intoxicating spirit of camaraderie. It deludes and mesmerizes both the strong and the weak with its lies about life, false promises, and convincing proofs. Moving to oppress its victims, it then becomes blasphemous and demonic, even claiming dominion over humanity and the environment.

Any number of visible entities—including human institutions, governments, causes, and ideologies—may incarnate this type of invisible, oppressive reality, which takes on a spiritual life of its own transcending the reasoning of individuals. Isaiah 13 and Rev 17–18 name this evil power "Babylon." Flat-footed approaches of literalism reify Babylon as nothing but an ancient empire or a future world order. In reality, apocalyptic literature's critique of Babylon applies equally to present-day idolatrous cultures, hubristic ideologies, and imperial theologies.

As the power of Babylon swells, it may carry to prominence an individual hubristic tyrant, insolent and skilled in intrigue. The Bible's apocalyptic texts name this pretentious, deluded figure in different ways. He is the "worthless shepherd" (Zech 11:17), the "son of Dawn" (Isa 14:12), the boastful "little horn" (Dan 7:8), the "lawless one" (2 Thess 2:3), the "beast" (Rev 13:1-10). He functions as a false messiah, that is, an "antimessiah."

The apocalyptic literature takes evil with utmost seriousness, refusing to minimize the threat of the invisible systems of subjugation and the idolatrous, mind-numbing principalities of the world, or, indeed, of any of the other terrifying forces of chaos and mayhem in our experience. The terrifying monsters with multiple heads and horns in the apocalyptic texts cannot be mistaken for minor quirks and anomalies in the workings of existence. They are obvious terrors that demand honest recognition.

Although taking evil seriously, the apocalyptic imagination also reveals a grand solution to the problem of evil, with all its accompanying terror and horror. It contextualizes evil within a cosmic plan of God for all of existence. God's cosmic prerogative and divine timetable for history's end define the place of evil in the world and set a fixed time for its ultimate defeat. Because evil and chaos are often rampant, only *the wise*—those informed by the apocalyptic imagination—confidently know that God's cosmic timetable for earth's history takes evil fully into account.

Apocalypticism's promise of evil's ultimate defeat raises serious theological issues and problems, particularly the problem of understanding divine retribution and judgment. In the apocalyptic imagination, evil's downfall comes through a massive exercise of divine wrath, which takes on generalized, global proportions, jolting and disrupting human life and the natural environment (e.g., Matt 7:24-27; 24:36-39).

A search for understanding about God's apocalyptic wrath begins with tracing biblical cross-references. For starters, Revelation's wrathful trumpet and bowl judgments become intelligible in light of their echoing of the Egyptian plagues of the exodus. If the exodus is their governing paradigm, these disasters must mean a stop to oppression and a liberation of God's people, not gratuitous destruction and terror.

Again, when earth's people hide from the "wrath of the Lamb" in Rev 6:16-17, their question "Who is able to stand?" echoes key Hebrew prophetic texts. Cross-references in Amos 5:18-20; 7:2, 5; Joel 2:11; and Mal 3:2 help interpret the question through their combined witnesses to a profound theological burden. Despite all wishful thinking, the status quo cannot withstand the advent of transcendent reality on earth unscathed and will be able to experience it only as wrath. As Amos warns, most people have not thought through what God's tangible appearance would really mean for them: "Why do you want the day of the Lord? / It is darkness, not light" (Amos 5:18*bc*).

Or again, when Mark 13:8 speaks of wrathful, chaos-laden "birth pangs," it echoes a variety of mythic poems in the Bible where God engages primordial chaos in creation related work (e.g., Ps 29; Job 38). In mythic poetry, primordial chaos is God's needed construction material in birthing new creative order into existence.

The notion that a cosmic unraveling and release of chaos prepares for an awesome new creation of existence relates directly to a Christian theological concept termed the "paschal mystery."

This theological mystery turns on the paradox that full, new life sometimes comes only through an experience of radical death. First Corinthians 15:36 is one apocalyptic passage expressing the notion: "Fool! What you sow does not come to life unless it dies."

Readers completely abuse the apocalyptic mystery of 1 Cor 15 if they make it a death wish for creation or a cause for gloating over others' pending doom. Paul elsewhere argues that Christians themselves must die to their old selves, as symbolized by the rite of baptism (Rom 6:4-7). Paul's image of baptism helps clarify apocalyptic judgment: The waters of chaos and death engulf the person undergoing baptism, who then emerges alive to God as a new creation.

Everyone familiar with great mythic epics or masterpieces of fantasy knows what a cause of celebration even a preliminary wrathful destruction of the powers of evil in existence can be. A scene from J. R. R. Tolkien's *The Two Towers,* the second book of *The Lord of the Rings* trilogy, may serve as an example.[5]

A proud host of monstrous Orcs and wild Half-orcs—soldiers of the evil wizard Saruman—has marched forth to conquer and burn neighboring, peaceable lands. Final victory comes within their grasp at an Armageddon-like battle at Helm's Deep. Suddenly, however, fear and wonder fall upon them. Rushing back through a valley, they pack it like swarming flies.

"Upon a ridge appeared a rider, clad in white, shining in the rising sun." It is the good wizard, Gandalf, a messianic figure. "The White Rider was upon them, and the terror of his coming filled the enemy with madness." In a state of sheer terror, the Orcs dropped their swords and spears and fled "like a black smoke driven by a mounting wind."

The scene evokes a reaction of joy and victory among the protagonists, a reaction which the reader shares also. The action plot of the narrative leaves no doubt that the Orcs' destruction is cause for pure celebration. They represent an ominous force of chaos and destruction in the world. Their continued existence would lead to tremendous ruin and suffering.

Our reaction as readers moves from a sense of relief and joy to a sense of awe in contemplating the Orcs' demise. Their defeat and complete destruction comes supernaturally, apart from human agency, and, between the lines of the book, suggests something of God's power, purpose, and perspective.

APOCALYPTIC TEXTS AND LIBERATION

In recent decades, the apocalyptic literature of the Bible has attracted the attention and close study of scholars oriented on liberation, including liberation of women, the poor, and the natural environment.[6] Scholars with this focus have done well to latch on to apocalyptic texts, for they are a golden theological resource on this area, revealing much about God's concern for liberation on earth.

The apocalyptic vision of the reign of God largely defines salvation in social and political terms rather than in individualistic and spiritual terms. Far from an ethereal realm populated by angels and human souls, God's coming reign, according to the apocalyptic imagination, entails heaven's expression as a visible, concrete reality here on earth. When realized, it will mean a tangible renewal of human government, economics, culture, and society. All God's people from all history's eras will gather into a community of living, embodied persons characterized by complete political and economic justice.

Isaiah 61 provides one good example of apocalypticism's core emphasis on reversing oppressive economic and social conditions. It proclaims a coming "favorable year" of liberation alongside a divine "day of vengeance" (v. 2). The "favorable year" is divine salvation envisioned as a biblical year of Jubilee, when all land was supposed to revert to its original owners and all slaves to their families. The phrase "proclaim liberty" in verse 1 of Isa 61 is the same diction used in Lev 25:10, where a Jubilee time of concrete, economic release is stipulated to occur every fiftieth year in Israel.

Salvation in the apocalyptic imagination also means ecological liberation. This perspective often gets lost, especially since popular Christian writers repeatedly call attention to an apocalyptic rapture that snatches the faithful away from the earth, abandoning it to disaster. Visualized in this way, apocalypticism appears to disparage nature. The impression is completely distorted. The apocalyptic imagination of the Bible moves in the opposite direction, emphasizing a "rapturing" of transcendent paradise down to the terrestrial plane.

I mentioned earlier the recurring apocalyptic image of a river of paradise irrigating God's renewed earth. Joel 3:18, Zech 14:8, and Rev 22:1 all use this image to emphasize God's apocalyptic design of positive environmental transformation. Apocalyptic texts characteristically draw on mythological images of Eden such as this to drive home that salvation entails an ideal relationship between humanity and the natural environment.

The ideal vision for society and the environment of apocalyptic texts represents a quantum leap beyond current conditions, offering a "competing vision" of how life might be lived. Human beings' present relationships with one another and with nature fall radically short of their ideal state in God's reign. Reading the apocalyptic texts of the Bible highlights this disparity, providing an implicit critique of the status quo.

Further leverage for social and political critique comes out of apocalyptic literature's insight into evil, especially transpersonal evil. Such evil reaches critical mass only at the end of days, but it also has preliminary incarnations throughout history. It could be present today in modern North America, for example, when blind consumerism wreaks havoc on the environment, when systematic bullying in public schools boomerangs in violent retaliation, or when embedded racism lands a disproportionate number of African Americans on death row.

Ward Ewing aptly notes how Revelation's insight into transpersonal, systemic evil provides grounds for critiquing the United States' foreign relations. The spirit of the "beast" of the Apocalypse appears not only in the Pax Romana of Revelation's milieu but also in our contemporary Pax Americana.

> Consider the spirit of America. As a nation we often desire to be number one, not one among equals. In our pride, at times we impose our will on other countries by military or economic force instead of seeking a common good through negotiation, dialogue and respectful nurturing. To achieve our own goals of security and material prosperity, we form alliances with all sorts of foreign governments, including oppressive dictatorships.[7]

Given society's present failings, social action and resistance would seem the most appropriate real-life application of apocalypticism's alternative vision of reality. In dreams begins responsibility. This is the stance of liberation-minded interpreters, at any rate, who reject arguments that apocalyptic rhetoric is "consolation language" at best and an excuse for passivity at worst.

Apocalyptic beliefs are no reason for apathy and inaction. Furthermore, they do not function merely as an opiate, that is, as psychological compensation for the oppressed and persecuted.

If in the apocalyptic imagination true justice is only a coming, postapocalyptic reality, the need for activism in the present at first does appear questionable. After all, only a thunderous intervention of heaven will suffice to set things right on earth. The goal of God's apocalyptic intervention, however, is the fruition of ideals long embedded in biblical tradition. What God realizes fully in the future is what would bring humanity the most fulfillment in the here and now. According to the apocalyptic imagination, it would be counterintuitive not to agitate for as much of this ethic and lifestyle in the present as possible.

Similar reflections correct the notion that apocalypticism reduces ethics to self-serving behavior in the face of imminent divine judgment. Apocalyptic judgment is less about each soul's "just desserts" than about a climactic Jubilee, which transforms human life in community. The apocalyptic Jubilee, our literature asserts, will be a time for people to restore and respect each other's dignity and full humanity. Rather than reap rewards at the eschaton, readers should expect to abandon selfishness and reorient their desires.

Apocalyptic visions make sense of life and help compose and orient readers, but their impetus is outward, toward witness and involvement, not inward, toward comfort and sedation. Theories of psychological compensation and emotional catharsis risk missing apocalypticism's action imperatives. In the book of Zechariah, expectations of God's reign on earth call for concrete action and sacrifice, putting aside personal goals to focus on God's work of rebuilding Jerusalem's temple (Zech 1:16; 4:9). At a later time, visions of doomsday prompt a call from the prophet Joel to drop everything and gather the community for lamentation at the temple: "Blow the trumpet in Zion; / sanctify a fast; / call a solemn assembly" (Joel 2:15).

Although only God can fully defeat the forces of Armageddon, apocalyptic texts understand them to be present in daily life already in preliminary form. Given their insidious, mesmerizing nature, the apocalyptic literature calls its readers to discernment and proactive social intervention. Even great sacrifice and heroic, life-risking action may be necessary (e.g., Dan 3:17-18).

That is what the book of Revelation means with its repeated summons for the reader to be a "conqueror" (e.g., Rev 2:7, 11, 17, 26; 21:7). The Apocalypse summons each member of John's churches to stick his or her neck out to a dangerous, even deadly, extent.[8]

CHAPTER 4

THE SOCIAL WORLDS BEHIND THE APOCALYPTIC LITERATURE

The visionary and symbolic language of apocalyptic literature presents a special challenge to uncovering its circumstances of composition. Literary characters—"Isaiah" and "Daniel"—proclaim the visions of Isa 24 and Dan 7, not historical figures. The identities of the actual authors are veiled. Apocalyptic texts typically also blur clues to their original settings. When the first authors of Isa 24:10 and Dan 7:7 spoke of "the city of chaos" and "a fourth beast," they doubtless envisaged specific instantiations of these transcendent symbols. However, they did not pass this specific historical information on to later readers.

Despite the paucity of historical controls, the fantastic images and radical expectations of apocalyptic texts have provoked various scholarly reconstructions of their origins. There have been many false leads. Hard evidence, mentioned in the preceding chapters, contradicts commonplace attempts to "explain" apocalyptic literature based on a divide between the powerless and the powerful or an influx of Persian religion into early Judaism.

Some apocalyptic groups do emerge, or at least land, at society's fringe and, at points, foreign (Mesopotamian and Persian) traditions did influence apocalyptic literature's development. These accidental facts do not fit many apocalyptic texts, however. Biblical apocalyptic literature often betrays the hands of central, power-holding authors. Most apocalyptic texts of the Bible display strong continuities with authentic Israelite traditions.

In recent years, new scrutiny of the biblical texts combined with methods and data from the social sciences has yielded improved, more critical understandings of the concrete milieus of apocalypticism. The observations of social scientists (noted earlier) about "millennial groups," which display radical, deviant beliefs parallel to biblical apocalyptic texts, have been of decisive assistance. Occurring across many cultures, millennial groups have distinct religious plans and programs and characteristic ways of organizing their life and interacting with society. Study of these groups provides biblical interpreters with illuminating social-scientific models that fit the data of the Bible's apocalyptic literature.

THE RISE OF APOCALYPTIC GROUPS

Social scientists concur that apocalypticism, at least in its origins, is a group phenomenon, not the idiosyncratic thinking of isolated individuals. Apocalyptic belief presupposes a network of like-minded adherents, a millennial group. In the social-scientific sense, the terms *millennialism* and *millennial group* refer to the social dimensions of apocalypticism, what is happening "on the ground" behind the apocalyptic imagination.

The argument for speaking of groups—not mere individuals—behind apocalyptic ideas and texts is tightly bound up with the observation that apocalypticism is a worldview—what sociologists call a symbolic universe, sheltering canopy, or plausibility structure. A symbolic universe is an overarching constellation of meaning, which lends credence and justification to the lifestyle entailed in belonging to a given social world.

The particular symbolic universe of apocalypticism sharply distinguishes between celestial and earthly reality, perceives a radical divide between cosmic forces of good and evil, and expects an imminent, supernatural advent of a glorious new era.

Initially, isolated individuals can be catalysts for such symbolic thinking, but an entire new "sheltering canopy" soon needs supporting social structures. A symbolic universe is something that a group of people must actively maintain.

Group life makes a new symbolic universe convincing to people by explicitly linking it to patterns of group behavior. As new converts join an esoteric group, a process of socialization incorporates its beliefs and social patterns into their daily lives. Ongoing life in association with group members actively and powerfully reinforces these communal perceptions and patterns. The community's symbolic imagination appears ever more inevitable to adherents, who may eventually become ready to die for it.

There are some caveats to this general picture.[1] First, although various authors have defined *millennialism* in rather specific and elaborate ways, I intend the term only to designate the social dimension of apocalypticism. Millennialism need not involve a mass movement, a religion of the oppressed, or an armed rebellion, as presupposed in some scholars' definitions. The term *millennial* is an adjective for a social phenomenon, parallel to the adjective *apocalyptic,* which applies to a literary genre and a worldview.

Second, over time apocalyptic ideas and language became increasingly widespread and diffuse within early Judaism. As apocalyptic thoughts captured the imaginations of more people, apocalyptic writing and thinking released its moorings in insular, tight-knit groups. Thus, numerous Jews in the Second Temple period maintained a generalized apocalyptic worldview without belonging to a defined millennial group or movement. (Even then, of course, apocalypticism remained a group phenomenon in the sense that many people, not just isolated individuals, believed in it.)

Social-scientific evidence garnered by ethnographers helps us envision the origins of millennial groups in Israel. As noted in chapter 1, a group's thought world moves in apocalyptic directions as its traditional images, values, and aspirations reconfigure into a new, eschatologically charged vision of reality. As one might almost predict, the traditional creation mythology of the group provides key building blocks forming the new world vision. Mythology's concern with "protology" mirrors apocalypticism's focus on "eschatology."

Mythical episodes often stand outside history, describing the fabled primordial time of beginnings (protology). Apocalyptic eschatology, in a parallel manner, also transcends history's venue. It envisions history headed for a massive collision with a celestial realm, which stands ontologically distinct from it and sovereign over it. As the collision nears, the celestial, archetypal realm becomes increasingly concrete and visible. Heaven's impact is felt universally and incontestably, and ushers in a permanent reign of God among humanity.

The course of human history is no longer the arena of God's saving work in apocalyptic literature, as it is in all standard biblical genres, including stories, prophecies, psalms, and wisdom sayings. Rather, the coming collision between the realms of earth and heaven terminates history. Only then can God begin the re-creative work of setting creation right and establishing paradise on earth.

Vibrant mythology reappears in the apocalyptic imagination, but transformed in three key ways. First, in apocalypticism, mythic images are newly revealed. They come to consciousness not through stories retold repeatedly in culture, but through unique heavenly visions or portents. They build up a new plausibility structure, which deviates from what is given and is usually taken for granted in the social order.

Second, mythic images no longer undergird and legitimize general human experience in their new apocalyptic role. Rather, they emerge at the end of history as constituent elements of the end-time drama and the transformation of the cosmos. In some apocalyptic texts, dramatic players in earth's final hour transparently reflect mythic prototypes. In others, mythic imagery becomes concrete in human experience, able to engage humanity realistically and directly.

Third, as it envisions mythology (with all of its "binary oppositions") becoming concrete and eschatological, the apocalyptic imagination increasingly perceives things in terms of dualisms. The ambiguities of normal existence recede into the background, as an all-illumining light is cast on everything. In the glare of this light, evil shows its true colors, polarized against all forces for good. Humanity fissions into irreconcilable opposites: goats versus sheep, weeds versus crops, the foolish versus the wise. The present era reveals its innate spiritual catastrophe, falling hopelessly short of the ideal, God-centered life of the age to come.

The normal course of terrestrial history unfolds in shades of gray, but the apocalyptic imagination reveals a transcendent backdrop to this process where all is painted in the absolute, mythic colors of black and white. Transcendental forces shaping reality are so embedded in human structures that most people are largely ignorant of their existence. The apocalyptic imagination, however, arises as a mirror revealing in full, schematic clarity all that enslaves and annihilates human beings. It shows the full dimensions of the forces at work amid humanity to oppose salvation, which heaven will shortly intervene on earth to destroy.

Helge S. Kvanvig puts it this way:

> What separates the apocalyptical literature from the earlier Old Testament traditions is the adoption of the dual perception of reality found in the myths. . . . The crisis in reality is no longer seen as a crisis begun and ended in this world, but ultimately brought about through the intervention of divine beings, and solved through the destruction of these beings. This is exemplified by the demonic kings and kingdoms in the Book of Daniel fighting against the holy ones.[2]

VARIOUS BIBLICAL TEXTS, VARIOUS APOCALYPTIC GROUPS

The apocalyptic transformation of traditional ideals and mythic images can occur in a wide variety of groups under multiple sets of circumstances. Even groups in power, who do not feel resentment like those in a setting of deprivation, are live candidates.[3] A group need only to bear traditions that express a profound sense of hope, traditions open to an ideal, transcendent reality.

The apocalyptic imagination of biblical texts does not supply hope in its absence, but derives from a profound apprehension of hope. It expresses a stubborn refusal to accept mundane, banal reality as hope's fulfillment. So much more seems promised by the innate witness of such symbols as prophecies of old and liturgies at Jerusalem's temple.

A potential millennial group must be minimally predisposed, in that members must have a notion of the forward movement of history and believe in a transcendent God capable of intervening in human affairs. The various groups behind the writings of the

Bible all share this predisposition. Beyond this, various external circumstances and events often further predispose apocalypticism's development. Milieus where events contradict expectations or where things seem unstable provide especially fertile conditions. At such times, a new worldview helps explain things: why things seem out of kilter, why God's reign seems so distant, or why human efforts at improving life appear stalled or thwarted.

Social scientists have observed that an influential figure, such as a visionary, a teacher, or a preacher, is often a catalyst in the rise of millennial groups. Such a figure may be especially familiar with the traditions and writings of the group, and helps bring them to focus in a new world vision. He or she often seizes upon the ancient myths of the group, projecting them into the end time and the ideal future beyond history.

In some cases, the catalytic element in millennialism's development is not the rise of a human leader but the discovery of a powerful literary work or the occurrence of an awesome portent in nature. Alternatively, reports of supernatural events or the arrival of a messiah on earth may be what stimulates a group's new apocalyptic imagination.

If a human figure is a catalyst of millennialism, he or she may come from any number of roles within society. These figures are sometimes malcontents and rebels, but certainly not always. Often they are societal leaders, as when Native American chiefs, such as Sitting Bull and Smohalla, promulgated the apocalyptic Ghost Dance. At other times, wealthy nobles, bureaucrats, and civic reformers have instigated the rise of new millennial groups. Even central priests in society have been catalyst figures in the rise of millennialism. Examples include Savonarola in fifteenth-century Florence, Mendieta in sixteenth-century New Spain, and Te Ua in nineteenth-century New Zealand.

If a catalyst figure has helped organize a millennial group, he or she may continue as its leader or principal teacher. An inner clique of special disciples may surround him or her, helping to instruct and manage an outer group of followers. The group may grow as new members join through processes of induction and initiation.

Millennial groups use varying means to secure the commitment of new initiates, sometimes requiring them to sell possessions or break away from prior personal relationships. These requirements help solidify a worldview of imminent cosmic upheaval—a conviction that the present world is passing away along with its dominant forms and networks.

As time goes on, the overall character, leadership, and composition of millennial groups may change. Tensions and conflicts sometimes strain a group's inner harmony so that factions split off or leaders are overthrown. A millennial group's expectations and behaviors may diminish or intensify, sometimes altering its relationships to external society.

If time disconfirms specific apocalyptic expectations, a group's membership may dwindle and its activities become routine. Alternatively, if conditions are favorable in a society, the worldview of a circumscribed millennial group can spread to become the basis of a mass movement. Rich and powerful members of the group may or may not choose to leave under such circumstances.

Millennial groups organize a way of life and a program for action in response to the goals of their apocalyptic vision and their understanding of God's blueprint for realizing those goals.[4] They develop practical plans for living in the final days of the universe, which may be either passive or active. A passive program focuses mainly on organizing the inner life of the group. An active program organizes collective preparations for the end times, such as the stockpiling of supplies or the construction of rafts, shelters, or bunkers. Collective action sometimes aims to jump-start apocalyptic events, using such means as special rituals or even the taking up of arms.

A cross-cultural survey reveals that millennial groups may occupy a variety of social locations.[5] Some millennial groups arise within power-holding sectors of society. They operate within central institutions, which maintain traditional values and uphold the social and political order. The apocalyptic Prophet Dance movement, organized by the chiefs of the Coast Salish tribes of Canada, is one example. Another is the Irvingite Catholic Apostolic Church of nineteenth-century Britain, whose leaders were aristocrats and members of Parliament. Members of such groups may use central power and authority to rally society around their leadership during apocalyptic scares, when dooms-day feels near.

Other millennial groups operate at society's fringe. Society's dominant culture views them as "doomsday cults," which threaten social stability. In medieval Europe, the poor and the destitute sometimes massed together to flog themselves in expectation of a sudden, apocalyptic judgment. In modern times, fringe sects make the news when they offer predictions of Armageddon or engage in extreme behaviors. Two publicized examples from the 1990s are the Hyoo-go movement in Korea and the Order of the Solar Temple in Switzerland and Canada.

Times when two cultures come into contact and conflict may be especially ripe for apocalypticism's development. Under such conditions, millennial groups may appear on either side of the conflict. In other words, millennialism may be as much the religion of oppressors as it is of the oppressed.

When millennialism arises on the side of an elite, expansionist society, it may justify efforts to colonize other peoples. Too often, western colonizers have put Christian apocalypticism to this sad misuse. Colluding with the Spanish monarchy, millennial Franciscan groups took part in Spain's sixteenth-century conquests in America. Apocalyptically oriented missionaries worked to subdue and convert American natives ("pagans"), so that God would allow the end times to begin. An apocalyptic program of preparing earth for the reign of God also drove English Puritan colonization of North America in the seventeenth century. For the Puritan clergy, coming to the New World and establishing a model society was a means to usher in the world to come.

Millennialism is sometimes a religion of imperialism, but at other times, it is a worldview of dominated or colonized peoples. The 1870 apocalyptic Ghost Dance movement, for example, arose within a dominated Native American culture, on the periphery of North American society. Blaming European Americans for the breakdown of traditional Paiute culture, the earliest Ghost Dance religion specifically targeted "whites" for judgment in an imminent huge earthquake.

Within cultures under alien domination, apocalypticism may nonetheless be a "central," establishment worldview if the indigenous society's leadership embraces it. Thus, millennialism had a central influence in Florentine politics and policy amidst a fifteenth-century military crisis with invading French armies. In parallel manner, the apocalyptic "cargo cults" of twentieth-century Melanesia often performed central social functions amid the pressures of western colonization. The leaders of such millennial cults were usually "big men," having high social status.

Clearly, millennial groups may arise amid a variety of possible external milieus. Interpreters must not force the apocalyptic literature of the Bible into one narrow mold, such as "consolation literature," "resistance texts," or "crisis genre." Rather, readers should be willing to follow the evidence of an apocalyptic writing about its social context and authorship, even if this evidence points to authors within establishment, priestly, or bureaucratic ranks. Rather than assuming a factious conflict behind all apocalyptic texts, readers should consider alternative scenarios in which millennialism supports central institutions and unites competing groups.

PART TWO

READING THE APOCALYPTIC TEXTS OF THE BIBLE

CHAPTER 5

EARLY APOCALYPTIC TEXTS AMONG THE PROPHETIC BOOKS

Mention *apocalypse* and scholars of the Hebrew Bible think of Daniel, but several earlier Scriptures also betray some form of apocalyptic imagination. Historical critics of the Bible saw this as early as the nineteenth century. In his commentary on Isaiah in 1892, for example, Bernhard Duhm noted that the author of Isa 24–27 could as well have written Daniel.

The biblical literature resembling Daniel and other apocalypses emerges starting in the Babylonian exile and the Persian-era restoration. The best examples are late prophetic texts in Ezekiel, Zechariah, Joel, Isaiah, and Malachi. In what follows, I survey these texts. In some cases, such as Zechariah, an apocalyptic imagination pervades almost the entire book. In others, such as Isaiah and Ezekiel, apocalyptic ideas and expectations come up only in specific sections.

I make no claim that prophetic writings in books such as Joel and Malachi are full-blown "apocalypses." Many of these eschatological texts lack the formal literary motifs and genre features found in later Hellenistic writings such as Daniel and *1 Enoch*. The regularities and accepted markers of the later literature only developed with time. For this reason, scholars have found it hard to agree on whether, and in what sense, the writings examined in this chapter are indeed apocalyptic. Despite the confusion and lack of consensus, the label "early apocalyptic," or "protoapocalyptic," is appropriate here.

The presence of Hellenistic genre features should not be the deciding factor in identifying an apocalyptic perspective in texts. As argued in part 1 of this volume, a new symbolic universe that appears apocalyptic arose and developed in Israel long before the advent of the recognized characteristics of the Hellenistic apocalypses. Some Persian-period Israelite texts exhibit this burgeoning new perceptual framework, with its radical concerns and orientations differing from standard Israelite prophecy. A focus on perceptions and scope, rather than on formal features that may convey them, allows me to apply a broad concept of apocalypticism in discussing some late biblical prophecy under the rubric of this chapter.

No ultimate essence or fixed motifs characterize the Persian-period apocalyptic writings. However, to use Ludwig Wittgenstein's terminology, they do bear an undeniable "family resemblance" to each other and to later, full-blown apocalypses. Their new apocalyptic imagination gropes to unveil transcendent reality, including celestial glory and terrestrial evil. It sees history approaching a crisis when the powers of heaven will intervene on earth with universal, incontestable consequences. It claims a new eon is coming, which appears otherworldly in comparison to life as readers now know it. In this new eon, mythological ideals of international and environmental harmony will become tangibly real on the planet.

As noted in the previous section, under the right conditions, an apocalyptic worldview can arise in any group. At various points in human history, groups of aristocrats, sages, priests, nuns, monks, and laborers have developed an apocalyptic imagination. The exact form and coloring of their new symbolic universe varies, depending on the group's specific traditions and their nostalgic image of the ideal past.

As it happens, all of the apocalyptic prophets to be examined in this section were also priests, or at least close associates of priests. In fact, they were members of three distinct priestly lines in ancient Israel, often at odds with one another. How we know will become clear as we proceed. What matters for now is that our visionaries' membership in different priestly lineages provides a convenient way of organizing our discussion.

The first three bodies of apocalyptic literature—texts from Ezekiel, Zechariah, and Joel—were written by "Zadokite" priests. Their apocalyptic worldview builds especially on the traditions of the Holiness Source of the Pentateuch. Next, texts within the prophetic collection of Isaiah authored by "Aaronide" priests are treated. The apocalyptic imagination here builds on the Psalms and the Priestly Source of the Pentateuch. Finally, the book of Malachi comes from the Levitical tribe of priests. Malachi's traditions are akin to those of the book of Deuteronomy.

A few introductory words about these priestly lineages are in order.

Zadokite priests, by the time of the writing of the Bible's early apocalyptic texts, were those controlling the Israelite chief priesthood and supervising other priests at Jerusalem. We know this based on the identities and genealogies of restoration leaders, who returned to Judah from Babylonian exile. Zadokite priests traced descent back to Zadok, one of King David's two chief priests (2 Sam 8:17).

The priestly line of the Zadokites was a subsection of a larger family of priests tracing decent to Aaron. Priests within this larger family are Aaronides. While some biblical writings highlight the Zadokites, others speak of Aaronides as Israel's basic group of clerics with rights to sacrifice at the temple. The book of Malachi (Mal 3:3), with other late traditions of the Bible, views Aaronide priests as members of the wider circle of the "descendants of Levi."

The Levites are a third descent-group of priests, members of the tribe of Levi. Some major biblical sources describe the Levites as a minor clergy, with no altar rights. Other biblical texts downplay distinctions between the Levites and other priestly lines.

Under King David, the Levites had a chief priest, Abiathar, representing them in Jerusalem alongside Zadok. Abiathar came into conflict with David's son Solomon, however, and was dismissed from service in Jerusalem (1 Kgs 2:26-27).

SELECTED TEXTS WITHIN EZEKIEL

The Bible's reports about the prophet Ezekiel have long disturbed and awed readers. God breaches Ezekiel's earthly experience, seizing control of the prophet's speech and actions. At God's mercy, the spirit transports Ezekiel up and down the Fertile Crescent and backward and forward in time. In the process, he witnesses God's unveiling of Israel's core corruption and God's powerful plans to set things right. Most significantly, Ezekiel's visionary gaze penetrates beyond that of other mortals to glimpse the dangerous glory of God's very presence.

Ezekiel and the editors of his book lived in a momentous era during the sixth century B.C.E., when the Babylonian empire was destroying and exiling Judah. The Babylonian ruler Nebuchadnezzar II expatriated an initial group of Judahites in 597 B.C.E., and destroyed Jerusalem a decade later. These were pivotal times religiously, as well as politically. Old forms of religious expression were vanishing, while new literary and scribal modes of religion began to flower. One burgeoning new mode of religious life revolved around the advent of written Scripture.

Adapting to life in Babylonian exile after 597 B.C.E., Ezekiel and his group pioneered a new, scribal mode of religious existence and prophetic activity. Instead of working primarily with group memory and oral tradition, they focused on studying theological precepts preserved in writing. They replaced spoken prophetic announcements of God's Word with literary artistry as their primary medium of prophetic communication.

The religious and prophetic shift toward scribalism in Ezekiel's time helps explain the Bible's complicated portrayal of the prophet. Ezekiel's behavior—such as his incapacity at speech for half the book—makes for confusing literal autobiography. Ezekiel's odd and complex activities make for quite meaningful reading, however, if approached as careful artwork, as literary and metaphorical illustration. The book's abstract, literary portrait of Ezekiel presents his whole life as a prophetic and theological message.

Ezekiel's many apocalyptic qualities might first appear obvious. He is preoccupied with the celestial and divine, developing images of the transcendent that became foundational in later, full-blown apocalyptic writings. Ezekiel's cosmic-sized tree, with its top in the clouds (Ezek 31), and his set of four living creatures guarding God's throne (Ezek 1:4-14) reappear in Daniel and Revelation respectively. Today's popular accounts of the end-time battle of Armageddon regularly refer to Ezek 38–39 and its prophecy of Gog's future invasion of Israel. The core of this vision, at least, probably goes back to the exilic period and Ezekiel himself.

It is significant to find these signs of nascent apocalypticism as early as Ezekiel, around 593 to 571 B.C.E. during the Babylonian exile. Ezekiel and his immediate followers recorded their texts well before the time of other apocalyptic writings, such as those in Zechariah, Joel, and Daniel. Yet, with few exceptions, modern scholars have overlooked Ezekiel's role as the earliest known apocalyptic visionary in Israel.

Part of the problem has been Ezekiel's role as a central priest of his society. Many modern scholars think of priests as traditionalists and guardians of the status quo. They find it hard to imagine them prophesying about God overturning the present world. Ethnographic and cross-cultural studies of central priests in many cultures, however, show that they are fully capable of an apocalyptic imagination.

Ezekiel was a priest by birth (Ezek 1:3), associated with upper-echelon clerics in charge at the Jerusalem temple—the Zadokites. When the Babylonians picked deportees, such as Ezekiel, to exile from Jerusalem in 597 B.C.E., they chose from among the cream of society. The Zadokites were the first priests on their list, taking their place alongside other prominent Judahite deportees.

The way Ezekiel's book highlights the Zadokites assures us he was among their number (cf. Ezek 44:15-16). The many priestly concerns in his writings provide confirmation. Among these are concerns about purity and holiness (e.g., Ezek 4:14; 18:6; 20:12; 36:25; 43:7-9, 12). These concerns even dominate the increasingly apocalyptic sections of the book.

The cultic purity of Israel's land is a huge concern after God slays the apocalyptic army of Gog of Magog. According to Ezek 39:11-16, Israel devotes seven months of work and commissions a professional group of investigators to bury Gog's evil horde and cleanse the land. The short section uses the Hebrew term for ceremonial cleansing three times (vv. 12, 14, 16).

Ezekiel's preoccupation with the land's purity comes straight from sacral traditions of the Zadokite priests now preserved in one of the sources of the Pentateuch known as the Holiness Source.[1] The Holiness Source conceives of the entire country of Israel as God's sacred dwelling place, which the people must keep ceremonially and ethically clean. One text of the source states, "You shall not defile the land in which you live, in which I also dwell; for I the LORD dwell among the Israelites" (Num 35:34). The presence of corpses is a particular source of the land's defilement (see the Holiness texts of Lev 22:1-9 and Num 5:2-3).

Since Ezekiel and his followers were Zadokite priests from Jerusalem's temple establishment, they were well educated and thoroughly familiar with Israelite and general Near Eastern lore and mythic poetry. Ezekiel's priestly, cosmopolitan training strongly informs the literary character of his book, which frequently uses rich metaphors and mythic images to portray and interpret the times.[2]

Metaphors and mythic archetypes are particularly prominent in Ezekiel's oracles against the foreign nations (Ezek 25–32), where he blasts the inner character of Israel's international enemies. Using mythic paradigms to paint the true colors of Israel's enemies allowed Ezekiel to justify their judgment. He could not hold them responsible for obeying God's unique covenant with his own nation, but they could surely see how closely they mirrored widespread mythic paradigms of narcissism, hubris, and self-destruction.

Ezekiel's priestly and scribal affinity for myths and archetypes strongly predisposed him toward apocalyptic thinking. Ever since the work of Hermann Gunkel (1895), scholars have recognized the central place in apocalypticism's rise of imagery and discourse from ancient Near Eastern myth.[3] Gunkel demonstrated in particular how the Near Eastern mythology of the gods' creation of the universe out of watery chaos played a pivotal role in early Jewish and Christian apocalyptic writings.

The apocalyptic imagination draws heavily on the primordial images of mythology to build its picture of the end times, especially its idea of a resurgence of primeval chaos followed by God's new creation. One can even define *apocalypticism* accurately as creation myth metamorphosed to focus on creation's end and rebirth. Thus, D. E. Aune states, "[Apocalyptic] eschatology is a

96

mythical mode of understanding the complete realization of sal-vation as a *future* event."[4]

An illustration from the oracle against Egypt in Ezek 31 shows how Ezekiel's use of mythological symbols often borders on apoc-alyptic thinking. In Ezek 31, the prophet describes the hubris and downfall of world superpowers using the image of the "cosmic tree." Orientalists and ethnographers have observed the cosmic-tree image in many cultures, where it is an archetypal symbol of creation and world order.

Nourished by the mythological waters of creation, Ezekiel's cosmic tree towers above the clouds (vv. 3-4). It shelters all great nations as well as earth's birds and animals under its shade (vv. 6, 17). God has it cut down, however, due to its haughty loftiness. Once felled, its branches fall on earth's mountains and valleys (v. 12) while all the nations quake (v. 16).

Like later apocalyptic texts, Ezek 31 describes God structuring earthly existence in a fixed way. God presets reality along the lines of the cosmic tree, so that human hubris inevitably, auto-matically, brings a mighty downfall. Ezekiel 31 approaches an apocalyptic type of determinism.

Ezekiel 31 further resembles later apocalypticism in its dual-ism. The cosmic tree is a transcendent model, which Ezekiel depicts controlling the nations and events of history. Picturing hubristic nations, such as Assyria and Egypt, as reflexes of a cos-mic model, he reduces them to mere shadows of an archetype that molds their fate. Later apocalyptic texts commonly picture earthly realities mirroring heavenly archetypes in this way (e.g., Dan 7; 10:20).

Ezekiel 31 falls short of apocalypticism, however, in that it never describes the cosmic tree taking physical form and actually invading the historical plane of reality. In later apocalyptic texts, mythological forms become physical realities on earth (e.g., Dan 4:13-14). In Ezek 31, by contrast, heaven's supernatural interven-tion in history is unnecessary. Historical figures, such as Nabopolassar ("the prince of the nations," v. 11), unknowingly fulfill heaven's dictates.

Other mythological texts in Ezekiel go beyond Ezek 31, cross-ing the line into apocalyptic thinking. The oracles of Ezek 38–39 provide the best examples. In these oracles, mythology takes on realistic form at earth's final, cataclysmic battle.

In the end times, according to Ezek 38–39, earth's superpowers mass against Mount Zion. They advance like a storm, like a cloud covering the land. God's people dwell securely and peaceably, unaware of any threat. They are back in their land, having experienced God's reversal of the many wrongs that led to their punishment and exile. God, however, has not yet reversed Nebuchadnezzar's sack of Jerusalem and the temple. Now is God's chance, for the armies of Magog and its allies form a surrogate for Babylon—indeed, for all God's enemies.

The dark hordes of Gog are completely ignorant of what they are facing in attacking Mount Zion. In Ezekiel's end-time war, Jerusalem physically becomes the mythological, transcendent cosmic mountain.

The mythical archetype of a cosmic mountain is widespread. It is common in the myths and legends of world cultures in general and of Near Easterners in particular. It is the axis point of the world, where earth and heaven intersect. The gods meet in council there, amid lush gardens, shining stones, and freshwater springs that issue forth rivers irrigating the world. The image was well known to Zadokite priests (cf. Ezek 28:13-14; 47:1-12; Ps 46:4-7; Zech 14:8-9).

In the end times, according to Ezek 38–39, Mount Zion becomes a physical, realistic cosmic mountain. It forms a cosmic center, at earth's "navel" (Ezek 38:12). It rises atop a mountainous land, personally possessed by God (38:21).

Mount Zion is supernaturally fortified. Attempting combat within its highlands disorients the enemy, whose swords turn "against their comrades." God is prepared to defend the holy mountain with "pestilence and bloodshed," with "torrential rains and hailstones, fire and sulfur" (38:21-22).

Zion upholds cosmic order and puts down mayhem and chaos. When Gog of Magog attacks Zion, all earth's foundations shake, and the world reverts to precreation chaos. "The mountains shall be thrown down," according to Ezek 38:20, "and the cliffs shall fall, and every wall shall tumble to the ground." Miraculously, God's people wait safely amid all the havoc. They need only to be still and know that God will defend the holy mountain. God will display God's holiness in the eyes of the entire world (Ezek 38:23).

A canonical approach to this section of Scripture will not fail to notice the summary verses of Ezek 39:21-29, which the Bible appends to Ezekiel's apocalypse. Adding this summary helps the reader put the radical fervor of Ezekiel's apocalyptic prophecies into a long-term perspective. It focuses the reader's attention away from end-time battles and onto the preceding era of history, when God restores God's people to faithful living. In light of God's future salvation, God's people should live securely in the here and now (v. 26). They should reflect God's holiness (v. 27) and know God's grace (v. 28).

Ethnographers and other social scientists have described several cases of priestly apocalypticism that illuminate the social background of Ezekiel's end-time visions. As in Ezekiel's case, society's central priesthood played a leading role in the apocalyptic Mamaia cult in Polynesia. Their priestly apocalyptic program centered on worship at the traditional sanctuary of Opoa, and on revitalizing traditional cult rituals and traditions.

In another case, in the southern Sudan in the 1920s, a "leopard-skin" priest named Gwek led the Lau Nuer people in an apocalyptic uprising. Gwek's family and followers built the Pyramid of Dengkur, a central cult site for the Lau.

Yet another apocalyptic group, the Irvingites—a nineteenth-century, British apocalyptic sect—had a socially central, liturgically oriented background. The Irvingites came from the upper strata of British society and had profound priestly preoccupations, including concerns for liturgy, incense, and altars.[5]

THE BOOK OF ZECHARIAH

In 539 B.C.E., Cyrus II of Persia conquered Babylon, paving the way home for interested Judean exiles. Repatriating subject peoples was part of Cyrus's policy of tolerance. His goal was promoting goodwill in the Persian empire.

Shortly after Cyrus's victory, and armed with an edict permitting the rebuilding of the Jerusalem temple, an initial group of returnees traveled to Judah—now the Persian province of Yehud. Their leader was Sheshbazzar, a Persian-appointed governor (Ezra 5:13-16).[6]

Reconstruction work in Jerusalem began under Sheshbazzar, but stalled (Ezra 4:1-5, 24). The Jerusalem temple remained in ruins for the rest of Cyrus's reign, the days of his son, Cambyses II, and on through the accession of the Persian ruler Darius I, in 522 B.C.E. The frustrating gridlock persisted despite a second return of exiles under a new Persian governor, Zerubbabel, and a chief priest, Joshua. Zerubbabel represented the royal line of King David in Jerusalem, while Joshua represented the Zadokite priesthood.

The oracles and vision cycle of the first half of Zechariah, chapters 1–8, date to a period beginning in 520 B.C.E. (Zech 1:1, 7), the second year of Darius's reign. This section of the book confronts the continued failures at reconstruction in Jerusalem, revealing God at work to rebuild both God's temple and God's people. It understands Jerusalem's rebuilding program as directly connected with the end times. Zechariah and his supporters envision that nothing short of the world's transformation and God's reign on earth will begin with completion of their restorative work.

Zechariah's prophecies continued at least until the fourth year of Darius, 518 B.C.E. (Zech 7:1). The temple was completed and dedicated a few years later, in 516. After this time, in all likelihood, the prophet's supporters and disciples took up and continued his prophetic work.

The book of Zechariah experienced growth beyond its original core, first through editorial supplements to Zech 1–8, and eventually through the addition of the second part of Zechariah, chapters 9–14.

Compared to earlier chapters, the prophetic and apocalyptic writings in Zechariah's second half are less unified and harder to situate historically. More focused on tribulation than the book's earlier texts, they deal with wicked community leaders, attacking nations, and other severe communal tests.

Modern interpreters agree that Zechariah has two distinct parts, but have no consensus about how the sections relate to each other. Many interpreters see them as contradictory writings, the first with a "realized eschatology" and the second taking a future-oriented, apocalyptic stance. They view the radical, apocalyptic oracles of Zech 9–14 as different in kind from the priestly, establishment ideals that come out so clearly earlier in the book. Zechariah advocated rebuilding the temple, they reason, so he must have expected exilic prophecies, like those of Ezekiel, to find fulfillment in present, mundane circumstances. He must have expected Israel's messianic hopes to be realized in Zerubbabel, the contemporary governor.

This point of view finds little supporting evidence in Zechariah itself. If Zechariah actually had mistakenly pinned his messianic hopes on Zerubbabel, it would be hard to imagine how his prophecies ever emerged as authoritative Scripture. Zerubbabel was no messiah!

Arguments that Zech 1–8 is about realized eschatology are similarly baseless. They assume temple circles focus strictly on maintaining a community's stability through repeated acts of worship and sacrifice. They suppose temple circles scarcely promote apocalyptic visions of catastrophic disruption and the world's renewal.

I could not disagree more.

The sacred precincts and liturgical symbols of the Jerusalem temple were icons: windows or portals into the transcendent. Remember, Zion symbolized the cosmic mountain. To approach the temple on Mount Zion meant leaving behind the world's agonies, such as drought and hunger, and entering God's lush garden. It meant sloughing off moral ambiguity and earthly compromise and entering an ethically pure realm. Zion permitted no mixing of chaos and paradise, good and evil.

The symbolism of Zion, rightly appreciated, does not ratify and uphold a stable status quo. It calls the present world order radically into question.

Members of the central cult establishment at Jerusalem must often have felt the discrepancy between mundane, historical experience and the symbols and mythological ideals of the temple on Zion. The priests experienced God's grace in the prayers, rituals, and sacrifices of the temple, and thirsted for more.

The symbolism and iconography of the temple jarred the mind, provoking visions and expectations of paradise on earth and the ennoblement of humanity. Such an ultimate salvation was far from reality in the here and now. Might it come through God's eschatological intervention?

A cycle of eight visions, infused with the symbols of the Jerusalem temple, forms the core of Zech 1–8. The scenes, spatial organization, and movement of the visions are bound up with temple elements. These elements are the building blocks of an apocalyptic imagination. They include altars (Zech 1:18-19), priestly garb (Zech 3:5), and lampstands (Zech 4:2). Temple foundations and stone bases (Zech 4:7) appear as offhand references, too. So do temple activities and procedures, including sacred judicial proceedings (Zech 3:1-4) and ceremonial cursings (Zech 5:1-4).

One example is Zechariah's second vision (Zech 1:18-21), where the four horns of the temple's altar come alive as the four corners of the cosmos, subject to God's judgment. Appearing as agents of God's destruction, four blacksmiths smash the horns, thus expelling all arrogant powers in creation opposed to God's coming reign on earth.

The vision of Zech 1:18-21 lacks the gory details of some full-blown apocalypses but clearly depicts God's final, apocalyptic battle. God's supernatural agents destroy the forces of evil grouped as a totality, an encapsulation of hubristic power, like Gog in Ezekiel. The vision thus prepares the way for God to dwell in Jerusalem's midst.

In the fifth vision of Zech 4, the temple structure, which was then still under construction, comes alive as an apocalyptic focal point. It is no coincidence that chapter 4 stands at the center of Zechariah's vision cycle. In the imminent era of salvation, the temple will transmute into the physical navel of the cosmos, from which God will reign over "the whole earth" (v. 14).

Within the vision, traditional temple symbols reveal an apocalyptic signification. Zerubbabel recovers and handles a holy stone in verse 7, perhaps the stone in the first temple that supported the ark of the covenant. The stone's mythic symbolism now takes on physical reality, however, as the people shout "Grace, grace to it!" As Tigchelaar's research suggests, it becomes the primeval stone—the starting point of God's re-creation of the cosmos. Its end-time function in the temple will be to permanently cap the subterranean forces of watery chaos.[7]

The temple lampstand of the vision (v. 2) also transmutes into a transcendent reality. The stand's seven lamps become God's omniscient eyes, "which range through the whole earth" (v. 10b). In the coming era, God is supernaturally present on Mount Zion (also see Zech 2:5, 10-11; 3:2; 8:2-3). God's glory emanates from the temple, flooding the world in light.

The textual world of Zech 4 makes theological claims about the notion of "witness." Readers are roused "as one is wakened from sleep" (v. 1) to discover a prospective role in God's project to radiate light over the world. There is a remarkable interdependence in the vision between God and representatives of the faithful community. Just as the olive trees provide the oil for the seven lamps, so God's outreach to humankind is a shared endeavor with human leaders.

Space precludes elaborating the many links connecting the two halves of the book of Zechariah. Zechariah 9–14 surely comes from the continuing school of the visionary responsible for the book's first eight chapters. Texts such as Zech 9:7 and 13:1-2 continue the group's original central-priestly concern with ritual and moral purity (Zech 2:12; 3:4, 9; 5:1-4; 8:3). Texts such as Zech 12:3, 8 and 14:10, 16 strongly reiterate the earlier chapters' theme of Jerusalem's emergence in the end times as God's cosmic mountain.

Perhaps no shared theme binds the two halves of Zechariah together more tightly than messianism. The hope for an ideal Davidic figure to rule over God's renewed community begins at the heart of Zechariah's vision cycle. As we have seen, Zech 4 presents a vision of olive trees. They are God's ideal representatives, a royal figure and priest sharing leadership of God's people. Zechariah looks forward with anticipation here to an expected royal prince and high priest of God's coming reign: "the two anointed ones who stand by the Lord of the whole earth" (Zech 4:14).

At first, Zechariah probably hoped that the contemporary governor, Zerubbabel, would be one of the olive trees (Zech 4:6-10a). Such hopes never materialized, however, and Zechariah soon abandoned using messianic language to refer to Zerubbabel.

Instead, in editorial additions to his prophecies, he and his supporters began expressing their hopes for a future Davidic ruler using the term "the Branch." The term comes from earlier prophecy, where it symbolized Israel's hopes for an ideal descendant of David who would bring justice and righteousness to earth (Jer 23:5; 33:15; cf. Isa 4:2). Zechariah is probably especially indebted for the term to his priestly predecessor Ezekiel (see Ezek 17:22-24, a messianic allegory).

In a divine oracle in Zech 3:8, God reminds Zechariah's temple colleagues that, in God's coming reign, they will have to share power with "my servant the Branch." Zechariah's group supports the temple priesthood, but it must not lose its radical messianic vision.

Zechariah 6:11-14 also stresses the advent of the Branch. The prophet orders two crowns made as eschatological symbols. One is to sit in the restored temple, awaiting the imminent arrival of "a man whose name is Branch" (v. 12).

The second half of Zechariah renews the book's original hopes for a coming, ideal scion of King David. Among the passages that were later added to chapters 1–8 is the celebrated messianic prophecy of Zech 9:9-10. The text looks forward to the entrance into Jerusalem of a coming king. Echoing Ps 45:4, the king rides on for the cause of truth, meekness, and righteousness. As in Ps 72:8, his advent ushers in God's reign "from sea to sea, / and from the River to the ends of the earth" (v. 10).

Zechariah 12 envisions a future era in which the house of David "shall be like God, like the angel of the LORD" (v. 8). This section of the chapter probably looks forward to an end-time Davidic ruler whose reign will perfectly reflect the will of God.

The subsequent verses of the chapter speak in elevated terms of "one whom they have pierced" (v. 10), a figure who becomes the object of heavy mourning. The original sense of this reference is beyond recovery. The present literary structure of Zechariah suggests an interpretation, however, by balancing and expanding verse 10 with a parallel text in Zech 13:7-9. The latter text describes a coming "shepherd" of God, who rules as God's associate. He is struck down as the tribulations of the end times begin. I have laid out arguments elsewhere that these passages near the end of Zechariah paint a literary portrait of a dying messiah.[8]

As with Ezekiel, Zechariah and his followers were central priests in society. Zechariah was the grandson of the priest Iddo (Zech 1:1; Ezra 5:1; 6:14), who led the return of an exiled priestly group back to Yehud. Apparently, Zechariah eventually headed Iddo's priestly household (Neh 12:4, 16). Zechariah's texts lean heavily on Ezekiel's Zadokite language and restoration program, strongly suggesting Zechariah and his supporters were Zadokites themselves. For example, see Ezek 43:1-5 ǁ Zech 1:16. Also see Ezek 40:3 ǁ Zech 2:1-2, and Ezek 37:24-27; 43:7-9 ǁ Zech 2:10; 8:3.

History provides various parallel examples of apocalyptic programs of rebuilding and purifying, which aim to pave the way for

God's end-time work. Savonarola, a statesman and lawgiver in fifteenth-century Florence, pursued a civic plan preparing his city for a central role in God's imminent reign. Like Zechariah, he aimed to build a new sacral order in Florence that would usher in the new age.

Apocalyptic fervor likewise impelled many early colonial leaders in America, such as Cotton Mather and Increase Mather. They traveled to New England to institute a pure theocracy with a Christlike governor, John Winthrop, so God's reign would come.[9]

THE BOOK OF JOEL

Joel, like Zechariah, is an early apocalyptic book among the Minor Prophets collection of the Hebrew Bible. Beautifully composed and organized, the book also possesses a mood of urgency and suspense that quickly captivates the reader.

In a hot, Arabian desert windstorm (sirocco) and locust plague, Joel and his audience caught a glimpse of looming world catastrophe. The insight raised basic questions for them about the human condition and about God's end-time strategy for redeeming humanity and nature. The earlier eighth-century Minor Prophets, such as Amos and Hosea, had not probed these far-reaching questions.

The scale of the devastating ecological catastrophe at the heart of the book of Joel provokes the same searching questions about God's plan for creation that confront modern people who have experienced a major terrorist assault. A growing number of people in the world today know something of what Joel, together with his audience, was experiencing in the wake of drought and locust plague.

Joel is not a very difficult book to read, but its striking combination of interests and language has often puzzled interpreters. Scholars wonder how Joel's concern with locusts and environmental disaster relates to his fears of end-time judgment. Does a devastating locust plague really have much to do with the idea of evil hordes attacking God's people in Jerusalem? Interpreters also regularly puzzle over how Joel's apocalyptic language, which focuses on historical crisis and disruption, fits in with his priestly and liturgical language, which elsewhere often seems to emphasize divine order, stability, and regularity in the world.

The question of when to date the book of Joel has been another ongoing issue for its interpreters, principally due to the lack of overt historical references in Joel's text. Joel does describe a particular, individual disaster, but plagues of drought and locusts have regularly afflicted the area of Palestine up through modern times. Even if scholars could agree that a literal locust catastrophe was the impetus behind Joel's apocalyptic oracles, they would be hard pressed to pinpoint and date the particular event at issue.

Compounding the problem of fixing a historical setting for Joel, critical scholars have regularly interpreted the mix of interests and language in the book as evidence of different authors from different times.

I believe scholars often make the problems of Joel's inner consistency and its place in Israel's history more complicated than they really are. The picture of Joel's reactions and activities throughout the book is a consistent one, customary for a temple priest at a time of plague or other disaster.

At a time of communal disaster, Joel gathers the people to lament and petition God at the temple. The disaster at issue begins as a sirocco combines with huge swarms of locusts, which eat all the land's vegetation, desolating it. As terrible as this present destruction was, Joel envisioned that it was a mere harbinger, or portent, of much worse: apocalyptic doomsday. Horrified, he asked the people to turn to God for mercy before it was too late. Given this inner logic to the book, a critical dissection of Joel into disparate fragments is unnecessary.

An exact dating of the locust disaster and Joel's reaction to it is impossible, but several clues suggest the appropriate time range falls in the several decades after the mid–fifth century B.C.E. The book presupposes the political scenario of Judah after the Babylonian exile, when it functioned under the local supervision of priests and governors. Since its depictions of disaster presuppose standing city walls (2:8-9), the book probably fits best in the decades after Nehemiah's time.

The key to understanding the literary structure of Joel is to understand the prophet's fear that the contemporary locust plague and sirocco is a harbinger of the apocalyptic judgment day. Joel's structure reflects and develops this belief by a pattern of doubled descriptions. First, there is a double description of desolation. Two separate sections depict first the contemporary environmental catastrophe and then the threatened apocalyptic judgment. The two sections share a strong resemblance, since Joel uses the images and language of locusts and siroccos to portray the horror of apocalyptic crisis and judgment.

Descriptions of public lamentation and fasting in the temple strategically follow each description of desolation. This doubled description of communal rites of repentance and prayer in the temple shows Joel's priestly response to the massive crises he faced.

God responds positively to the liturgical activities of the people, and a double picture of deliverance emerges. Joel first delivers a priestly oracle promising deliverance from the immediate ecological crisis. An elaborate promise of apocalyptic salvation follows, concluding the book. The apocalyptic conclusion is actually a series of passages promising divine protection of the faithful through the crises of the end times and into the start of a new era of paradise. God defeats the powers of evil arrayed against God's people, and ushers in the millennial age.

The following outline of Joel summarizes this structure based on doubled descriptions:

Joel 1:1-12	(A) Ecological Desolation
Joel 1:13-20	(B) Temple Rites and Lamentation
Joel 2:1-11	(A') Apocalyptic Desolation
Joel 2:12-17	(B') Temple Rites and Lamentation
Joel 2:18-27	(C) Oracle of Immediate Deliverance
Joel 2:28–3:21	(C') Promises of Apocalyptic Deliverance

Joel especially follows Ezekiel's example, reusing the same specific prophetic and apocalyptic motifs. Like this priestly, apocalyptic visionary of the Babylonian exile, Joel was likely a Zadokite priest.

Joel expresses Ezekiel's recurring concern that Israel recognize God's identity and power (Joel 3:17; cf. Ezek 36:11; 39:28). Repeating Ezek 30:2-3, Joel cries, "Alas for the day! / For the day of the LORD is near" (Joel 1:15). Echoing Ezek 38, he expresses fear of an attack by a northern army on restored Judah (Joel 2:20; Ezek 38:1-9). Further, he speaks of the outpouring of God's spirit in the end times (Joel 2:28) in the same manner as Ezekiel (Ezek 39:29). Again, Joel's stream of paradise flowing out of the temple to water the land in the new age (Joel 3:18) comes straight from Ezek 47:1-12.

It seems doubtful that Joel's fears of an imminent apocalypse would have sprung so quickly to mind amid the locust plague if Ezekiel's previous apocalyptic warnings were not well known to him and his colleagues. Study of Ezekiel predisposed Joel's group for developing their own version of apocalyptic imagination when the locust plague hit.

Ezekiel is not the only Hebrew Scripture to which Joel refers. Even by a conservative reckoning, at least half a dozen citations of biblical texts appear in Joel's three chapters. Joel incontestably cites Isa 13:6; Zeph 1:14-15; Jonah 4:2; Ps 79:10; Isa 45:5; and Amos 1:2. Beyond these examples, Joel has more than twenty other probable references to previously composed scriptural texts.

This observation confirms a relatively late postexilic dating for Joel, when the Scriptures that he cites were available to him in writing. It also refreshes our memory about the key place of traditional themes and values in the rise of the apocalyptic imagination. Joel provides a fine example of how an apocalyptic worldview normally maintains strong roots in the traditions and authentic symbols of the group within which it comes to life.

The apocalyptic imagination arose within the biblical tradition as a coherent rearrangement of Israel's traditional symbol store. The new symbolic universe of apocalyptic works, such as Joel, grew out of the traditional symbols and themes of Israel's emerging corpus of authoritative Scripture. The new worldview was both ontologically comprehensive and eschatologically charged.

Joel's unique way of experiencing reality through a comprehensive new rearrangement of biblical sayings and symbols could not have developed much earlier than it did in Israel's history. Given its dependence on established, authoritative writings, it makes sense that the apocalyptic imagination only arose within Israel at a late period, that is, the period during and after the exile.

The book of Joel focuses theologically on God's prerogative and control in the world. Neither human beings nor a blind principle of determinism, but the hand of God guides history for Joel. The fate of the world is in God's hand, whether God is judging and undoing humanity and creation or preserving faithful survivors and reshaping the world into a thing of beauty.

God first appears in Joel's visions leading forces of judgment against an ill-prepared complacent people. "The LORD utters his voice / at the head of his army; / how vast is his host!" (2:11). Jarred into wakefulness and radical conversion, the people recognize their total dependence on God's mercy (2:13).

God attends to their assembly of worship and hears their lament. Retaining complete, cosmic prerogative, God switches sides, moving to defend God's people. Mercifully, God's roar no longer sounds from before enemy troops but from atop Mount Zion, God's holy mountain.

> The LORD roars from Zion,
>> and utters his voice from Jerusalem,
>> and the heavens and the earth shake.
> But the LORD is a refuge for his people,
>> a stronghold for the people of Israel. (Joel 3:16)

In the end, God's spirit pours out on everyone, regardless of factors such as age, gender, and social status (Joel 2:28). "Everyone who calls on the name of the LORD shall be saved" (Joel 2:32). Further, God's faithful community finds itself immersed in the active presence of the holiness of God. Delivered, renewed Jerusalem blazes with God's transforming presence, so that Joel 3:17 becomes true for all to see:

> So you shall know that I, the LORD your God,
>> dwell in Zion, my holy mountain.
> And Jerusalem shall be holy,
>> and strangers shall never again pass through it.

Joel's ideal vision of end-time salvation forms an implicit exhortation to readers about how to live now, in the mundane world. No doubt, this relevance for everyday life in large measure ensured that the community of the faithful preserved Joel's apocalyptic visions. While readers of Joel lack the power to usher in the end-time vision, they can order their present lives in conformity with its claims about authentic, fully human living—for example, its vision of a fully engaged worship and a radically inclusive community.

From the themes, traditions, and structure of the book of Joel, its social background is all but transparent. Joel operated from within the ranks of the central priests of the postexilic temple in Jerusalem. These priests in power—the Zadokites—viewed a contemporary plague crisis as a portent of a looming eschatological crisis. They responded in conformity with their priestly roles in society.

Along with his colleagues within the central temple establishment, Joel responds to what he fears is an end-time crisis just as he would to a mundane one. He convenes a national lament ceremony and liturgy for fasting and prayer to God. Along with the other central priests of his group, he uses cultic means and rituals to awaken the people to the apocalyptic significance of the present crisis and to have them call on God for salvation in the midst of it (Joel 1:13-14; 2:12-17).

The literary forms and language of the book strongly reflect this ceremonial action-plan for surviving the eschaton, especially the pervasive liturgical language of lamentation, including descriptions of disaster, petitions to God, and oracles of salvation.

Joel's references to Ezekiel, especially his allusion to the attack of a "northern army" in Joel 2:20, suggest he understood himself as a student of Ezekiel's prophecy. He was well aware of Ezekiel's apocalyptic vision of an end-time assault on Jerusalem from the north (Ezek 38–39). His knowledge of Ezekiel, and of related texts such as Zechariah, predisposed him to expect the eschaton when a major ecological disaster hit. When he faced a sirocco and locust plague, he and his priestly colleagues believed the end of days had entered their field of vision.

Natural upheavals have shocked similarly predisposed groups into expecting doomsday at other times and places in world history. Famines and plagues in thirteenth- and fourteenth-century Europe, for example, strongly boosted the strength of apocalyptic movements there. The first flagellant movements in Italy arose in the wake of a famine in 1258 and the outbreak of the plague in 1259. People joined in, believing famine and plague heralded a coming final judgment. They flagellated themselves publicly in large numbers as a way of expressing repentance in the face of God's coming wrath.

The cross-cultural evidence shows an outbreak of plague or catastrophe can jar groups from any strata of society into expecting doomsday. Powerful and rich figures are no exception. The spread of plague to Antwerp in 1530, for example, motivated many wealthy and influential figures to join the Spiritual Liberty apocalyptic group. These upper-echelon figures included well-to-do merchants and even the jeweler of the French king Francis I.

At the outbreak of plague in the Spanish New World of the sixteenth century, a fear of apocalyptic doom gripped groups among Spanish colonizers in America. The case is significant, since it shows the pain and suffering involved in a plague is not what motivates the rise of apocalypticism. It was physically healthy groups among the Spaniards, predisposed by Franciscan apocalyptic traditions, which interpreted the plague as a harbinger of doomsday. Apocalyptic beliefs and fears did not arise among the millions of suffering natives, who died from the contagious diseases brought by the Spaniards. Their native traditions did not predispose them to interpret the plague as an apocalyptic omen in this way.

SELECTED TEXTS WITHIN ISAIAH

The historical figure of Isaiah, son of Amoz, prophesied many of the sayings in Isa 1–39 in Jerusalem in the eighth century B.C.E. The book bearing his name, however, contains many additional prophecies from at least two subsequent eras. The apocalyptic passages of the book occur in these additional prophecies.

The beautiful prophetic poems of Isa 40–55 come from the exilic era in Babylonia, from somewhat later than Ezekiel's exilic prophecies. The prophecies and early apocalyptic texts of Isa 56–66 and Isa 24–27 date still later. The book of Isaiah grew to include these passages only during the postexilic Persian era, beginning at Zechariah's time and continuing as late as the time of Joel.

Although many texts in Isaiah are contemporary with the prophets Ezekiel and Zechariah, they differ from the writings of these figures. Ezekiel and Zechariah interact with specific audiences in Babylonia and Yehud. Their prophecies name specific dates when they were revealed. This is not the case for the late parts of Isaiah. Although its exilic and postexilic components obviously had specific audiences and dates, the present canonical shape of Isaiah has obliterated them. The voice of Isa 40–66 addresses circumstances in the exile and beyond but speaks as if it belonged to the original Isaiah of Jerusalem.

The rhetorical strategy of the book of Isaiah clearly aims to present its literary contents as one unified body, associated with a single literary persona. Only chapters 1–39 name and describe him, but the persona of Isaiah stamps its impress in the entire book. The book, in its received form, presents a singular, prophetic perspective gazing out from the preexilic period. It looks ahead to the far future, anticipating the course of God's work in fulfilling God's purposes.

The present holistic form of Isaiah, in which a single prophetic persona speaks throughout, guides readers in interpreting the book's contents. For one thing, it invites readers to appreciate some strong lines of continuity within the expanse of the book.

One major continuing theme of Isaiah is God's eternal promise to preserve Mount Zion and God's people, even through the worst of calamities. God's word to the people throughout Isaiah is "Do not fear!" (e.g., Isa 7:4; 10:24; 35:4; 37:6; 40:9; 41:10, 13-14; 43:1, 5). It is an oracle of assurance and salvation associated with biblical promises of God's unconditional love and God's protection of Abraham's descendants (Gen 15:1; 26:24; Exod 14:13).

God's unconditional love for Zion's people does not preclude severe divine chastisements (cf. 2 Sam 7:12-16). From the start of the book, the people's unrighteousness brings God's judgment in the form of invasions: first by a Syria-Ephraim coalition, then by Assyria, and finally by Babylon.

Judgment comes in full force, but a remnant of the people always survives. A holy seed of incredible potential always remains within the smoldering stump left by God's judgment (cf. Isa 6:13). Isaiah's investment of hopes in a remnant creates a strong momentum of promise in the book, orienting Israel toward the future.

Throughout periods of judgment, God always maintains a safety net for Judah so at least a remnant survives. The people intermittently sink toward destruction, but God's commitment to Zion eventually buoys them up. The book of Isaiah, in its present canonical shape, shows how this dynamic plays itself out over time. Its rhetorical structure presents Israel's life with God as a cyclical progression through troughs and peaks.

The progression is forward moving; one senses it has a goal (a *telos*). God's commitment to Zion is for some greater purpose than periodic disappointment. The prophetic persona of Isaiah looks toward the future with hopes that God's unconditional commitment to Zion's people will ultimately not just buoy them up but catapult them into glory. Images of God's salvation and glory from the psalms partly inform these hopes. The psalms were a major influence in the Isaiah tradition.

The hopes of the Isaiah persona for eschatological fulfillment of God's purposes for Israel come to full poetic and mythological expression in Isa 40–55. This second section of the book beautifully depicts the *telos* of Isaiah's cyclical picture of Israel's life with God.

The poems in Second Isaiah date to the late exilic period, when Cyrus was about to repatriate the Judean captives. As Cyrus's liberation came, the bearers of Isaiah's prophetic hopes found their deepest aspirations on the verge of fulfillment. With hardship and dependence behind them, they were free to begin the restoration.

The reality on the ground in Yehud did not match the tidal wave of expectation that had been building force within the Isaiah tradition, however. As the restoration began, Jerusalem, the temple, and the cities of the land were still in ruins (Isa 58:12; 61:4; 64:10-11; 63:18). The Isaiah school discovered that for their heightened eschatological expectations to see fulfillment, God would have to act, directly and supernaturally. Indeed, only an apocalyptic intervention of God would bring their transcendental hopes to birth.

The school of Isaiah now produced additional texts, beyond those of Isa 40–55. In these new writings, an apocalyptic imagination comes to expression. The imagination had its building blocks in the Isaiah group's own store of writings, especially the writings in Second Isaiah. Crucial building blocks, as well, came out of the psalms and the Pentateuch's priestly writings. These sources had always informed the writings of the Isaiah tradition and continued to do so as it moved in an apocalyptic direction. One example of the appearance of apocalypticism in the tradition occurs in Isa 63:1-6.

As Isa 63:1-6 opens, the reader overhears city guards of Jerusalem in earnest conversation about an approaching stranger. He is no ordinary figure, but splendidly robed and marching in great might. Furthermore, his garments are stained crimson as if from battle.

The passage quickly assumes the form of an interrogation of

the figure by the sentinels, and we hear the mighty trooper answering his challengers in the first person. He never says so plainly, but his language about his divine attributes and violent deeds make clear he is the well-known Divine Warrior.

The Divine Warrior image is a traditional one, common in Israel's poetic accounts of creation and its songs about the conquest of the land of Canaan. The LORD overthrew the mythological forces of chaos to create the cosmos. The LORD commands the host of heaven, and supernaturally defeats all earthly enemies with thunder, hail, and torrential rain.

Directly echoing the earlier Isaiah poetry of chapters 40–55, the Warrior of Isa 63:1-6 makes clear his identity as Israel's righteous savior. God is one who speaks in righteousness (v. 1; cf. Isa 45:19, 23), "announcing vindication." God's nature is incomparable, the divine work of salvation requiring no assistance (vv. 3, 5; cf. Isa 41:28; 44:8; 45:5-6, 14). Israel's enemies will now drink the chalice of God's wrath (v. 6; cf. Isa 51:21-23).

As these strong verbal echoes of Isa 40–55 make clear, the earlier prophetic promises of the Isaiah school are finally coming to concrete fulfillment. In Isa 63, an apocalyptic imagination is emerging before our eyes.

Isaiah 63:1-6 is rich with traditional motifs and language, providing many clues about other building blocks of this imagination. Tellingly, the traditional psalms of Israel's temple worship loom large directly behind our text's imagery. Psalm 24:7-10 has the same image of God approaching Jerusalem after victory over the forces of chaos. God approaches "strong and mighty, . . . mighty in battle" (Ps 24:8). Psalms 44:3 and 98:1 both have the same image of God's mighty arm achieving victory. The psalms are also a possible source of the image of God's punishment as a cup of wrath (Pss 60:3; 75:8).

While the psalms in general have inspired Isa 63:1-6, Ps 60:5-12 must have been of particular import. Psalm 60 is a communal lament, used in the preexilic temple in situations of national defeat. In the face of calamity, the people complain and petition God in verses 1-5. God, through a priest or prophet in the temple, returns a saving word in verses 6-8, using the poetic image of the Divine Warrior. The image, with its rich mythological and archetypal allusions, becomes concrete and eschatological in Isa 63.

Psalm 60 emphasizes that its Warrior images are metaphors.

114

God's helmet is actually the Israelite tribe of Ephraim, and God's scepter is Judah (Ps 60:7). The people's literal desire is that God will empower "our armies" (Ps 60:10).

Things are otherwise in Isa 63. God acts alone and directly (Isa 63:3, 5), not through Israel. The scope of victory is broader than in the psalm. Overcoming humanly impossible odds, God defeats injustice and victimization on a grand (universal and cosmic) scale.

Verse 8 of Ps 60 uses the Warrior image to put preexilic nations, contemporary with Israel, in their places: Moab, a basin to bathe the feet; Edom, a servant to whom sandals are thrown; Philistia, the theme of a victory song. In Isa 63, by contrast, the adversaries are no longer mundane, historical nations. The Isaiah group picks up the image of Edom (especially from the prayer for victory in Ps 60:9-12) but hears a symbolic, universal connotation.

"Edom" is now the archetypal enemy of Israel. Isaiah 63 takes it as a collective embodiment of evil similar to Ezekiel's "Gog" (cf. Isa 34; Mal 1:2-5). As Joseph Blenkinsopp argues, toward the end of the Isaiah tradition Edom becomes the "evil empire *par excellence*," embodying "the idea of chaos."[10]

In Ps 60:12, the congregation concludes their prayer with confidence that God will, metaphorically speaking, "tread down our foes." Isaiah 63:6 reuses the image. God's actions in Isaiah, however, are no metaphor. The depiction of God's unrelenting wrath and massive bloodshed in Isaiah can only refer to God's end-time purge of all injustice from the world. Zechariah 10:5 uses the same verb to picture the end-time annihilation of forces hostile to God.

Texts in the final eleven chapters of Isaiah, such as Isa 63:1-6, contain a great deal of apocalyptic imagination, but so do the texts of Isa 24–27. These chapters are frequently even called "Isaiah's Apocalypse," a rubric tracing back to Bernhard Duhm (1892) and Rudolph Smend (1884).

Many scholars continue to raise questions about calling Isa 24–27 apocalyptic. Their caution is legitimate, since the chapters lack many standard literary motifs and radical features of the full-blown Hellenistic apocalypses. An incipient apocalyptic world-view (perceptual framework) seems apparent from many of the section's images, however, including images of embodied evil, divine invasion, and otherworldly salvation. God's coming reign on earth even ends death. Mythological images of creation at home in the psalms of the temple and in the priestly documents of the Bible come alive as end-time realities here, just as in Isa 63.

Isaiah 24 describes a great, cosmic unraveling. There comes apart all God's primeval work in Gen 1–11, particularly the work pictured in the P source (that is, the priestly portions of the Pentateuch highlighting creation, unconditional covenant, and ritual organization) of these chapters. Earth's inhabitants have so "polluted" the world that it languishes and withers (Isa 24:4-5). In reaction, the literary persona of Isaiah cries out, "I pine away. Woe is me!" (Isa 24:16c).

Earth's pollution is so bad that God revokes the eternal promise made after Noah's flood (Gen 9:1-17, P). God's undoing of the "everlasting covenant" with Noah is incredible (Isa 24:5; Gen 9:16 P). It spells the end of earth's mundane, postdiluvian history. Apparently, God decides to remake the world to save it from itself.

Events proceed backward, behind Noah's covenant, as God follows through with the decision. Isaiah 24:1 announces, "The LORD is about to lay waste the earth and make it desolate, / and he will twist its surface and scatter its inhabitants." To accomplish this, the primordial chaos of the flood returns. Exactly as in Gen 7:11 (P; also see Gen 8:2), God opens the "windows of heaven" (floodgates of the sky) and the foundations of earth tremble (Isa 24:18). Finally, the "city" of the enemies of God reverts to the precreation mode of Gen 1:2, to "the city of chaos" (Isa 24:10).

With the world tottering on the brink of oblivion, God's saving work of re-creation begins. As with Noah's flood, a remnant remains after the deluge. They are the righteous remnant the Isaiah persona always longed for.

Isaiah's righteous survivors emerge in a new world, where

> the LORD of hosts will reign
>   on Mount Zion and in Jerusalem,
> and . . . will manifest his glory.
> (Isa 24:23; cf. Isa 52:7; Ps 97:1)

God's glory comes to earth physically, resulting in a qualitatively more wondrous creation. It so brightly manifests itself on earth, in fact, that the moon is abashed and the sun ashamed.

These brief surveys of Isa 63:1-6 and Isa 24 provide only a sampling of the rich apocalyptic strain in the Isaiah tradition. I hope that it is enough of a taste to prompt the reader to further exploration of this intriguing corpus of Scripture. Rather than probe further, I turn to a little scholarly detective work on the identity of the visionaries behind the book of Isaiah's apocalyptic texts.

First, strong clues signal a group of authors, rather than an individual. These clues come in oblique references in scattered texts of Isaiah. Isaiah 62:6-7 may refer to the group metaphorically, calling them "sentinels." Isaiah 66:5 similarly describes a whole group of those who preserve and hold fast to God's Word. Again, in Isa 35:3-4, another apocalyptic passage in Isaiah, God commands a plurality of prophets to encourage God's people.

The Isaiah group's prophetic poetry is well crafted, suggesting group members composed their sayings and visions in writing. They may have distributed them from the beginning in association with the prophetic corpus of Isaiah of Jerusalem. Issuing their work in purely written form would have made a strategy of pseudonymity viable—it made the idea of an "Isaiah persona" work.

Their Isaianic language and ideals give pride of place to God's unconditional love of Zion and its people, a theme they drew from the psalms and the J and P sources of the Pentateuch. (The J source is the portion of the Pentateuch that always refers to God as YHWH, JHWH in German.) Indeed the language and motifs of the psalms and of the P source pervade the writings of the Isaiah school, as we have seen in our sample probes.

A priestly community associated with the theology and liturgy of the Jerusalem temple would be the most likely carriers of such traditions. As his commissioning experience within the temple demonstrates, Isaiah of Jerusalem himself operated within such priestly circles (Isa 6).

At significant points, the thinking and theology of the Isaiah school differs from the traditions of Ezekiel and the Holiness Source of the Pentateuch. It is thus unlikely that the group members were Zadokites. Rather, they probably counted themselves among the wider priestly circle of the descendants of Aaron.[11]

The unconditional promises and archetypal ideals of their traditions burst alive with apocalyptic fervor in the period of uncertainty at the end of the exile. Historians and social scientists have observed apocalyptic radicalization within similar groups when basic expectations have mounted as the world changed rapidly.

Apocalyptic expectations built steadily starting in eleventh-century Europe, for example, at a time coinciding with expanding social and economic horizons. They were strongest among people with access to means and power, who saw new possibilities for undreamed-of wealth.[12]

The Isaiah group strained to overcome serious opposition to their apocalyptic program within the postexilic community of Yehud. Their writings of the postexilic period have a sharp polemical edge, clearly visible in passages such as Isa 57:3-13; 65:1-7, 11-15; 66:3-4, 17. God's physical, concrete salvation is at hand but delayed due to the sin of opponents (e.g., Isa 59:1-2).

Scholars have creatively reconstructed specific factions within the society of Yehud as the target of attack, even suggesting temple leaders and temple theology as the enemy. Paul Hanson identifies the opponents of our texts as postexilic Zadokite priests, the followers of Ezekiel.[13] The texts of Isaiah, however, lack evidence supporting such speculations.

It is more likely that the Isaiah school was attacking common religious practices in their wider community. They particularly objected to practices falling outside the traditional precepts of their Zion theology, especially God's sole prerogative to receive Israel's worship. Isaiah of Jerusalem could as easily have mounted the same polemics against his own contemporaries. They committed the very offenses blasted in the third part of Isaiah, including spiritualism, fertility rituals, and rites in which children were sacrificed to Molech (cf. 2 Kgs 18:4).

Brooks Schramm recently devoted a full-length study to identifying the opponents in the late polemics of the Isaiah tradition. He concludes, that the group behind Isaiah's apocalyptic texts is continuing a battle—also waged by priestly sources of the Pentateuch—against an age-old "syncretistic" worship of Yahweh in Israel. By a syncretistic practice of worship, Schramm means worshiping multiple deities alongside of Yahweh. This was often the majority religious practice in ancient Israel, whereas biblical traditions, including Zion theology, were in the minority.

Schramm writes, "All of the cultic practices attacked by Third Isaiah are summarily condemned not only by the pre-exilic prophets but also by the Pentateuch. . . . Third Isaiah and the 'priestly' Pentateuch, at least in regard to these basic cultic issues, are in total agreement."[14]

THE BOOK OF MALACHI

The little book of Malachi is underappreciated today. The only aspect of the book familiar to many people is its prophecy—cited by Jesus (Matt 11:14; 17:11-12)—that the coming of God's messenger, Elijah, will precede the start of God's reign on earth. But Malachi deserves more attention because it advocates a set of theological traditions rare among the Bible's apocalyptic writings. The prophet and his circle strongly support the traditions of the Sinai covenant and the book of Deuteronomy. These Sinai-oriented traditions make a unique contribution to the Bible's apocalyptic imagination.

Malachi makes no direct claims of a unique perspective, and says nothing up front about a unique group of authors. Even the Hebrew name *Malachi*, which means "my messenger," may be no proper name at all but merely a descriptive title. Some scholars even doubt Malachi's status as a distinctive, independent book of the Bible. They view it instead as an appendix to Zechariah, attached by editors using the same superscription—"An Oracle" (Mal 1:1)—that interlocks Zechariah's major sections (Zech 9:1 and 12:1).

A close reading of Malachi quickly dispels the theory. Malachi is no mere appendix to Zechariah, and stark differences separate the traditions of the books. Malachi's introduction by the term *oracle,* moreover, bears little significance since a variety of postexilic groups could have used various forms of this superscription to introduce their writings. Canonical shaping of Malachi as a separate biblical book was no arbitrary process. It reflects Malachi's distinctiveness.

The germ of truth in the appendix theory is that Malachi does follow Zechariah chronologically, coming many decades after his work. The contents of his book presuppose the completion of Zechariah's temple. So too, they presuppose the waning of Zechariah's religious influence on his priestly colleagues.

By Malachi's time, perhaps the mid-fifth century B.C.E., Zechariah's apocalyptic enthusiasm at the rebuilding of the temple had worn off. Despite revivals in various periods, the people and priests had lapsed in faithfulness and become mechanical in worship. The temple might as well have remained in ruins, since the worship of Malachi's time was corrupt. The way was clearly not yet paved for the advent of God's apocalyptic salvation.

Malachi and his supporters confront this situation in their writings, using the language of back-and-forth dispute and legal prosecution. Malachi particularly targets the priests currently in charge, who are not living up to their priestly calling (Mal 1:6; 2:1). Indeed, they are guilty of holding God in disdain (Mal 1:13). "Oh, that someone among you would shut the temple doors, so that you would not kindle fires on my altar in vain! I have no pleasure in you, says the LORD" (Mal 1:10).

Malachi's hopes and fears about his situation are decidedly apocalyptic. Divine justice will triumph with fullness, he proclaims, despite his audience's complaints and skepticism at the delay of God's appearance (Mal 2:17). God is about to send a supernatural messenger to prepare for the LORD's coming to his temple (Mal 3:1; cf. 4:5). That coming will be "sudden" (Mal 3:1) and more than people bargain for (Mal 3:2).

God's messenger is about to purge and purify the community like "a refiner's fire" and "fullers' soap" (Mal 3:2). Afterwards, God draws near for judgment. The marginalized are uplifted and ideal balance comes to the covenant community (Mal 3:5). An ideal obedience ("fear") of the LORD finally appears on earth (cf. Deut 5:29; 6:2, 13; 10:12; 13:4).

Malachi 3:16–4:3 envisions a moral dualism within Yehud. Those who reject community and discipleship face a terrifying end. They will experience God's apocalyptic day as a furnace, burning up all earth's stubble (Mal 4:1). Things are entirely different, however, for those who fear God's name. They are destined to become God's "special possession," fulfilling God's ancient covenantal promises at Sinai (Mal 3:17; Deut 7:6; 26:18; Exod 19:5). They will experience an unheard of display of righteousness throughout the entire earth (Mal 4:2).

Like our other biblical examples, Malachi's apocalyptic imagination developed out of the symbol store of his group's unique biblical traditions. Scholars disagree, however, on how to characterize these traditions. Part of the problem is deciphering Malachi's orientation toward priestly theology, especially since he is preoccupied with priesthood but harshly criticizes priests. Another is untangling Malachi's somewhat confusing terminology for priests.

Malachi's background and orientation become clear when one realizes his affinity with Deuteronomy's traditions and related traditions of the Sinai covenant.

Malachi's "messenger," whose imminent advent prepares for God's apocalyptic day, stands firmly in Deuteronomy's tradition of "a prophet like Moses" (Deut 18:15-19). Malachi's complaint about unacceptable sacrificial animals, which are "blind" and "lame," also closely reflects Deuteronomy's thought and language (Mal 1:8; Deut 15:21). Again, his emphasis on allegiance to "one God" (Mal 2:10) fits the famous words of the Shema in Deut 6:4.

Malachi presents an ideal vision of the priesthood in Mal 2:4-7, which provides his criteria for judging his priestly opponents. There is little doubt about its origins. His standard speaks of a special covenant with Levi, reflecting the same idea in Deut 18:5; 33:8-11. Jeremiah 33:20-22, a text heavily influenced by Deuteronomy, knows of this covenant as well.

Malachi's ideal standard holds the Levites responsible for bearing and transmitting "Torah." They are also responsible for teaching the people. This vision of Levitical priesthood comes straight from Deuteronomic texts such as Deut 17:8-11, 18; 31:9; 33:10.

Malachi holds all priests responsible to the covenant with Levi, just as Deuteronomy does. (Aaron too was a Levite, he argues.) In preparation for God's reign on earth, God's apocalyptic messenger will subject all priests to the covenant's test. Malachi 3:3 thus foretells how the messenger "will purify the descendants of Levi," that is, both Aaronides and Levites. Contemporary priests who mock God will disappear as dross. Those aligned with Levi's covenant will emerge from the refining cleansed.

Malachi's preoccupation with priesthood and particularly his trenchant appeal to Deuteronomy's ideal vision for the descendants of Levi are the clue to his role in society. Malachi and his followers were most likely Levites operating within temple worship in Yehud. In attacking temple priests, Malachi probably admonishes colleagues from sibling priesthood branches: the Aaronides and the Zadokites.

Further textual evidence supports Malachi's identification as a Levite. For one thing, just as the ideal Levitical priest is the "messenger of the LORD" (Mal 2:7), Malachi's name means "[the LORD's] messenger." It is hard to believe that this is a mere coincidence.

More telltale support comes at Mal 2:10. Speaking in the first person, Malachi asks the temple priests, "Have we not all one father [namely, Levi]?" In this rhetorical question, Malachi practically declares himself a Levite. A full-length study of Malachi by Carol Bechtel Reynolds supports the conclusion that Malachi upholds Deuteronomic tradition as a Levite. She states:

> Even at its most eschatological moments, the book of Malachi remains the work of a Levitical priest prophesying against rival Aaronid priests. In both language and form, the prophetic author draws upon his [Sinai oriented] heritage. The separation of the faithful from the "evildoers" . . . echoes a similar division of the house in Exod 32:26-35, where Moses asks, "Who is on the LORD's side," and the sons of Levi rally to their ultimate act of faithfulness.[15]

The Levites were subordinate ministers at the temple in the postexilic period. Among other duties, they worked at various scribal projects and were in charge of temple music and psalms (Ps 135:19-20; 1 Chr 6:31-32; 16:4-37; 2 Chr 8:14). As Levites, Malachi and his supporters would have shared responsibility for worship at the temple with the Zadokites and Aaronides. Although subordinate in status, they worked among establishment circles rather than at society's periphery.

Researchers have documented cross-cultural parallels to Malachi, where an apocalyptic imagination develops amid a quarrel between power-sharing factions at the center of a society. One case occurred in Indonesia in 1825–1830, when thousands of Javanese people became convinced the *Ratu Adil*, a messiah, was on earth.[16] Prince Dipanagara of Java's royal family appeared to be this figure. Supported by many followers, including royal relatives and palace troops, Prince Dipanagara led an apocalyptic military revolt against the Dutch colonizers of Java.

Group members knew they would encounter opposition, however, even among their own people. The *Ratu Adil* was destined to appear at a time of great wickedness and to confront powerful forces of darkness.

Besides the Dutch, the opponents of the group ended up including a powerful faction loyal to Dipanagara's worldly brother. The quarrel between the two parties began while both brothers were still at court in Yogyakarta. It eventually became so intolerable, that Dipanagara withdrew before expanding his followers into a huge military force.

CHAPTER 6

THE BOOK
OF DANIEL

ISSUES IN READING

The book of Daniel is a fascinating collection of compelling stories and vibrant visions associated with Daniel and his friends, Hananiah, Mishael, and Azariah, wise and faithful Judean exiles serving as court officials for a series of foreign kings. The apocalyptic imagination of the stories at court pokes fun at human arrogance, especially pretensions to might and size. The sweeping, apocalyptic perspective of the visions raises the purview of readers above current events and pressing concerns, to illumine history's course and God in control.

The earlier portions of the Daniel collection, the tales of suspense and intrigue at court in Dan 1–6, come from late Persian and early Hellenistic times. Perhaps these tales were assembled between 350 and 200 B.C.E. It is difficult to be more precise than that. What is clear is that this part of Daniel originated long after the period it portrays. Daniel's cycle of court tales came together two or three centuries after the book's literary setting, that is, the period of Israel's Babylonian exile and of Babylon's defeat by the Persians (ca. 605–536 B.C.E.).

The book of Daniel reached its final form even later, in the years leading up to 164 B.C.E. This was the period of the outrageous persecutions of the Jews by the Seleucid leader Antiochus IV Epiphanes. It was the period, too, of the successful revolt of the Maccabean militants of Judea against Antiochus's oppressive rule. Coming from this late in history, during the Maccabean revolt, Daniel is the latest book of the Hebrew Bible.

Those who first composed and treasured the tales and visions of the book were likely courtiers themselves, similar to Daniel and his companions (see the final section below). They would have been Diaspora Judeans working as bureaucrats and sages far from their native land of Israel. The group wove the book of Daniel together over time, initially against the backdrop of Diaspora court life. Later they, or their successors, greatly expanded the collection in Jerusalem, during the Maccabean crisis.

Turning from the Bible's prophetic texts to enter the world of the book of Daniel requires readers to make some adjustments. Much late Israelite prophecy exhibits a nascent apocalyptic imagination, but Dan 7–12 takes the form of a full-blown apocalypse. Readers of the book, especially of chapters 7–12, should brace themselves. They must be prepared to encounter everything from nightmarish monsters to the blazing advent on earth of the celestial "Son of Man." They will have to wrestle with symbol-rich calculations of the end of time, perceptions that challenge workaday understandings of the world, and an awesome vista of the "Ancient of Days" seated for the final judgment.

Unlike prophetic literature, such as Isaiah or Ezekiel, Daniel lacks any core of oracles or writings by an actual, historical prophet. Throughout the book, the figure of Daniel is a literary character, the hero of a work of historical fiction. Stories about this ancient worthy communicate theological claims in the book, just as they do in other Hellenistic apocalypses. Other literary heroes in apocalypses of the period include such celebrated characters as Adam, Enoch, Noah, and Abraham.

The book has the following outline:

Part I: Court Tales

Daniel 1	Dedication amid a Foreign Court
Daniel 2	Nebuchadnezzar's Dream
Daniel 3	The Fiery Furnace
Daniel 4	The Felling of the High Tree
Daniel 5	Belshazzar's Feast
Daniel 6	Daniel in the Lion's Den

Part II: Visions

Daniel 7	The Four Beasts and the Ancient of Days
Daniel 8	The Ram, Goat, and Little Horn
Daniel 9	Seventy Weeks of Years
Daniel 10–12	The Final, Panoramic Revelation

The first half of Daniel contains folktales about the hero Daniel and his three companions. In some of these, conflicts at court endanger the heroes and they almost become martyrs. Other tales involve contests at court, in which the heroes outshine their competitors.

Far from mere children's stories, the tales of Dan 1–6 call readers to radically revision reality. They fortify readers to doggedly follow God when it is far from practical and prudent. Daniel is such a golden, larger-than-life figure in chapters 1–6 precisely to provide hope for readers that revolutionary discipleship is possible even in a world outrageously ignorant of heaven's ways.

There are dreams and visions aplenty for Daniel to unravel in chapters 1–6, but nothing as surreal as in chapters 7–12. Facing the four major visions of the book's second half, Daniel loses his golden status as heroic interpreter. Words cannot capture the realities that now confront him, and he stands baffled, even bewildered. Fortunately, mediating angels are present to help. They interpret the visions of Dan 7–12 for our hero, as is characteristic of Hellenistic apocalypses.

The visions of Dan 7–12 disclose a dualistic, heavenly world and an imminent culmination to mundane life. They provide a wide-screen view of history, revealing God's blueprint for its course and conclusion. They contain pulsing images on a mythic scale, and have a keen interest in such matters as angels and the resurrection of the dead. They predict the ultimate triumph of good over evil.

Beware of domesticating the apocalyptic symbols and images of Daniel. An apocalyptic vision is not merely an allegory or a coded description of everyday politics. Rather, the apocalyptic imagination discloses a separate, transcendent backdrop to earthly affairs. It argues that heavenly forces care for God's people, whereas dark powers propel the claims and conquests of those who are blind to God and God's ways. Humans are mistaken in thinking their doings are autonomous and purely earthbound. Earth's dominant structures and systems are far less plausible and justifiable than earth's rulers would have us believe.

In Daniel, the heavenly court is intimately engaged in the daily unfolding events of earthly geopolitics. People and powers on earth do not act in autonomous isolation.

Take Dan 10 for example. Verses 12-13 and verse 20 make clear that heaven gets involved when an empire such as Persia gains sway over God's people. As long as Persia held Israel in its grip, various angels worked in shifts to restrain its power. With God's large-scale plans in mind, they intervened and kept in place limits on the severity of Israel's servitude.

A close look at angels elsewhere in Daniel confirms the book's expectation of heaven's radical intervention in earth's affairs. These beings are real players in space and time. To demythologize them—treat them as mere metaphors or coded ciphers—is an injustice to the text, which never finds it necessary to "interpret" them as something other than what they seem.

Other transcendent phenomena appear on earth in Daniel. In chapter 5, Belshazzar turns pale at seeing a floating hand writing doomful words on his palace wall. In Dan 3, a visible supernatural figure intervenes to save Daniel's three companions from Nebuchadnezzar's fiery furnace. The king sees the figure amid the raging flames, and declares he "has the appearance of a god" (v. 25).

Some particularly superb examples of a literal, supernatural intervention of heaven on earth occur in Dan 4. In verse 13 (cf. v. 23), for instance, a supernatural figure—a "holy watcher"—descends from heaven to the earthly sphere. Nowhere does the chapter treat the figure as a cipher or code term needing interpretation. Rather, the text's plain sense envisions a transcendent entity literally invading space/time and arranging the downfall of

Nebuchadnezzar. As John Collins correctly perceives, "The watcher is a mythic-realistic figure; he is not interpreted as a symbol for something else."[1]

Other signs of transcendent reality invading earth pervade Dan 4. Nebuchadnezzar learns of his imminent downfall, while in a waking state, on the roof of his palace. An audible voice announces his fate to him directly (vv. 31-32). The supernatural word takes effect "immediately," with no human instrumentality (v. 33). The king becomes a beast with a beast's mind, an observable transformation. As Collins notes, this is no allegory.[2] According to verse 33, his hair grows into the feathers or wings of eagles, and his nails become like the claws of birds.

The apocalyptic symbolic universe of the Daniel group emerged out of the unique roles of group members as wise advisors and learned interpreters in foreign courts. As professional, royal sages and scholars, the members of the group operated within the rubric of what scholars call "mantic wisdom." Mantic wisdom is the skill of sages in figuring out hidden or obscure revelations, such as omens or dreams. The traditions and habits of mantic wisdom were familiar in both Israel and the wider ancient Near East. The figure of Joseph in Genesis is the best biblical example of such a wise man highly skilled at unraveling mysteries.

Several qualities and preoccupations of mantic wisdom make it a veritable hotbed for the birth of an apocalyptic imagination. Consider the following characteristics, for example.

Manticism is concerned with hidden patterns and structures underlying mundane reality. Interpreting divine revelations in various forms, it peers into the future to reveal what lies ahead. Among groups treasuring scriptural traditions, mantic wisdom may take a particularly interesting turn. It may wrestle with how the unfulfilled ideals and prophecies of Scripture may eventually find definitive realization.

The scholarly training and mantic roles of the Daniel group meant its members were intimately familiar with Israelite and ancient Near Eastern mythological imagery as well as with biblical traditions. Both visionary, mythic images and verbal, written Scripture provided key building blocks for the book of Daniel's apocalyptic imagination.

Interpreters widely recognize the key role of Israelite and Near Eastern mythological imagery in Daniel's visions.[3] In the apocalyptic world of Daniel, as in Ezekiel and Isaiah, mythic symbols of creation make a strong showing.

Examples abound. Daniel 2 envisions a huge stone growing to become a cosmic-sized mountain that fills the earth. Daniel 4 envisions the fall of a cosmic-sized tree, leaving the creatures of earth homeless. As in Ezek 31, the tree is an archetypal image known from legends and dreams across numerous cultures.

Daniel 7 allows the reader to peer into the sea of chaos lying outside the created order. Daniel recalls, "I . . . saw in my vision by night the four winds of heaven stirring up the great sea" (v. 2). This is the same great aqueous Abyss, stirred by the winds of heaven, found at the beginning of the Genesis creation story (Gen 1:2).

Interpreters usually recognize the central place of visionary archetypes and mythic motifs in mantic wisdom, but, in cases such as Daniel, mantic inquiry also focused on Scripture. Scriptures—especially long unfulfilled Scriptures—provided the Daniel group with fascinating puzzles for study and decipherment. Inscribed and archived, the words of Israel's past prophets became a puzzle of God ripe for untangling.

Michael Fishbane deserves credit for the insight that Daniel's apocalypticism has natural roots in a "mantic" study of Scripture. Fishbane writes:

> [Daniel] 9–12 . . . presents an imposing concatenation of prophetic authorities. . . . Certainly, a proclivity to compose such a prophetic patchwork attests both to a scholarly attentiveness to authoritative sources received in the prophetic *traditum* and to a sense of apocalyptic immediacy. And, surely, just this is the desired impact of the concatenation upon the reader. By strategically and cumulatively assembling numerous prophetic pronouncements the author leads us into the mental world of wise believers, Daniel's ["wise ones"; Dan 1:4; 11:33, 35, and 12:3], and the tangle of authoritative texts which encoded their universe and provided an atmosphere of confidence in the inevitability of the apocalyptic forecast.[4]

An apocalyptic imagination took shape as the Daniel group pored over the Scriptures, especially lapsed or unfulfilled prophecies. In their study and interpretation of the texts, biblical citations and echoes rearranged and realigned themselves in their minds as a new universe of meaning. This innovative symbolic universe boasted a new capacity for understanding God's ordering of historical time and God's saving plans for restoring balance on earth.

TRACING SCRIPTURAL ALLUSIONS IN DANIEL

Already in the court tales of Dan 1–6, fascinating allusions and echoes of earlier biblical texts appear. John G. Gammie has studied the sources behind Daniel and concluded that the court stories betray a clear "allusive" or "anthological" style.[5] God's preservation of Daniel's three friends in the fiery furnace (Dan 3) recalls the words of Isa 43:2cd, "when you walk through fire you shall not be burned, / and the flame shall not consume you." Daniel 6:21-24 has a similar relationship to Ps 57:4-6.

Daniel 4's image of a huge tree in earth's midst sheltering all life echoes the same picture in Ezek 31. God's removal of Nebuchadnezzar's reason in the same chapter (see Dan 4:16, 36) echoes a different genre of scripture, the wisdom of Job 12:12-25. Verses 24-25 of Job 12 in particular declare,

> [God] strips understanding from the leaders of the earth,
>   and makes them wander in a pathless waste.
> They grope in the dark without light;
>   the makes them stagger like a drunkard.

The demise at night of the arrogant Belshazzar in Dan 5:30 echoes the insight of Job 34:16-30. Verses 24-25 of the passage read,

> [God] shatters the mighty without investigation,
>   and sets others in their place.
> Thus, knowing their works,
>   he overturns them in the night, and they are crushed.

The authors of Daniel's court tales made especially concentrated use of the vocabulary and theological ideas of Isa 40–55. The evidence includes the following verbal echoes and allusions: Dan 2:22 ‖ Isa 45:7a; Dan 4:35 ‖ Isa 40:17a; Dan 5:23 ‖ Isa 46:7; and Dan 6:26 ‖ Isa 49:18. Among the theological notions borrowed from Isaiah, Dan 1–6 emphasizes the powerlessness of manufactured idols and the complete incapacity of the soothsayers and enchanters of foreign gods.

In addition, the court tales portray the figure of Daniel with language associated with Isaiah's Suffering Servant. God's spirit, for example, is said to rest on both persons (Dan 4:8, 9, 18; 5:11 ‖ Isa 42:1). The effect is to exhort faithful readers to model themselves on the character of Isaiah's servant, especially as they, like Daniel, grapple with life lived amid those who do not know God.

The Daniel group seems to have mined Scripture even more heavily as their apocalyptic imagination developed and found expression in Daniel's second half. Scholars have identified multiple scriptural allusions particularly in chapters 9–12. Such references occur, for example, in Dan 11:10, 22, 26-27, 30-31, 33, 35-36, 40, 45; 12:1-4, 7, 9-10, 12.

To document just one instance, note the pervasive influence of Isa 10:22-23 on Dan 11. The chapter, in its military descriptions, echoes Isaiah's language about a "flood" or "rush" of destruction. Appearing in Dan 11:10, 22, 26, and 40, the echoes dominate this section of the book.

It is especially telling that the figure of Daniel in chapter 9—at the center of the book's apocalyptic vision cycle—appears wrestling with the interpretation of Scripture. As the passage opens, he has been studying Jeremiah and noting the book's prophecies about the duration of the exile. According to Jer 25:11-12 and 29:10, God decreed that Jerusalem would lay desolated for seventy years, after which God would end the exile.

Discerning that the time of divine favor should be at hand, Daniel implores God to action in a remarkable prayer full of allusions to previous Scripture. It is a liturgical conglomeration pieced together out of 1 Kgs 8; Ezra 9:6-15; and Neh 9:6-37. It attempts to provide the exact sort of confession required for the exile's end by earlier texts such as Deut 30:1-10; 1 Kgs 8:46-53; and Jer 29:10-14.

As Daniel finishes his moving prayer, the angel Gabriel appears to him and offers a fascinating and complex interpretation of Jeremiah's prophecy about a seventy-year period of exile (Dan 9:20-27). The interests of the critical reader immediately perk. What is happening?

A complex, learned explication of Jeremiah's prophecy would not really have been relevant in the literary setting of Daniel's life and times. In the Persian period, the exiles would have been satisfied with a plain, straight reading of Jeremiah. The text's plain sense was, in fact, about to be realized. Just about seventy years after the Babylonian destruction of Jerusalem, the Jerusalem temple was rebuilt by repatriated exiles under Zechariah's prodding. The project was complete in 519 B.C.E.

If its literary and theological goal were merely accurate depiction of the Persian period, Dan 9 would have simply had Gabriel assure the exiles that the temple was about to be rebuilt. They would see it rededicated in 519. That Gabriel's message is far more complex than this assures us that something else is going on in Dan 9.

With its complex, new interpretation of Jeremiah's seventy years, the text is wrestling with problems from a later date, years after the start of the Persian period. Questions about the true end of the exile, and what the faithful would have to do to participate, arose especially in Hellenistic times. Even in modern times, the faithful still await God's full restoration of God's people.

God's promised favor toward Jerusalem after seventy years of desolation never fully materialized. This was clear by Hellenistic times, when Jerusalem was languishing under the oppressive rule of Antiochus IV. It remained clear for those who preserved Daniel as Scripture, continuing to treasure the book long after Antiochus's demise. Daniel 9 grapples with this vexing situation.

It exhorts faithful readers to confession and prayer, such as that modeled in Dan 9:3-19. Further, it assures the faithful that Jeremiah's prophetic promise will see a vastly more substantial fulfillment than the one experienced in 519 B.C.E. Jeremiah's word has a "fuller," apocalyptic sense yet to come about.

Verses 20-27 of Dan 9 represent the new, mantic interpretation of Jer 25:11-12 and 29:10 by the Hellenistic group that composed Dan 7–12. This interpretation arose in the times of Antiochus, though its significance transcends its period of origin. In this section, Scriptures from Jeremiah and other texts reconfigure in an imaginative new apocalyptic assemblage.

Daniel, under the tutelage of the angel Gabriel, discerns a new apocalyptic significance to Jeremiah's number "seventy." Key to the expanded understanding is the notion of cycles of Sabbaths and Jubilees in the Pentateuch, especially Lev 25:1-17. The Daniel group was well aware from studying the Pentateuch of Sabbath cycles of varying durations, including cycles of seven days, seven years, and even seven-times-seven years.

Before Jeremiah's time, Chronicles already conceived of Jeremiah's number "seventy" as a set of Sabbath cycles (2 Chr 36:21; cf. Lev 26:34-39). This idea served as a springboard for Dan 9's rethinking of Jeremiah. If Jer 25:11-12 and 29:10 were about a Sabbath rest, the "70 years" at issue might be a figural expression for seventy Sabbatical cycles, that is, 70 weeks of years—490 years. (A "week" in this case is a unit of measure equaling seven years.)

According to Dan 9, Israel would have to wait that full stretch of years until God's ultimate restoration and renewal of God's people came about. That stretch of time would contain distinct messianic events and apocalyptic tribulations.

Multiple scriptural references and allusions supply the basis for Dan 9's blueprint of events and tribulations leading up to the end of the seventy Sabbatical cycles.[6] The mantic reflections of the chapter extend well beyond interpretation of Jeremiah and Leviticus. Verses 20-27 are a pastiche of scriptural echoes.

Verse 26 predicts a special anointed one, or Messiah, to appear in an era following Jerusalem's restoration. The appearance of this figure, even after years of waiting, does not mark God's immediate advent. According to the verse, the figure will tragically be cut down and disappear. The notion that God's special servant is destined to be cut off echoes key scriptures such as Zech 13:7-9 and Isa 52:13–53:12.

The end of verse 26 forecasts that Jerusalem and the temple are to be destroyed again. The language echoes Isa 10:22b-23, "Destruction is decreed, overflowing with righteousness. For the Lord GOD of hosts will make a full end, as decreed." Both Isaiah and Daniel refer specifically to a flood of judgment and to a decreed destruction.

Verse 27 of Dan 9 also uses the language of Isa 10:22-23. It states that an evil leader will reign in the end times, but meet the same fate predicted for Jerusalem in verse 26.

This end-time antagonist appears to be modeled in part on the hubristic tyrant of Ezek 28:11-19. Like Ezekiel's despot, Daniel's antagonist has international connections, profanes the sanctuaries of his territory, and ends up appalling all onlookers. Both figures meet an abysmal fate. Motifs from Ezek 7 also color Dan 9:27.

CONTENTS AND THEOLOGICAL HIGHLIGHTS

Daniel contains texts of differing genres, which readers should approach with differing expectations. It is a mistake to read the court tales of chapters 1–6 as straight history. Rather, keep an eye out for their literary artistry and their outrageous humor. The tales' mockery of the bloated egos and predictable banality of the imperial rulers of the earth is especially entertaining. The theological claim behind this caricature is that in God's eyes the mighty pretensions of earth's superpowers are preposterous.

One example of the humor of the tales is the lengthy enumeration of officials and musical instruments in Dan 3.[7] The chapter repeatedly rehearses the automatic obeisance before Nebuchadnezzar's giant idol of every type of Babylonian political official the very moment an inflated ensemble of instruments sounds. The effect is to mercilessly satirize pagan worship as purely mechanistic and mindless. Idolaters emerge as automatons, cowardly and pathetic.

Many of the apocalyptic visions of Dan 7–12 offer panoramic views of earthly history. World powers rise and fall, as history progresses along God's divine timetable. Often the exact identities of the superpowers in question are ambiguous. At times, however—in chapter 8, for example—known ancient Near East empires are explicitly in view.

Readers new to the study of Daniel may not have a firm grip on the historical sequence in which Babylonia was succeeded by Persia, which in turn was succeeded by the Hellenistic empire of Alexander the Great and the kingdoms of the Ptolomies and Seleucids. Having a historical time line handy will help in reading Daniel's political visions.

Although the book of Daniel divides in half rather neatly, interpreters are often too quick to isolate Daniel's court tales from its apocalyptic visions. There are good reasons to think an ongoing group of mantic sages authored all Daniel's various components. If so, one would expect strong lines of continuity to run through Daniel's twelve chapters, and, in fact, this is what careful readers find.

The court tales already reveal an emerging apocalyptic imagination. Nebuchadnezzar's two dreams, for example, closely resemble the symbolic night visions of full-blown apocalyptic literature. Such dream visions in apocalypses often form the media of divine revelation about a coming crisis. They generally contain esoteric, deviant knowledge, which clashes with mundane, public understandings of the world, just as Nebuchadnezzar's two dreams do.

The dream vision of Dan 4 shows further particular tendencies toward apocalypticism. It contains a metaphysical dualism, revealing a supernatural, heavenly world where God is in charge and angelic "watchers" decide earth's fate in council. It claims that God predetermines earth's political history, a point illustrated by heaven's orchestration of preset phases in Nebuchadnezzar's reign. It emphasizes the larger point of heaven's sole prerogative to control everything on earth, a message summarized by verses 3 and 34, which frame the chapter.

Not only the framing verses but also multiple statements within chapter 4 drive home this bottom line: Dominion belongs to God. The reader cannot help but draw the apocalyptic inference. God can establish God's permanent reign on earth at whatever point seems fitting.

The dream vision of Dan 2 is even more apocalyptically oriented than that of chapter 4. By the same token, chapter 2 forms an even stronger link with chapters 7–12. The vision of the chapter appears to have made an indelible imprint on the Daniel group's collective imagination.

Daniel 2 works out a blueprint for earth's history that permanently guided the group's thinking. Of all the court tales, this chapter most nearly approximates the apocalyptic eschatology of Daniel's later chapters, where God preordains the reigns of a sequence of kingdoms leading ultimately to earth's final destiny.

At the climax of chapter 2's dream vision, a stone strikes and crushes a great statue representing the mighty superpowers of the world. This rock is the realm of God, which puts an end to all earth's kingdoms, becomes a great mountain filling the earth, and endures forever. It is hard to imagine a more blatant apocalypse. God's reign invades earth supernaturally and thunderously, putting a stop to history and establishing itself as a new creation.

Daniel Berrigan expresses the dynamic of the chapter lyrically.

Unto itself, final, definitive, of God, nothing can supplant the rock nor anticipate it, nor presume to possess it. No power or principality or empire or military or economic or religious power avails to sway it from its appointment with destiny and destiny's God. Nothing can allow or forbid it place, or dictate its form or duration.[8]

Other facets of Dan 1–6 besides the dream visions anticipate apocalyptic motifs and themes in chapters 7–12. The hubris and folly of the various rulers in the court tales is an example. Their narcissism and pomposity foreshadows the wickedness of end-time leaders yet to come.

The arrogant leadership of the court tales is mostly just preposterous and comedic, but in the apocalyptic visions it reemerges as something grim and demonic. As the court tales reveal, the insolence of rulers is never just humorous. It bears the seeds of spiritual abomination. This is clear in chapter 3, where Nebuchadnezzar imposes a tailor-made religious observance as a means of universal ideological control. It is clearer in chapter 5, in Belshazzar's obscene misuse of temple vessels. Belshazzar's arrogance and blasphemy at his infamous feast are especially close to the desolating sacrilege perpetrated by the horrible, despotic tyrant of Daniel's later, fully apocalyptic chapters.

A central theological concern in both parts of Daniel is prodding readers' imaginations. Daniel dethrones the claims and prerogatives of earth's military, economic, and political systems, reimaging them as a tenuous mix of iron and clay (Dan 2:33, 41-43). Though they stand beautiful as a huge tree, providing shelter and food for all manner of life, they are liable to be chopped down in a moment (Dan 4). In place of human pretension and arrogance, Daniel imagines a supernatural hand, inscribing a message to shatter all expectations (Dan 5:5-6).

This apocalyptic insight summons readers to responsibility and engagement. They must oppose all earthly claims to divine entitlement and infallibility. They must stand against all attempts at ideological control and all displays of might that pervert human community and the natural world (e.g., Dan 3:12; 6:10). In the process, readers' new apocalyptic imagination will likely come up against official resistance and retaliation. At such times, the response of Daniel's three colleagues is appropriate.

If our God whom we serve is able to deliver us from the furnace of blazing fire and out of your hand, O king, let him deliver us. But if not, be it known to you, O king, that we will not serve your gods and we will not worship the golden statue that you have set up. (Dan 3:17-18)

By exposing human efforts at universal utopia as prone to perversion and inhumanity, Daniel refocuses readers' hopes for salvation on the promised reign of God. In place of self-deifying images of authority, the text reveals a crashing stone that topples everything and becomes a new creation (Dan 2:34-35, 44).

God's reign makes its epiphany on the clouds of heaven for all to see (Dan 7:13). At its arrival, all resistance to salvation is permanently defeated, and all peoples, nations, and languages serve God (Dan 7:14). A huge reunion of God's people of all times takes place, including faithful persons newly awakened from death (Dan 12:1-3). This new community of God will "fill the whole earth" and "endure forever" (Dan 2:35, 44).

The authors that collected and composed the texts of Daniel were sages, preoccupied with gaining wisdom. It makes sense that their collected texts are concerned with communicating wisdom, particularly wise guidance in discerning the spirits of the times. The book of Daniel intends to help readers see below the surface of their historical situation into the spiritual dynamics that animate it.

The presupposition is that demonic power tends not to remain purely ethereal but incorporates itself into earthly structures. Furthermore, the demonic tends to present itself as wondrous, beneficent, and even salvific. According to Dan 8:25 (NLT), the despotic end-time ruler to come "will be a master of deception, defeating many by catching them off guard." Only wise instruction and training will allow this type of evil to be exposed and resisted when it surfaces. Daniel 12:10*b* affirms that in the end times, "none of the wicked shall understand, but those who are wise shall understand."

Helge Kvanvig captures the theology succinctly:

The demonic power puts on a mask. It has its own makeup, presenting itself in the image of . . . God. Humans will find the demonic power beautiful, reasonable, and in the time of confusion, trustworthy.

The apocalypses were given to the believers for two reasons:

Firstly, the visions unmask the diabolic power, displaying it in all its cruelty. Secondly, the visions will give the key to understand the nature of the tribulations, of the end time.[9]

The wisdom of Daniel for discerning the times has relevance not only for doomsday at history's end but also for many prior occasions in human life and history. The doomful pattern of the apocalypse emerges repeatedly in a minor key within history before reaching its final crescendo. These instances are all remarkably, even genetically, parallel. Most readers of Daniel through the centuries will never see the final apocalypse, but many will experience various prefigurements, or "microcosms," of the end of days.

The original authors of Daniel experienced such a foretaste of the end times. Antiochus, with all his outrageous persecutions and sacrileges, appeared to them as none other than the boastful little Antimessiah of doomsday, the apocalyptic "little horn" of Dan 7:8, 11, 20-21, and 24-26.

They announce as much in chapter 8, which speaks of an evil "little horn" of the Hellenistic period that all scholars identify with Antiochus. Antiochus's persecutions, however, never amounted to the culminating horrors of the end of days. They formed only an apocalyptic "eruption," a harbinger and prefigurement of a fuller form of the same events yet to find fulfillment.

Those who preserved Daniel as Scripture recognized that the sort of preliminary eruption that happened at the time of Antiochus could happen repeatedly in history. Generations to come might well see a whole variety of miniature apocalyptic outbursts before God's reign finally comes in fullness. One reason the faithful have treasured the writings of Daniel is their wise insight into the schematic form of such eruptions. Knowing the scheme helps readers recognize doomful, apocalyptic crises when they surface. By recognizing them, they can respond accordingly.

In playful, ornithological terms, one might distinguish two types of apocalyptic birds. When apocalyptic fears arise in society, one can play the part of the apocalyptic *rooster* or the role of the apocalyptic *owl*. Study of Daniel helps readers know when to take on one of the two roles.

There are times in history when it is good to take the perspective of a cautious owl, unwilling to get agitated by speculative predictions and alarmist cries of impending doom. The well-known Y2K crisis at the turn of the twenty-first century is a case in point. Despite the rhetoric in some quarters, there was no reason to retreat to bunkers and await the world's end at that juncture.

At other times in history, it has been appropriate to be an apocalyptic rooster. At the fall of Jerusalem in 70 C.E., the reign of Queen Mary I in sixteenth-century England, and the Nazi Holocaust of the twentieth century, apocalyptic dynamics were at play, at least in embryonic form. In such circumstances, it was appropriate to drop everything and confront doomful times. When one is up against evil on a massive scale, one cannot go about business as usual. Comfortable Bible readers from suburbia in the U.S. may forget this, but my international students from Sudan and elsewhere in the world understand it intimately.

The approach to reading Daniel that I am advocating is unabashedly oriented toward the future. It treasures Daniel as a forward-pointing key for discerning the times. It sees Daniel's texts as eschatological prophecy rather than reportage of long past events. In particular, it sees the panoramic outlines of history in the visions of Dan 7–12 as having as much to do with future, unrealized events as with a retrospective *(ex eventu)* rehearsal of ancient history.

READING DANIEL AS CANONICAL SCRIPTURE

By the start of the twentieth century, a radical criticism of Daniel emerged that seemed to push modern, historical-critical assumptions to an extreme. In this approach, the apocalyptic visions of Dan 7–12 look backward rather than forward. They are a retrospective review of history, written after the fact to assure ancient readers that God is in control of history, guiding it according to a predetermined plan. The message aims at consolation and encouragement—needful help for the book's first readers, afflicted Jews in the time of Antiochus.

S. R. Driver adumbrates this modern reading perspective in his commentary on Daniel, a volume of the Cambridge Bible for Schools and Colleges: "The general aim of the visions attributed to Daniel in [chapters 7–12] is to shew, with increasing detail and distinctness, that as the course of history, so far as it has hitherto gone, has been in accordance with God's predetermined plan, so it is not less part of His plan that the trial of the saints should not continue indefinitely."[10] For Driver, the visions of Dan 7–12 are primarily about what has hitherto transpired. They *retrofit* Daniel with a detailed foreknowledge in order to assure readers that they are safe in God's hands.

Paul L. Redditt takes a similar position in his recent commentary on Daniel. He also reads Daniel as a review of history, which the writers expected to culminate in their own times: the era of Antiochus. He sees Daniel's purpose as a call for readers to learn from the past and live accordingly in the present. Writing a century after Driver's time, Redditt still claims:

> Daniel is less a book about the future than about the past and present. The book casts a look back from the Maccabean period to the centuries and empires that preceded it and gave a new reading for its own day. . . . It came to say that no human empire was golden, no human institutions deserved ultimate allegiance. Such insights are its real legacy to the twentieth century.[11]

The stance of Driver and Redditt has a venerable, archaic pedigree. It is as old as the third-century work of Porphyry and the eighteenth-century work of the deist, Anthony Collins. Porphyry, a rationalist attacked by Saint Jerome, argued Daniel was a Maccabean forgery. The forger passed the book off as future-oriented prophecy, when in fact it was a retrospective rehearsal of history. Anthony Collins, another famous rationalist, revived Porphyry's theory during the Enlightenment, in 1727.

Modern historical interpretation of Daniel is fully appropriate. It contributes to the book's understanding, helping to explain its historical references and its original milieu. The book did take shape in Maccabean times, and there is no denying that its authors experienced the events around them as an apocalyptic crisis. It would be a mistake to force readers of Daniel to choose a purely future-oriented reading strategy, and reject a modern, historical interpretation.

It is equally a mistake to historicize the text, pushing historical criticism to an extreme. To imagine that historical references exhaust Daniel's meaning would be to lose the prophetic quality of the text as a scriptural message about the future, a future lying open before contemporary readers. All the monstrous beasts of

Dan 7 and 8 would end up as creatures that have already come and gone. The contemporary reader would be off the hook, since these beasts no longer roam the earth. In the twenty-first century, Daniel's monsters would be of taxidermic interest only.

If a resolute historicizing approach is correct, then premodern interpreters of Daniel, such as Jerome, Josephus, and even Jesus, are fundamentally mistaken. Most premodern readers of Daniel, contrary to the rationalist critics, have assumed the book is primarily a message about events to come. They have understood it as a witness to the future—a guide for discerning the times and epochs as they unfold.

In a subsequent chapter, we shall look closely at Jesus' apocalyptic discourse found in Matt 24 and its parallels. Because Matt 24 explicitly cites Daniel, it gives us a good idea of Daniel's meaning for early Christian communities at about 85 C.E.

This meaning is plainly oriented to the future. Matthew 24:15-21 warns readers about what to do when they see "the desolating sacrilege standing in the holy place, as was spoken of by the prophet Daniel" (v. 15; cf. Dan 9:27; 11:31; 12:11). Matthew 24:30 promises that after the sacrileges and tribulations of the end times, Daniel's "Son of Man" will come on the clouds of heaven (Dan 7:9-14, 22). The "Son of Man" is Jesus at his second coming here, an event eagerly anticipated by the Matthew community.

The first-century Jewish historian Josephus, writing about 90 C.E., also understood Daniel to be about "things that are future." He says so plainly in his *Antiquities of the Jews,* in describing the meaning of Nebuchadnezzar's dream of a great stone that crushes all earth's kingdoms.

In book 10 (10.203-18), Josephus writes, "Daniel did also declare the meaning of the stone to the king; but I do not think it proper to relate it; since I have only undertaken to describe things past or present, but not things that are future." The reticence of Josephus to interpret the stone probably stems from fear of his Roman patrons. He doubtless believed that Dan 2 might well be a prophecy of the Roman Empire's destruction.

From about the same time as Josephus, the book of 4 Ezra also interprets Daniel's visions as future-oriented prophecy. In 4 Ezra 12:10-36, an interpreting angel speaks of Daniel to help clarify a recent divine revelation. In verse 11, the angel states, "The eagle which you saw coming up from the sea is the fourth kingdom which appeared in a vision to your brother Daniel." The context makes clear that the eagle is Rome, not some prior empire. The author of 4 Ezra is interpreting Daniel's fourth beast as a prophecy pointing ahead to his own Roman era.

It is hard to believe these disparate, early interpretations of Daniel were all oblivious to the book's obvious literary sense. Premodern interpreters were not uncritical readers. They labored tirelessly over the minutest details of scripture. They would surely have noticed if the book's scope was limited solely to the Maccabean period.

Close study of Daniel's content and shape led them to the opposite conclusion. They concluded that the book's images and imagination burst the bounds of its original historical milieu. Second-century events had not exhausted its prophetic insights.

If Daniel's symbols and images were solely about Maccabean times, it would be hard to understand why the faithful ever preserved Daniel as Scripture. The claim of the book is that the world ends at the demise of the last monster of chapter 7. If rationalist, historicist interpreters are correct, and Daniel's fourth beast is a coded cipher for Hellenism, then there is a real problem. History did not end at that point!

History has *disconfirmed* any prophecy of the world's end with the Hellenistic kingdom of Antiochus. Daniel's vision, under this interpretation, is blatantly false prophecy. No group would treasure such a false prophecy as Scripture.

In light of the positive reception of the book by synagogue and church as *true* prophecy, it behooves us to recheck its contents and shape. Daniel's meaning for those who preserved it as Scripture has obviously transcended a domesticated, historicist sense. What inherent qualities of the book made this possible?

There is no question of doubting modern criticism's discovery that Dan 7–12 comes from Hellenistic times, from a group expecting the advent of God's apocalyptic reign within their lifetimes. The first students of Daniel's visions doubtless applied them directly to their own Hellenistic age. The question at issue turns on whether Daniel's visions reify their symbols and archetypes as sharply as some modern critics claim. If they do not, we can inquire whether an alternative reading is possible—one in which the apocalyptic visions of the book possess a more profound, more imaginative vitality than often suggested.

As a sample probe, let us look at the two comparable visions of monstrous animals found in Dan 8 and Dan 7.

As noted above, Dan 8 has a specific focus on the Hellenistic age. The chapter bears witness that the primitive Daniel group saw the age of Antiochus as an apocalyptic eruption in history—perhaps *the climactic* eruption. Antiochus's blasphemies seemed to be more than God could allow without thunderously intervening.

The vision describes a succession of two beasts, the second of which sprouts a series of horns. First comes a ram with two horns (v. 3), which verse 20 identifies as Medo-Persia (the Achaemenid Empire, whose chief peoples were the Persians and the Medes). Then a shaggy male goat with a conspicuous horn appears (v. 5), overcoming the ram. Verse 21 identifies the goat as Greece, and its prominent horn as the Greek Empire's first king, Alexander the Great.

Four horns sprout to replace Alexander (v. 8), representing Alexander's four generals who divvied up his empire (v. 22). The vision goes no farther than the Hellenistic period. It ends with the rise to power of a horrible little horn (v. 9), which verses 23-25 identify as an arrogant and despotic ruler—doubtless Antiochus, who came to the throne in the Seleucid part of Alexander's empire in 175 B.C.E.

The vision of Dan 7 is related, but not without key differences. It contains a similar series of beasts but includes two additional animals. It speaks of earthly empires, but not nearly as specifically as chapter 8. It leaves open for interpretation all decisions about which empires go with which beasts.

If the Daniel group had an opinion about how the archetypal beasts of chapter 7 are instantiated on earth, they did not express it in writing. They simply recorded a succession of monsters, extending from a lion with eagle's wings (v. 4), to a fierce bear (v. 5), to a leopard with four wings and four heads (v. 6), to a dreadful fourth beast with ten horns (v. 7). A final little boastful horn arises at the conclusion of the sequence (v. 8).

The expansive qualities of Dan 7 that extend beyond the narrower specificities of Dan 8 already reveal how the book of Daniel earned recognition as forward-pointing prophecy, transcending its original historical milieu. I suggest that Dan 7's inherent qualities of transcendence, mysteriousness, and historical ambiguity account for how it came to be handed down as Scripture.

The Daniel group possessed chapter 7 as an authoritative prophecy and doubtless hoped its glorious conclusion—in which God's reign trumps the boastful little horn of the end times—applied to their own day. They doubtless hoped the fourth beast of chapter 7 was Greece, another version of Dan 8's male goat. If so, the little horn of Dan 7:8, 25 would be Antiochus, the despot of Dan 8:9 whom they wished overthrown. Many modern interpreters see no other possibility for reading Dan 7 than this. They argue that any other reading is eisegesis.

Chapter 7 of Daniel, however, never reifies the text by making these specific identifications. This is fortunate, for history has proved that the original interpretive stance of the Daniel group was premature. They experienced a close brush with apocalyptic chaos, not the culmination of history. Daniel 7, with its "elastic, spongy" quality, fit these times in a preliminary fashion, but would have to wait longer for a definitive fulfillment.

For various New Testament texts, Daniel's fourth beast is more accurately identified with Rome than with Greece. First John 2:18 and 2 Thess 2:3-5, for example, warn their Roman-era audiences that Daniel's end-time antimessiah (Dan 7:8, 25) is still on the horizon. Yet, even the apocalyptic expectations of the early Christians proved premature. Still today, God's reign on a re-created earth remains a future hope. History awaits some sort of revival of Daniel's fourth beast before any final apocalyptic drama can transpire.

Further close study of Dan 7 reveals substantial interpretive obstacles to the Daniel group's hopes for a speedy apocalypse. The Daniel group, in fact, would have had to do some impressive interpretive "gymnastics" to get the sequence of monsters in chapter 7 to culminate in Hellenistic, Maccabean times. That the monsters of the chapter resist being "nabbed by the tail" in this way is further evidence of the text's inherent vitality that led the faithful to value it as a prophetic witness.

For Greece to be the final beast of the sequence in chapter 7, the Daniel group would have needed to split up Medo-Persia into two successive empires. They would have had to understand verse 5 of chapter 7 to refer to Media and verse 6 to Persia, leaving Greece as the climactic beast. This interpretive move is completely counterintuitive. Daniel 8:20 specifically conceived of Medo-Persia as a single beast: the ram with two horns of verse 3.

Given the facts of chapter 8, it is heavy-handed to split up Medo-Persia and spread it out over two separate beasts in chapter 7.

If Medo-Persia is not split into two beasts, then the third beast (v. 6) of Dan 7—not the fourth and final one—is the Hellenistic empire of Alexander the Great. This identification fits the imagery of verse 6 well. One strains to imagine why Persia would have four heads, as the leopard-beast of the verse does. The image of four heads, by contrast, is a natural fit for Alexander's empire. The empire ended up divided in four by Alexander's generals, Cassander, Lysimachus, Seleucus, and Ptolemy.

Comparison with chapter 8 confirms this close fit with Alexander's Diadochi. The four-headed leopard of Dan 7:6 is analogous to the four-horned goat of Dan 8:8. In both cases, there is a fourfold grouping of bodily appendages atop a symbolic beast. Daniel 8:22 specifically aligns these four appendages with the four successor kingdoms of Alexander's Greek empire.

It is the third beast of Dan 7—not the fourth—that most closely fits the Hellenistic world contemporaneous with the original Daniel group. They could have guessed their experience was only a prefigurement of the ultimate apocalypse. Present-day readers should get on guard. The earth is not yet free from Daniel's fourth, final monster!

GROUP ORIGINS AND SOCIAL BACKGROUND

The two halves of the book of Daniel share significant continuities. The second half of Daniel, in fact, interprets and develops specific themes and subject matter from the book's first half. At a minimum, we can safely assume the authors of Dan 7–12 treasured the court tales of Dan 1–6, finding them especially relevant to their group circle and circumstances. The suggestion is unavoidable that the authors of both halves of the book of Daniel were members of a continuing group that composed the stories and visions of the book of Daniel over many decades.

These authors may well have been people with lifestyles and daily challenges similar or identical to the characters in the court tales of the book. They treasured the court tales because they spoke directly to their needs and problems. Like Daniel and his three friends, the group lived as expatriates in the Diaspora. Like the character Daniel, a wise man and royal official in Babylon, they found careers in service of foreign rulers. They likely served as attendants, advisers, and mantic sages within the central, royal power structures of their foreign home.

Both major sections of the book of Daniel hint that their authors are wise men, mantic sages. Daniel 1:4 celebrates the protagonists of Daniel's court tales as "young men . . . versed in every branch of wisdom." Daniel 11:33, 35 and 12:3, 10 likewise celebrate "wise men." These verses within the book's second half specially esteem these figures, who will give instruction and understanding to their people during the end times, and shine bright as the sky at the resurrection of the dead.[12]

Mesopotamia had a tradition of mantic sages. The Daniel group likely operated as royal advisers or bureaucrats in the eastern Diaspora, in the tradition of this mantic wisdom of Babylon. They probably collected and edited the court tales of Dan 1–6 sometime during the third century B.C.E. This was the Hellenistic period. Specifically, it was a time when the Ptolemies—successors of Alexander the Great—ruled Judea.

Under conditions of relative support and benevolence in the context of service in a royal court, their early apocalypticism was calm and optimistic compared to what we find in Dan 7–12. They had an apocalyptic elitist character, rather than a revolutionary chiliast one. The members of the Daniel group were royal insiders, not members of some alienated fringe.

Life at court was competitive and full of pitfalls, but did not involve targeted persecution. The monarchs of the court tales expose Daniel and his companions to danger due primarily to royal inanity and incompetence. See, for example, the wonderfully comic depiction of Darius as a witless dupe in Dan 6:14-15. Darius, ruler of the known world, tears his hair out all night to come up with a plan for delivering Daniel from the famous lions' den. He makes feverish exertions but ends up exposed as besotted and paralyzed.

By the early second century (perhaps at the time the Seleucids captured Palestine from the Ptolemies), the Daniel group returned to Judea, their ancestral homeland, where they recorded the apocalyptic visions of Dan 7–12. At this period, after 198 B.C.E., their burgeoning apocalyptic imagination came increasingly into conflict with the viewpoint of their sponsors. As noted above, a deviant worldview will often encounter blank stares and punishing opposition from official quarters.

The writings of the Daniel group became less lighthearted and comedic as the new Seleucid rulers of Judea revealed their true colors. As Antiochus moved to Hellenize the Judeans, the Daniel writings took on a deadly seriousness and an ever more cosmological perspective. They become progressively more concerned with honestly revealing that God's reign will not come without horrible birth pangs. But it will come. A terrifying state of chaos preceded God's original creation of the cosmos. This chaos would reassert itself in the end times, but only to pave the way for God's new, re-creative work.

CHAPTER 7

APOCALYPTICISM AND THE JESUS GROUP

A straightforward reading of the New Testament quickly reveals an "Apocalyptic Jesus." Jesus, as the New Testament describes him, believed that God was about to overturn the world directly and decisively. He further expected to play a signal messianic role in God's imminent apocalyptic work. For example, Matt 24:37-39 reads: "For as the days of Noah were, so will be the coming of the Son of Man. . . . They knew nothing until the flood came and swept them all away." For other good examples of Jesus' apocalypticism, see Mark 8:38; 13:26; 14:62.

Jesus' messianic role was subject to great misunderstanding, so he carefully and subtly molded his disciples' thinking about it. He taught them that at the same time the role involved radical suffering, it was also miraculous and transcendent. The Messiah will be supernaturally involved in ushering in a new world of justice and peace on earth.

A lively scholarly debate has continued for over a century about whether Jesus of Nazareth—the actual Jesus of history—fits the picture of an apocalyptic messiah. Can historians reasonably conclude that Jesus, a Jewish peasant living in Palestine in the Roman era, expected an imminent, overpowering divine intervention that would turn the world on its head? Could he have understood himself as a transcendent, messianic protagonist in such an apocalyptic scenario?

Is this the most probable historical picture of Jesus?

Following in the footsteps of studies by Johannes Weiss in 1892 and Albert Schweitzer in 1901, many twentieth-century scholars accepted a paradigm of Jesus as an apocalyptic prophet. Not all scholars were convinced, however, and the debate has raged particularly strongly in the last two decades.

Present-day scholars—for example, the seventy-plus scholars of the Jesus Seminar—have intensively renewed interest in the historical Jesus. Researchers are now about evenly divided over the question of Jesus' apocalypticism. Prominent members of the Jesus Seminar, such as John Dominic Crossan, Marcus Borg, and Stephen Patterson, have written studies arguing that Jesus was not an apocalyptic messiah.[1]

Scholars debate Jesus' identity, in part, because the Bible is a highly complex database for historical research. To research Jesus, critical scholars have to weigh the relative historical value of the sources making up the New Testament. They probe behind the Bible's layers of interpretation to uncover the earliest reliable historical material about Jesus' life and teaching. It is painstaking and rather hypothetical work.

A set of criteria of authenticity aids this enterprise. Scholars disagree over many proposed criteria, but a few seem incontrovertibly useful. When two or three separate sources in the New Testament independently witness to a saying or deed of Jesus, it is impressive evidence that it is dominical (i.e., authentic to the Jesus of history and not an embellishment of later biblical writers).

For example, Mark and Luke independently preserve a parable of Jesus about slaves needing to be watchful when they do not know the hour of their master's return home (Mark 13:34-35; Luke 12:36-38). There is double reason to believe that the historical Jesus actually told such a parable, alerting people to be expectant about the imminent reign of God.

Likewise, when the Bible preserves something awkward or embarrassing about Jesus, such as an unfulfilled prophecy, it is hard to argue that interpreters and editors invented the information later for their own reasons. It is doubtful that the gospel writers would have invented Jesus' prediction to his missionary disciples in Matt 10:23 that "You will not have gone through all the towns of Israel before the Son of Man comes."

Evidence meeting such stringent criteria is rare, of course. Scholars often have to settle for data that is far less certain. Data that does pass such high tests of authenticity is exciting, however, because it allows for relatively solid conclusions about the historical Jesus.

Even when they agree they have uncovered reliable historical evidence about Jesus, scholars frequently wrestle with interpreting the evidence. Part of the problem is that Jesus so frequently used metaphorical and poetic language in teaching. He purposely puzzled audiences, pushing them to change their thinking and reevaluate their lives. His parables suggest a major crisis is looming, but they do not overtly describe what it is (e.g., Matt 7:27 ‖ Luke 6:49).

Too narrow an understanding of apocalypticism causes problems for other scholars in synthesizing a coherent Jesus. They doubt a coherent Jesus could be both a social critic and an apocalyptic visionary. If Jesus emphasized a coming, postapocalyptic justice, they ask, does that not preclude a focus on justice in this world?

A more critical and flexible understanding of Jesus' apocalypticism resolves this proposed tension. For Jesus, God's reign brings to reality all the traditional ideals of the Bible's lawgivers, prophets, and sages. God always intended these classic biblical norms to apply to communal life, and is now about to ensure that they will forever. The apocalyptic vision of God's reign thus presents a lifestyle to which the world should already aspire. It provides orientation and adrenaline for active social criticism in the here and now, whether the end times are imminent or somehow delayed.

To make headway in uncovering Jesus of Nazareth, scholars need a sound methodology. The best approach is to begin with an overall hypothesis about Jesus—a model or paradigm—and then test it against the evidence. Jesus' historical and social milieu must allow for the suggested paradigm, and the evidence from critical study of the New Testament must support it. The most reliable paradigm of Jesus will fit the evidence and integrate it consistently, in a persuasive and satisfying way. In what space is available here, let us begin to test the paradigm of the apocalyptic Jesus.

I will leave aside from the present discussion several basic features of Jesus' personality and place in society, including his role as miracle worker and healer and his identity as a wise teacher, teller of parables, and social critic. Scholars find it easy to accept that Jesus played these roles. Jesus' historical milieu incontestably allowed for them, and they are clear from the various sources of the New Testament.

Where scholars disagree hotly is about Jesus' apocalypticism and his consciousness about himself as a suffering, eschatological messiah. Did the historical Jesus really have an apocalyptic identity?

JESUS AS AN APOCALYPTIC HERALD

Continuing scholarly study of the Dead Sea Scrolls is shedding significant new light on Jesus' own understanding of his identity as the Messiah, forcing scholars to rethink long-held theories. The scrolls predate Jesus and his followers. They offer clear insight into the historical background of Jesus' life and ministry, revealing one set of messianic and apocalyptic beliefs within the complex and multifaceted early Judaism of late Hellenistic and early Roman times. The Dead Sea Scrolls make plain, in particular, the range of self-understandings possible for a person who believed that he was the messiah in Jesus' time.

Two hymns among the writings of Qumran have recently caught scholars' attention because they call into question common scholarly assumptions about the messianic expectations of Jesus' era. These messianic hymns—the "Self-Glorification Hymn" and a second, connected, responsorial hymn, calling the community to respond in thanks to the content of the first hymn— are part of the Qumran "Thanksgiving Scroll." The Scroll is a collection of psalms of thanksgiving to God used in the Dead Sea Scroll community.

The following scroll texts and fragments preserve the "Self-Glorification Hymn": 4QHe; 4Q491 frg. 11, col. 1, lines 5-11. The second, responsorial hymn occurs in 4QHa frg. 7, col. 1, lines

151

13-23 and col. 2, lines 1-14; 4Q491 frg. 11, col. 1, lines 13-16. These documents were composed at Qumran during the second half of the first century B.C.E., and thus predate Jesus' adult ministry by several decades. I shall refer to the hymns as Israel Knohl labels them and presents them in English translation: hymn 1, versions 1 and 2, and hymn 2, versions 1 and 2.[2]

The second, responsorial hymn celebrates a time of God's vindication and judgment of humanity in conjunction with the appearance of the Messiah. This time of epiphany makes God's reign obvious to the whole world, whose people now recognize the power of God's Messiah made known in might (hymn 2, version 2). God "casts down the haughty spirit." "Injustice is removed," its perpetrators consigned to "eternal destruction" (hymn 2, version 1, column 2).

There follows a time of world redemption, a shining new era of paradise. "Iniquity ends" and wickedness perishes. "Grief disappears" from people's hearts. "Groaning flees," and "terror ceases." Humankind instead experiences "healing for all times," along with "eternal blessing."

All this is evidence of a radical brand of messianism. According to these hymns, the coming to earth of the Messiah is an apocalyptic, cataclysmic event. This type of messianic understanding, the Dead Sea Scrolls reveal, was possible and extant at Jesus' time. Since early, pre-Christian Judaism knew of this type of messianism, an "apocalyptic Jesus" is within the bounds of historical possibility.

The biblical evidence connects the start of Jesus' ministry with the contemporary apocalyptic excitement occurring in the Judean wilderness at places such as Qumran. The connecting link is the figure of John the Baptizer.

John the Baptizer was like the covenanters of Qumran in key respects. Like them, he cherished priestly concerns (Luke 3:3; 5:33; 11:1) and was a descendent of priests (Luke 1:5). Radically critical of contemporary society, especially the Jerusalem aristocracy, he moved his ministry out to the wilderness just as they did (Luke 3:4).

The Baptizer was an apocalyptic prophet who announced God was about to impose God's rule on earth. He preached that the day of judgment was at hand, warning his audience of "the wrath to come." Already, according to the Baptizer, "the ax is lying at the root of the trees" (Matt 3:7, 10 ‖ Luke 3:7, 9). God was now sending the Messiah to separate the "wheat" and the "chaff," and to burn up the chaff "with unquenchable fire" (Matt 3:12 ‖ Luke 3:17).

According to every indication, Jesus of Nazareth carried on the program of John the Baptizer. Jesus' public ministry began after being baptized by John. It commenced with the very same message as the Baptizer, if the exact parallelism between Matt 3:2 and 4:17 is any guide. Indeed, Jesus likely viewed the Baptizer's proclamation of the reign of God as something already inaugurated (proleptically) in Jesus' ongoing work. Later, Jesus praises the Baptizer in glowing terms (Matt 11:11 ‖ Luke 7:28).

Jesus drew an apocalyptic orientation not only from association with the Baptizer but also from key apocalyptic texts of the Hebrew Bible.

Near the start of his ministry, according to Luke 4, Jesus identified his mission on earth as the program of one such apocalyptic passage, Isa 61. Identifying himself with the ideal speaker of Isa 61, he read the poetic passage to a synagogue in Nazareth. He then announced, "Today this scripture has been fulfilled in your hearing" (Luke 4:21).

Applying criteria of historical authenticity, there is strong reason to trust Jesus' affinity with the ideal voice of Isa 61. Two separate gospel sources, Luke 4:16-19 (special Luke material) and Matt 11:5 (Q source material; cf. also Matt 5:3 and the Qumran text known as 4Q521), show him drawing on Isa 61 to explain his messianic mission. (The Q source is the primitive source that scholars believe stands behind many virtually identical sayings in Matthew and Luke.) Jesus' personal identification with the message of Isa 61 is thus "doubly attested," and historically trustworthy.

Look closely at Isa 61. When Jesus steps into place as the poem's speaker, he takes on the role of an apocalyptic herald. Verse 2 summarizes Jesus' messianic program: to inaugurate the time of God's favor and the day of God's vengeance.

God's "day of vengeance," to which verse 2 refers, is the time when God battles all forces in creation that stubbornly oppose salvation. Cross-references in Isa 34:8 and 63:4 make this obvious. Isaiah 63:1-6 declares that on the "day of vengeance," God will trample down peoples in anger, crushing them in wrath.

Although God's apocalyptic appearance is a day of vengeance for the wicked, it is a comforting time of "favor" for God's covenant people. God's favor is concrete and physical—for the entire world to see—not ethereal. Isaiah 61:1 establishes this at the poem's start.

According to verse 1, God's servant comes to "proclaim liberty," an expression straight from Lev 25:10 and its legal/economic provision for a year of Jubilee. Jubilee time in Leviticus is about concrete, economic liberty, not ethereal feelings of liberty. When Isa 61 alludes to an ultimate, climactic Jubilee, it envisions God's restoration of covenant community on earth. It envisions God enacting a concrete, physical liberty that rocks the world.

Other source texts of the Gospels provide further evidence that the Jesus of history associated his earthly mission with the end times, the imminent arrival of the reign of God on earth.

At the start of the gospel of Mark, Jesus comes to Galilee, proclaiming the good news of God, and saying, "The time is fulfilled, and the kingdom of God has come near; repent, and believe in the good news" (Mark 1:15). The Q source independently attests the same expectation in a different context, namely, Jesus' sending of his twelve disciples to preach to the people of Israel. Central to the proclamation of the twelve is this very message, "The kingdom of heaven/God has come near" (Matt 10:7 ‖ Luke 9:2; 10:9, 11). We are safe in tracing this announcement back to Jesus of Nazareth, since it meets the criterion of double independent attestation.

The "kingdom of God," proclaimed by Jesus and the Jesus group, is an apocalyptic concept in diverse texts of ancient Judaism. In texts such as Dan 7:14; Psalm of Solomon 17:3; Testament of Moses 10:1; and Qumran texts 4Q246 and 4Q521, the concept clearly refers to God's unmistakable exercise of sovereign authority on earth, established by God's own initiative in coming and invading history.

Jesus is clear that God's reign is coming to earth whether human beings cooperate or not. Human beings are not instrumental in achieving it. In fact, Jesus expects many people to permanently reject his summons to prepare for God's intervention and judgment (Luke 10:11-12).

The focus on God's initiative and prerogative is no excuse for apathy and inaction, however. Jesus and the disciples earnestly summon people to repent and believe in what God is doing (Mark 1:15). The apocalyptic vision of God at work to bring all of previous history and revelation to culmination should orient people's thinking and living.

An additional piece of evidence that Jesus heralded an immediate apocalypse is the New Testament writers' struggle with the delay of his forecasts. A crisis of interpretation developed in primitive Christianity as time passed with no fulfillment of Jesus' apocalyptic expectations. Luke 19:11 betrays one interpretive technique in dealing with the crisis. The verse argues that Jesus' disciples were quite capable of misinterpreting him over the definite imminence of the end times.

The compiler of Mark deals with the ongoing nonfulfillment of Jesus' apocalyptic sayings in another way. He softens Mark 9:1 by placing it immediately before the account of the transfiguration. Giving the saying this editorial context implies that history has not disconfirmed it. Some of Jesus' contemporaries did live long enough to witness at least a "preview" of the reign of God in the events of Mark 9:2-10.

John 21:22-23 works hard to clarify yet another of Jesus' apocalyptic sayings. John's audience was undoubtedly upset by the death of the beloved disciple, whom they thought Jesus had promised would see the second coming (the Parousia). The editor clarifies that Jesus' traditional saying about the beloved disciple's life span was not a prediction but merely a hypothetical question. "If it is my will that he remain until I come, what is that to you?"

Based on such early Christian wrestlings with Jesus' traditional sayings, Dale C. Allison aptly concludes, "Clearly the sources betray the tacit awareness that Jesus and those around him erroneously hoped for a near end. This fact has far-reaching consequences."[3]

JESUS' CATASTROPHIC MESSIAHSHIP

The Gospels picture Jesus not only announcing God's coming reign but also playing the role of messianic protagonist in the imminent apocalypse. Jesus' messianic work, particularly his suffering and death, are key in ushering in God's apocalyptic rule on earth. Jesus slowly teaches the disciples that God's apocalyptic plans call for the Messiah to suffer and give up his life to atone for humankind.

155

Mark 8:31-32, for example, reads: "Then he began to teach them that the Son of Man must undergo great suffering, and be rejected by the elders, the chief priests, and the scribes, and be killed, and after three days rise again. He said all this quite openly."

Do these notions about Jesus' pivotal apocalyptic role trace back to Jesus himself? Is it historically accurate to say he viewed himself as a suffering messiah?

Many contemporary scholars believe the answer to be no.

In the mid-twentieth century, Rudolf Bultmann presented a classic case for their negative conclusion. Bultmann argued the historical Jesus was not conscious of being a dying and rising divine figure. He did not predict his suffering and death. It was only Jesus' disciples, after his death, who interpreted his life and work in terms of the Suffering Servant of Isa 53 and the super-natural, apocalyptic Son of Man of Daniel.

Bultmann writes, "The tradition of Jesus' sayings reveals no trace of a consciousness on his part of being the Servant of God of [Isaiah] 53. The messianic interpretation of [Isaiah] 53 was discovered in the Christian Church, and even in it evidently not immediately."[4]

We have already uncovered evidence contradicting Bultmann's position. Jesus' citation of Isa 61 near the start of his ministry shows he identified himself with the ideal protagonist of the Servant poems of the second half of the book of Isaiah. Although Isa 61 does not mention it, the larger collection of these poems connects the mission of God's ideal servant with a lifestyle of suffering and death.

Critical scholars argue that Isa 61 is from a separate, later source of Isaiah than the poems of the Suffering Servant in Isa 42:1-4; 49:1-6; 50:4-9; and 52:13–53:12. However, Jesus did not practice historical criticism. He would have had no reason to differentiate Isa 61 from its sibling Servant poems, where God's ideal servant suffers and dies in atonement for others.[5]

The Dead Sea Scrolls offer evidence further calling Bultmann's view into question. They reveal that the notion of an atoning mes-siah was a live concept within Jesus' historical milieu, not an innovation of post-Easter Christianity. The idea is unambiguous in the *Damascus Document*, which tells the covenant community of the end times that the messiah will "atone their iniquity better than through meal and sin-offerings" (CD 14:18-19).

A specifically messianic interpretation of Isaiah's Servant poems appears within the Dead Sea Scrolls in the unique pair of messianic hymns of the Qumran Thanksgiving Scroll introduced earlier. I have yet to describe the first hymn's contents. It is known as the "Self-Glorification Hymn," because its speaker presents himself in glorious terms. This self-presentation contrasts sharply with the language of most of the other psalms of the Thanksgiving Scroll. The speaker of the "Self-Glorification Hymn," it soon becomes apparent, is no ordinary member of the Qumran community but a messianic figure. He is at home in the heavenly realm and brings redemption to earth.

The speaker of the hymn may be an ideal, literary figure, sketched out by the Qumran group. Alternatively, the hymn's speaker may be an actual figure of history. Michael Wise argues that the followers of the well-known "teacher of righteousness" of the group composed the hymn pseudonymously, in his name, after his death.[6] In contrast, Israel Knohl suggests the speaker arose as a leader of the Qumran group in the time of King Herod. He was not the teacher of righteousness, but a subsequent Essene leader, believed by himself and the Qumran community to be the royal messiah of Israel.

What is interesting for our purposes is not the identification of the hymn's speaker but the messianic concepts of which he speaks. This messiah is clearly one whose character and mission are bound up with suffering. He describes himself as a radically despised and rejected figure. More than the rest of humanity, he has endured evil (lines 2-3, hymn 1, version 1).

Just as Isaiah's Suffering Servant is "despised and rejected by others" (Isa 53:3), so the Qumran messiah is "despised" and "rejected [by others]." Just as the Suffering Servant of Isaiah is "exalted and lifted up" (Isa 52:13; cf. Isa 53:10, 12), so God "magnifies" the Qumran messiah "to the clouds" (hymn 2, column 2, line 9). Unquestionably, the description of the Qumran messiah draws in part on the picture of the Servant figure of Isaiah, especially the picture in Isa 53.

Line 9 of version 2 of the "Self-Glorification Hymn" confirms this interpretation. The Qumran messiah states directly that he has "borne all afflictions." The link to the servant figure of Isaiah

is hard to deny. Isaiah 53:4 states, "Surely he has borne our infir-
mities, / and carried our diseases." Isaiah 53:11 adds, "My servant
shall make many righteous, / and he shall bear their iniquities."
The Suffering Servant of Isa 53 and the Qumran messiah of the
"Self-Glorification Hymn" both suffer vicariously for others, bearing their pain, sickness, and guilt.

On the basis of this evidence, Knohl concludes, "The speaker
in the first [Self-Glorification] hymn, who saw himself in terms of
the 'suffering servant' described by Isaiah, was regarded by his
community as someone who through his sufferings had atoned
for the sins of all the members of his sect."[7]

In light of the language and content of this Qumran hymn, it is
hard to defend the position of Bultmann and his contemporary
followers. The Qumran text reveals that the idea of a suffering
messiah was native to Jesus' milieu, not the invention of the post-
Easter church (i.e., the product of Christian reflection on the
meaning of Jesus' crucifixion). Since the notion of messianic
atonement and suffering was live in Jesus' historical context,
scholars must be willing to accept that Jesus believed himself to
be a suffering messiah if the biblical evidence points in that direction. Jesus of Nazareth, the historical figure himself, may have
understood suffering and dying as an integral part of his God-
given mission.

Even if God's messianic plan had not specified that the Messiah
must suffer (as in the "Self-Glorification Hymn"), public indifference and opposition to his message (e.g., Mark 4:4-7; 6:4; Matt
10:23; John 15:18) would surely have led Jesus to anticipate ending up despised and rejected. Up against opposition, he
responded along the lines of Isaiah's Servant poetry, shunning
active resistance and embracing human frailty. This response, he
surely concluded, would ultimately bring him messianic victory.

True victory, Jesus consistently taught, comes not through violent resistance but through turning the other cheek in the face of
violence (Matt 5:39 ‖ Luke 6:29), through taking up one's cross
(doubly attested: Mark 8:34; Matt 10:38 ‖ Luke 14:27), and
through losing one's life (doubly attested: Mark 8:35; Matt 10:39 ‖
Luke 17:33).

Several authentic glimpses within the Gospels into Jesus' words
and actions attest that he fits the paradigm of a catastrophic messiah—one who ushers in God's reign through suffering and death.

He fits the vision of the speaker of Qumran's "Self-Glorification Hymn." Mark, the earliest gospel, provides several clear glimpses of this, and we can begin with a few examples of them.

Within Jesus' parable of the wicked tenants, Mark 12:8 describes the tenants killing the vineyard owner's heir and casting him out of the vineyard. The parable overtly reflects Jesus' belief that his messianic mission from God will get him killed.

Matthew's and Luke's versions of the parable modify Mark 12:8, conforming it to the sequence of events of Jesus' passion. Had the early church invented Mark's version of the parable after Jesus' death, they would likely not have needed to make such adjustments. Mark's early version of the parable appears authentically dominical.

In Mark 14:27, Jesus quotes Zech 13:7, "strike the shepherd, and the sheep will be scattered." Zechariah 13, like Isa 53, anticipates that God's ideal servant will have to suffer and die. Beyond Isa 53, however, Zech 13:7-9 spells out specific trials and tribulations that follow in the wake of the Messiah's demise. Jesus is thus able to use this quote to account for both his imminent passion and the tribulation and displacement of the disciples it will provoke.

Jesus' reference to this Zecharian prophecy of messianic suffering is likely authentic. The *Damascus Document* at Qumran had already used the prophecy to interpret the death of an end-time leader (CD 19:5-10),[8] and the saying fits Jesus' habits of mind and speech. Jesus habitually spoke of himself as a shepherd (e.g., Matt 10:16; 15:24; 18:12-14). He also repeatedly identified key parts of his messianic mission with the sequence of themes and images in Zech 9–14 (Mark 11:1-10 ‖ Zech 9:9-10; Mark 11:15-17 ‖ Zech 14:20-21).

N. T. Wright states, "There should be no doubt that Jesus knew this whole passage [of Zech 9–14], and that he saw it as centrally constitutive of his own vocation, at the level not just of ideas but of agendas."[9]

Jesus' programmatic saying in Mark 10:45 may serve as a final example of Mark's witness on this topic. In the saying, Jesus announces the whole goal of his messianic mission is "to give his life a ransom for many" (cf. 1 Macc 2:50; 6:44). Scholars debate the authenticity of Mark 10:45, but it has in its favor a form and structure that are tightly parallel with Jesus' authentic saying in Matt 10:34-35.[10]

The Q source provides corroborating evidence of Jesus' catastrophic messianism, although its witness to the paradigm is less direct than in Mark.

Q attests, for example, that Jesus wrestled with the ironic fact that God's Messiah is humbled in the course of his life mission. Jesus laments the irony that "foxes have holes, and birds of the air have nests; but the Son of Man has nowhere to lay his head" (Matt 8:20 || Luke 9:58).

Q further attests a catastrophic messiahship by supporting the tradition of the Hebrew Bible that prophets tend to suffer rejection and martyrdom. Jesus laments over Jerusalem: "Jerusalem, Jerusalem, the city that kills the prophets and stones those who are sent to it!" (Matt 23:37 || Luke 13:34). For the same theme elsewhere in Q, see Matt 5:12 || Luke 6:23 and Matt 23:29-31 || Luke 11:47-48.

In other words, the paradigm of catastrophic messiahship fits the evidence of Mark and Q. Perhaps the firmest evidence that the paradigm fits the historical Jesus, however, comes from Jesus' actions and sayings at the Last Supper.

At his last supper, a day before his crucifixion, Jesus directly addresses his suffering and death. Several New Testament sources independently confirm that Jesus foresaw his passion on this occasion. They independently attest that, at least at this late point in his life, he interpreted his coming suffering and death in terms of a catastrophic messianic mission.

As part of the symbolism of the Last Supper, Jesus specifically presents the cup of wine as his own blood. "This is my blood of the covenant, which is poured out for many," he states in Mark 14:24. The words unmistakably announce he is going to his own death on behalf of the "many."

Three independent biblical texts verify that Jesus himself—the Jesus of history—linked the cup of wine with his own shed blood. The statement is triply attested. Along with Mark 14:24, see 1 Cor 11:25 and John 6:53. It is hard to imagine a stronger warrant for this saying's historicity.

N. T. Wright draws the following historical conclusion:

It emerges that Jesus, in prophetic style, identified the bread with his own body, and the wine with his own blood, and that he spoke about these in language which echoed the context of Passover, sacrifice, and covenant which the meal, in any case, must already have possessed. The synoptic tradition also indicates that Jesus said something about the climactic events being so close that this would be the last such meal he would share with his followers before the kingdom arrived.[11]

Having established that Jesus' messianic mission was consciously catastrophic, I need to reiterate that it was also both sane and dignified. Some scholars have had trouble reconciling a positive, ethical vision of Jesus with the thought that he was somehow suicidal, bent on a mission of self-destruction. Would not Jesus have been immoral or psychologically ill to pursue a cataclysmic messianism with death as its goal? The answer becomes clearer in light of the newly appreciated Qumran evidence.

The scrolls suggest that Jesus could have understood the life task of a suffering messiah as a divinely predetermined plan. God's preset messianic trajectory—clear already at Qumran decades before Jesus' birth—called for the Messiah to have to overcome his natural will to live and pursue a path that, though leading to suffering and even death, would achieve a great redemption for his people. Resigning oneself to such a plan would have been a fully sane and ethical act, as long as one understood oneself to be submitting to the ancient but harsh will of God for God's Messiah.

JESUS' TRANSCENDENT IDENTITY

The viewpoint of the New Testament writings is that Jesus' suffering and death are of benefit to humanity because of his unique, transcendent identity. The Jesus of the Gospels is consciously aware of his special, supernatural status. He betrays this at various points (e.g., Mark 12:35-37), but particularly in his oblique references to himself as Daniel's Son of Man (e.g., Matt 13:41; 25:31; Mark 13:26; 14:62; Luke 21:36).

The Son of Man, according to Dan 7, along with the Similitudes of Enoch (part of the Pseudepigrapha), is a heavenly figure of majesty, associated with the gathering together of God's people at the end of history and the initiation of God's reign.

Many modern scholars suppose that only subsequent to Jesus' life were his followers able, retrospectively, to apply ideas of a divine savior to him. Such ideas about Jesus, they assert, are implausible before the Christian movement expanded within the Hellenistic culture of the Roman Empire. This assumption seems considerably less likely in light of the evidence of the paired messianic hymns of Qumran that we have been studying.

Let us turn to the specific presentation of the supernatural, quasi-divine character of the messiah in these hymns.

The speaker of hymn 1, version 1 dwells in the holy council of heaven (lines 1-2), especially "beloved" of the heavenly "king," God (line 7). In fact, he sits enthroned in heaven (line 4). Version 2 (line 5) of the hymn is even more explicit. The speaker of the hymn has a heavenly throne, a "throne of power in the angelic council."

The members of the angelic council where the speaker has his throne are not his equals, but inferiors. "To my glory none can compare," he claims (version 1, lines 7-8). He asks rhetorically, "Who is like me among the angels *['ēlīm]*?" (version 1, line 5).

Israel Knohl notes that this claim of superiority to the angels is far from standard among the scrolls from Qumran. Normally, it is only God who occupies a "throne of power" surrounded by angelic ministers. Thus, Knohl writes, "The hero of the hymns claims divine status, . . . clearly comparing himself to the biblical God."[12]

An additional observation reinforces how radical the claims of this messiah really are. In line 5 of version 1, the speaker of the hymn actually appropriates to himself biblical language glorifying God. His words have a clear cross-reference in the Song of the Sea in Exod 15. Exodus 15:11 praises God as follows: "Who is like you, O LORD, among the gods *['ēlīm; TANAKH*: 'celestials,' NJB: 'holy ones']? / Who is like you, majestic in holiness?"

Finally, in the first hymn, the messianic speaker describes his human nature as radically transformed. He is no longer a standard, fleshly creature with normal, physical drives. In hymn 1, version 2 he states, "[My] desi[re] is not of the flesh, [for] everything precious to me is in the glory of the holy [hab]itation." The presence of such a being on earth is remarkable. It suggests something wonderful is about to happen in earth's history—perhaps a large-scale transformation of humankind's physical nature along the lines modeled by the messiah.

These statements about the messiah are radical, so radical that Knohl suggests they led at least one member of the Qumran community to mangle the Thanksgiving Scroll, which contained the messianic hymns. This would account for the disfigured condition in which the Thanksgiving Scroll was discovered in the twentieth century. Knohl surmises, "Such audacious use of [biblical language] could surely have led to the disfiguration of the copy of the Thanksgiving Scroll later."[13]

A separate text among the Dead Sea Scrolls, confirms that these radical messianic notions do not represent an isolated aberration within the thinking of the Qumran community. The document, labeled the "son of God" text (4Q246, cols. 1-2), is another instance where the group speaks about humans possessing, or at least claiming, divine attributes. It describes a human ruler of the end times, albeit an enemy ruler, whom people turn to and serve as the "son of God," the "son of the Most High."

To sum up, the notion of a transcendent, supernatural messiah is attested at Qumran. Since it was live among Jews in Palestine in the intertestamental period, Jesus and the original group of Palestinian Jews who surrounded him presumably had access to it. The biblical picture that Jesus regarded himself as Daniel's and Enoch's Son of Man is historically plausible.

Beyond being plausible, is it actually the case that Jesus was conscious of a transcendent identity? Does the paradigm fit the New Testament data? Perhaps the surest way to begin an answer is to return to the New Testament evidence about Jesus' last supper.

According to the evidence, directly after his words about the cup of wine at the Last Supper, Jesus emphasized something startling. The Last Supper anticipates the inbreaking of the reign of God with Jesus present in glory. We have double, independent attestation of this point.

After drinking the cup of wine at the supper, according to Mark 14:25, Jesus says, "I will never again drink of the fruit of the vine until that day when I drink it new in the kingdom of God." In the context of Jesus' passion experience, to speak of drinking the wine "new" in the "kingdom" on "that day" is to speak of drinking it vindicated as God's triumphant redeemer. As William Lane writes, "There is here a clear anticipation of the messianic banquet when the Passover fellowship with [Jesus'] followers will be renewed in the Kingdom of God."[14]

Jesus here looks beyond his death to a resumption of the Last Supper in God's reign. There, the supper will be completed and fulfilled as the much anticipated messianic banquet (cf. Luke

163

13:29; 14:15; 22:28-30). Presumably, Jesus understood himself as the transcendent host of that apocalyptic meal.

First Corinthians 11:26 independently attests to Jesus' concluding words at the Last Supper. After quoting words parallel to Mark 14:22-24, Paul paraphrases the substance of Mark 14:25 by saying the Eucharist aims to, "proclaim the Lord's death until he comes."

Paul appears to have known that Jesus concluded the Last Supper with a reference to serving as apocalyptic host of banquet fellowship in the reign of God. He believed this could involve nothing less than Jesus' second coming in transcendent glory to gather the faithful into that fellowship.

Let us turn now to make brief appraisals of some of Jesus' radical sayings about the Son of Man.

Although many scholars doubt the historical authenticity of the apocalyptic Son of Man sayings, good warrants support tracing several of them back to Jesus of Nazareth. Some of these sayings, in fact, are doubly attested in New Testament sources. A good example is the Son of Man saying in Mark 8:38, which is also attested in Q—Matt 10:32-33 ‖ Luke 12:8-9.

We begin with Mark 14:62. The verse presents Jesus making a brazen, public self-disclosure of transcendent glory at his trial before the Sanhedrin. The high priest asks Jesus directly, "Are you the Messiah?" and he responds in the affirmative. Jesus said, "I am; and

> 'you will see the Son of Man
> seated at the right hand of the Power,'
> and 'coming with the clouds of heaven.' "

Despite the doubts of scholars, the account may well be historically accurate. Jesus was crucified with the inscription "King of the Jews" over his head, as almost all historians concede. Thus, the authorities doubtless challenged him directly over the issue of messianic claims. Jesus would not have denied his messianic role when challenged in such a setting, so the question becomes whether the specific response recorded in Mark 14:62 is authentic or invented.

A key reason to believe it is authentic is its lack of literal fulfillment. Early Christians might have invented Jesus telling

Caiaphas he would see the Son of Man resurrected. Would they have invented a saying that Caiaphas would see him coming on the clouds to usher in God's reign?

If the statement is authentic, how can we understand Jesus' thinking? The likeliest answer is that Jesus drew his conclusions based on a commitment to the truth of Dan 7. He invested great stock in Daniel's vision that a transcendent Son of Man figure would vindicate the faithful at history's culmination (Dan 7:13-14). Understanding himself called by God as the Messiah, he confessed before Caiaphas his belief to be the figure of the Son of Man.

In light of the Qumran evidence, the belief is not incredible. The triumphal advent of Jesus as the Son of Man is the one event that would clarify and forever vindicate Jesus' mission of messianic humiliation and suffering. It would concretely realize all Jesus' apocalyptic hopes and dreams for humanity.

A second apocalyptic Son of Man saying claims historical authenticity. Two separate traditions of the New Testament attest to it. Both Mark 13:26-27 (‖ Matt 24:30-31) and 1 Thess 4:15-17 preserve an apocalyptic saying of Jesus similar to that of Mark 14:62. Based again on the scenario of Dan 7:13-14, Jesus affirms his transcendent identity and refers to his end-time triumph. This time, he connects his messianic triumph with forming an ideal, reunited community of the faithful on earth.

Speaking of the end times, Jesus in Mark 13:26-27 says that earth's people "will see 'the Son of Man coming in clouds' with great power and glory. Then he will send out the angels, and gather his elect from the four winds, from the ends of the earth to the ends of heaven."

Key elements of the saying are the Son of Man's descent from heaven, the appearance of accompanying angels, and the gathering together of the faithful. Drawing on a second, independent source, Matt 24:30-31 adds further features. In Matthew, there is a trumpet call and a reference to Zech 12:10-14. These features do not appear to be invented by Matthew, since they are found in the saying's independent appearance in 1 Thess 4:16 and Rev 1:7, respectively.

The authenticity of Jesus' statement in Mark and Matthew is bolstered by Paul's reference to it in 1 Thess 4:15-17. In the epistle, our earliest New Testament Scripture, Paul is explaining Jesus' return and his gathering of the faithful, both alive and deceased. He proceeds by referring to a special "word of the Lord" in his possession (v. 15).

Paul might conceivably mean some recent, prophetically revealed statement of the risen Lord. More likely, however, he is citing a teaching of the earthly Jesus preserved within primitive Christianity. Paul uses parallel wording and technique elsewhere to cite sayings of Jesus of Nazareth also preserved in the Gospels (e.g., Rom 14:14; 1 Cor 7:10; 9:14).

In all likelihood, Paul cites the same apocalyptic teaching of Jesus preserved in Mark 13:26-27 (‖ Matt 24:30-31). He repeats the key elements of the saying, including the idea of a descent from heaven. He refers to an archangel's call. Moreover, he specifically mentions the Lord's gathering of all believers. He goes beyond Mark and Matthew in specifying this as a "gathering" together of both the living and the dead.

Paul replaces Jesus' oblique reference to the Son of Man with direct references to Jesus as "Lord." Along with the early church, Paul has concluded that Jesus' references to the coming of the Son of Man were references to Jesus' own second coming, his Parousia.

Yet another of Jesus' apocalyptic sayings about the Son of Man is doubly, perhaps triply, attested. It must serve as our final piece of evidence that Jesus was aware of having a transcendent identity.

The Q source (Matt 24:42-44 ‖ Luke 12:39-40) and 1 Thess 5:2-4 preserve a poetic saying of Jesus about the suddenness of his apocalyptic triumph. According to Jesus, the event will fall as unexpectedly as the coming of a thief in the night. The book of Revelation apparently also knows of the saying (Rev 3:3; 16:15).

The Q source appears to preserve a slightly more original form of the saying than Paul does. In Q's form, Jesus tells a parable to motivate the disciples to watchfulness about God's reign. "If the owner of the house had known in what part of the night the thief was coming, he would have stayed awake and would not have let his house be broken into. You also must be ready!" In both Matt 24:44 and Luke 12:40, Jesus applies the parable directly to the apocalyptic advent of the Son of Man.

There is every reason to believe that Paul in 1 Thess 5:2-4 attests to the same saying. He uses the same poetic image for the same purpose of motivating his readers to wakefulness about Jesus' apocalyptic advent. It is doubtful Paul would have invented the thief metaphor for use in his present context. Its use creates the awkward paradox that Christians "not in darkness" (v. 4) are saved and vindicated specifically by a nighttime operative!

Paul adjusts Jesus' saying in at least two ways. He drops Jesus' language about the Son of Man, since he no longer needs to speak cryptically about Jesus' transcendent identity. He also makes a further application of the saying not originally present in the parable. Jesus' parable made a simple point about vigilance, but Paul adds the idea that a thief's appearance is generally unwelcome. There were false prophets in the Thessalonian church to which Paul wrote, and he believed the coming of Christ as a thief would spell their "sudden destruction" (v. 3).

CHAPTER 8

APOCALYPTIC WORLDS AND THE EARLY CHRISTIAN CHURCHES

Whatever one concludes about Jesus' own apocalyptic consciousness, it is certain that his disciples, after his death, interpreted his life and work in apocalyptic terms. Within decades after the crucifixion, many communities oriented on the worship of Jesus sprang up around the Roman Empire. Written correspondence with these communities, which date from as early as twenty-five years after the events of the Gospels, evidences a powerful apocalyptic orientation. Post-Easter Christian reflection on the meaning of Jesus concluded he had come on a catastrophic, messianic mission to usher in the reign of God on earth.

Readers of most any of the literary worlds of the New Testament encounter some form of an apocalyptic imagination. Many texts expect Jesus' quick return, to "put all his enemies under his feet" (1 Cor 15:25). The variety of first-century Christian writers holding this hope is clear from comparing texts such as Acts 3:19-21; Rom 13:11; Heb 10:37; Jas 5:8; 1 Pet 4:17; and Rev 22:20. Other scriptural authors, no less committed to an apocalyptic Jesus, modify the end-time scenario of primitive Christianity to allow for an increasingly likely delay of Jesus' second coming.

John 21:23 is an example of the latter viewpoint. As I mentioned earlier, the verse struggles to deal with the death of Jesus' beloved disciple before the Lord's Parousia. It protests that Jesus did not technically promise the beloved disciple that he would live to see the world's end, so his death does not disconfirm Jesus' word.

Although apocalypticism is simply a backdrop behind many New Testament writings, it moves center stage in several notable cases. The primary apocalyptic writing of the New Testament is Revelation, which is the topic of the next chapter. Now we turn to several celebrated apocalyptic texts within Paul's letters and the Synoptic Gospels.

Paul's best-known apocalyptic texts occur in letters he wrote to Christian communities in Greece—Corinth and Thessalonica. These early Pauline discourses elaborate an apocalyptic universe in order to deal with community problems. Paul writes to allay community members' anxiety at the death of loved ones and to counter the spread of false understandings about the end of days.

The most elaborate apocalyptic passage within the Gospels is the "little apocalypse," found in Mark 13 and its parallels in Matt 24 and Luke 21. The "little apocalypse" gathers into one discourse some of the most specific sayings within the Jesus tradition about the end times. Canonical shaping of this discourse over time came to terms with the delay of the Parousia. Shaping also reinforced a call to Christians to be wakeful about Jesus' return.

THE LETTERS OF PAUL

None of Paul's letters takes the strict form of an "apocalypse," with a heavenly intermediary granting an extended vision of archetypal symbols and heavenly reality. Paul did sometimes experience significant visions (see 2 Cor 12:1-4), but he makes no direct reference to them in his most "apocalyptic" passages, 1 Cor 15 and 1 Thess 4:13–5:11. At least in terms of literary genre, narrowly defined, the contents of his epistles differ from apocalypses such as the books of Daniel and Revelation.

Apocalyptic thoughts and themes dominate Paul's extant

writings, however. The death and resurrection of Jesus rearranges his thinking in a way quite comparable to the heavenly ascent of an apocalyptic visionary.[1] In light of the crucified and risen Jesus, Paul's thought is rife with the radical conviction that world history—indeed, creation itself—is experiencing a terrible and wonderful new departure. As J. Christiaan Becker puts it, an apocalyptic imagination provides "the master symbolism of Paul's thought."[2]

Along with the gospel events, the Hebrew Scriptures informed Paul's apocalyptic imagination. In this regard, Paul was less a visionary *seer* than an apocalyptic *teacher,* like the well-known teacher of righteousness at Qumran. As the Qumran community viewed their teacher of righteousness as having the interpretive key to the mysteries of Scripture, so Paul's Christian converts believed that he, as prophet and apostle, could interpret the true meaning of tradition. Enlightened by the teaching of Jesus Christ and the Holy Spirit, Paul had the wisdom and authority to show them how all of Scripture was coming to fulfillment in their lifetime.

Paul believes "the ends of the ages" have come upon him and his readers, and God's promised new creation has been inaugurated (1 Cor 10:11; Gal 6:15; 2 Cor 5:17). God's full transformation of humanity and the universe remains less than fully realized, however. This awaits Jesus' second coming (1 Cor 15:23; 1 Thess 3:13), which may occur at any time (1 Cor 15:51; 1 Thess 4:15). With Christ's return from heaven, the world will experience the resurrection of the dead and the re-creation of the cosmos (1 Thess 4:16-17; 1 Cor 15:19-20).

Hoping for Christ's speedy return, Paul prays, "Our Lord, come!" (Gk. *Maranatha;* 1 Cor 16:22). In the meantime, readers should begin to detach themselves from mundane lifestyles. "The present form of this world is passing away," he reminds them, along with its dominant social forms and cultural values (1 Cor 7:29-31).

Misconceptions about Paul's theology often hamper today's readers from properly appreciating and interpreting his apocalypticism. One long strain of interpretation—stretching from Augustine through Luther to Bultmann—has overemphasized the theme of individual salvation in Paul's thinking. This effectively underplays Paul's emphasis on cosmic redemption.

Just as commonly, interpreters misconstrue Paul's thinking and theology as mostly antithetical to the Hebrew Bible and its traditional biblical themes. Until recently, many scholars repeatedly asserted that Paul's theology of a suffering, atoning messiah was foreign both to the Hebrew Bible and to the Judaism of Paul's day. Since he advocated such alien views, Paul must primarily have been an innovator, proposing a radically new religious way of thinking.

No one doubts there is much that is new in Paul's thought compared to the Hebrew Bible. Noncanonical, Hellenistic apocalypses inform his spiritual and intellectual world, providing him with distinctive images of death, intermediate existence, judgment and punishment. The language of the moral philosophers of his day gives him a powerful new tool for meeting the pastoral needs of his readers. Downplaying the centrality of the Hebrew Bible in Paul's universe of meaning, however, is a mistake. It effectively prevents any solid foothold in the world of Paul's writings, which is awash in genuine scriptural themes and language.

Interpreting and appropriating Israel's canonical Scripture, including its core symbols and ideals, was fundamental to Paul's self-identity. His letters constantly cite and echo the Hebrew Bible. In fact, tracing Paul's scriptural allusions is generally a far more fruitful means of interpreting the world of his writings than unearthing the contours of his ancient historical context. His allusions to Scripture, specifically to the Greek Septuagint, form a crucial context of interpretation that remains accessible and relevant to modern readers, even when hypothetical details about the original circumstances of his letters do not.[3]

Tracing the scriptural building blocks of Paul's thought is nowhere more illuminating than in the case of his apocalyptic imagination. Paul's apocalyptic vision arose because a building momentum within the formation of Scripture prepared for it. Ripe social and political circumstances did not create it, nor was it borrowed from the eschatological spirit that infused the Roman Empire at the time. For Paul, the "ends of the ages" taking place around him was the fulfillment and climax of Hebrew Bible ideals, events, and prophecies.

Paul understood the Law and the Prophets to define God's ideals for human community and for the flourishing of righteousness on earth. Further, he read Israel's Scriptures as a sure witness to God's cosmic prerogative and redemptive purposes. Paul deduced from Scripture that God is at work to set things right and gather a faithful remnant to God's self. As the eschatological and apocalyptic texts of the Hebrew Bible attest, God will eventually achieve these goals by putting down all opposing forces on earth. God's people will not have to wait forever to see God's reign.

It can be no accident that Paul quotes Isaiah most frequently of all scriptural books (28 direct citations). Isaiah's prophecies point forward to a time when God will restore God's people at Mount Zion and reverse all wrongs so that Israel and the nations will recognize and worship God. Isaiah's powerful apocalyptic expectations of God's cosmic salvation must have been a foundational force informing Paul's apocalyptic imagination.

Paul believed the day of salvation prophesied by Isaiah and related Scriptures had dawned in his lifetime. He lived at a privileged moment in salvation history when Scripture's most powerful symbols and paradigms were blossoming, taking on concrete form. Biblical images and idioms assumed an apocalyptic configuration in his letters, as he and his audience came to grips with the realization that his small, newly formed house-churches actually embodied God's redemptive goals for human history.

The central place of authoritative Scripture in Paul's apocalypticism has an illuminating parallel in the style of the apocalyptic scrolls at Qumran. The messianic hymns of the Thanksgiving Scroll that we have examined, for example, consist of a veritable anthology of quotes and echoes of Isaiah and other biblical texts, just as Paul's apocalyptic imagination does. The writers of the Dead Sea Scrolls, like Paul and his supporters, saw Scripture's fundamental symbols and typologies coming to fulfillment in the life of their privileged, end-time community.

The passion and resurrection of Jesus Christ were the catalyst in focusing Paul's apocalyptic imagination, a key difference from apocalypticism at Qumran. For Paul and his supporters, the fact that God had just raised Christ from the dead changed everything. Paul would completely reject the idea that the resurrection was a one-time spiritual victory, said and done so we all can move forward. For him, the ramifications of the resurrection concretely challenge the physical basis of the world we inhabit—the entire created order.

Paul never conceived of the resurrection as an experience unique to Jesus, the Messiah. Far from merely an isolated messianic event, for Paul, as for other New Testament writers, Christ's resurrection was a harbinger of the end times. It signaled the general resurrection of all the dead, which Scripture anticipated at the climax of history. Christ's resurrection was, to use Paul's agricultural metaphor, "the first fruits of those who have died" (1 Cor 15:20). It presaged a whole resurrection "harvest."

As Dale Allison writes, "The resurrection of the dead, when it appears in Jewish sources, is a collective experience, not something that happens to an isolated individual (which is why some early Christians tried their best not to isolate Jesus' experience: Matt 27:51-53; 1 Cor 15:20; Col 1:18). Resurrection is also associated with a number of supernatural events, such as the last judgment, which clearly had not yet occurred [when the New Testament documents were written]."[4]

The cataclysmic work of Jesus Messiah, Paul was convinced, had inaugurated all for which the Law and the Prophets longed. Since Christ's crucifixion and victory over death mark the ends of the ages, Paul concluded that all Scripture's ideals and hopes were about to come into focus.

First Corinthians 15 provides an excellent glimpse into Paul's apocalyptic imagination and its scriptural building blocks. It is one of the earliest letters we have from him, and it shows the centrality of apocalypticism in his missionary work. Thus, it is well worth a brief examination.

By early in the year 50 C.E., Paul was extending his mission out of the Near East into Europe, starting with Greece. Working his way south from Macedonia through Athens, he met missionaries named Priscilla and Aquila in Corinth and joined them in preaching the gospel (Acts 18:2-4). Paul worked for a year and a half in Corinth, "planting" and "fathering" a network of house-churches (1 Cor 3:6; 4:15). He wrote 1 Corinthians to this Christian network around 54 C.E., after he had left Greece and moved across the Aegean Sea to Ephesus on his continuing missionary journeys.

Paul addresses several community problems in 1 Corinthians, but none more serious than the Corinthians' conflict over apocalypticism. Taking their misunderstandings about this topic with the utmost seriousness, Paul postpones pastoral instruction on it until chapter 15 at the letter's climax.

Under the influence of nonscriptural teachings (the "bad company" Paul mentions in 1 Cor 15:33), some Corinthian believers had developed a spiritual idealism that clashed hard with Paul's apocalypticism. The major conflict was over God's end-time redemption of the material world, especially the corporeal human body. Members of the community wondered why God would ever want to resurrect the body. To their "spiritual" way of thinking, bodies were little more than a source of weakness and sin. It would be better for the spirit to be rid of the body at death. As Richard Hays states, some Corinthians "were so spiritual that they found the notion of a resurrection *of the body* crass and embarrassing."[5]

Many Bible readers today awkwardly find themselves kindred spirits of the wayward Corinthian recipients of Paul's letter. They treat the resurrection of the body as a metaphor for spiritual transformation rather than something concrete. They comfort the bereaved with notions of ethereal, heavenly joys, whitewashing the cold, hard tragedy of the grave. Such thinking fits ancient Hellenistic dualism well, but not the witness of biblical literature.

Paul's extended instruction in chapter 15 counters the Corinthians' skepticism about the resurrection with a radical apocalyptic imagination. He affirms God's radical commitment to redeeming the physical and material quality of existence. In the course of his argument, Paul reveals how Scripture and scriptural interpretation form the basis of his symbol system.

The view of reality Paul presents arises directly from "the Scriptures," as he states twice at the beginning of his instruction (vv. 3, 4). He goes on to cite or echo well over a dozen Hebrew Bible passages as he works through the Corinthians' doubts. The number of references to Scripture is especially noteworthy, considering that Paul is writing not to Jews but to new believers who previously were mostly Gentiles (see 1 Cor 12:2).

The Hebrew Bible building blocks of 1 Cor 15 include at least the following references and allusions: Gen 2:17; 3:19 (v. 21); Dan 7:27 (v. 24); Ps 110:1 (v. 25); Ps 49:14 and Hab 2:5 (v. 26); Ps 8:6 (v. 27); Isa 22:13 (v. 32); Ps 14:1 (v. 36); Gen 1:11-12, 20-25 (vv. 38-39); Gen 1:14-18 and Dan 12:3 (vv. 40-41); Gen 2:7 (v. 45); Isa 27:13 (v. 52); Isa 25:7-8 (v. 54); and Hos 13:14 (v. 55).

Note the number of allusions to Gen 1–3, the biblical story of the world's creation and humanity's fall. Creation symbols figure strongly, because the apocalyptic imagination is preoccupied with setting creation right. The archetype of Adam particularly captivates Paul. Adam symbolizes for him the problem of sin and death within the present created order (v. 22). Further, for Paul, Adam incarnates the decay and weakness of the "natural body" to be rectified by God's apocalyptic work of resurrecting the dead with new imperishable bodies (vv. 44-45).

Other scriptural images inform elaborate messianic beliefs within Paul's apocalyptic imagination. Paul understands the Hebrew Scriptures to articulate and prophesy a catastrophic messianic mission to earth. The mission atones for humanity and presages the bodily resurrection of the dead. Citing what is probably an early Christian creed, Paul states, "Christ died for our sins in accordance with the scriptures" (v. 3). "He was raised on the third day in accordance with the scriptures" (v. 4).

Paul does not cite the specific Scriptures he has in mind, but he must be referring to texts such as Isa 53 and Ps 22. An ideal literary figure undergoes death and rescue in these texts, saving those around him in the process. Qumran's "Self-Glorification Hymn" envisages the same type of catastrophic messiah. It builds a messianic imagination out of the same scriptural echoes used by Paul and the early church, anticipating his worldview by well over half a century.

Just like Paul's messiah, the protagonist of the "Self-Glorification Hymn" has "borne all afflictions" (cf. Isa 53:4, 11). After his rejection and suffering, God "magnifies" the Qumran messiah "to the clouds" (cf. Isa 52:13; 53:10, 12). Paul's messianic use of Hebrew Scripture is far from unprecedented.

Paul's symbolic universe interweaves further biblical images from Psalms and Isaiah to depict an end-time, cosmic victory of God. It takes place at the second coming of the Messiah. At that time, God will defeat all enemies on earth, including death itself.

Psalm 110:1 contributes the ideal of an undisputed reign of God's Messiah. At its origins, the psalm referred to a reigning Davidic king, but after the monarchic era the only king in mind for those who preserved the psalm as Scripture was the Messiah. Paul reads the psalm in its scriptural, canonical sense when he deduces from it that the Messiah will decisively subdue all Zion's antagonists at the end of days (vv. 25, 27).

Isaiah 25:6-8 adds to Paul's scenario that when evil is finally

175

vanquished, an amazing new age will begin on earth. According to Isa 25, this new age will include a gathering of all peoples— Gentiles along with Jews—to feast at Mount Zion. Furthermore, God at that time will destroy "the shroud [of death]" that currently enfolds all nations. God will "swallow up death forever" (Isa 25:8; cf. 1 Cor 15:54). Under God's reign on earth, physical, embodied life will be possible without the threat of death.

Based on another text in Isaiah (27:12-13), Paul believes the sounding of a great trumpet will announce God's end-time gathering of all believers (v. 52; cf. Matt 24:31). Daniel 12:1-3 informs him that this grand eschatological ingathering includes the dead as well as the living (v. 52). Bodily resurrection is central to God's purposes for creation. The hyperspirituality of some Corinthians has completely led them astray.

Scripture supplies Paul the additional image that the faithful departed return to life completely transfigured (vv. 35-50). The resurrection is no crude resuscitation of corpses, as skeptics of the resurrection at Corinth supposed. Rather, God transforms the bodily existence of believers into a glorious new state. Daniel 12:3 states that the newly resurrected will "shine." They will become "like the stars forever" (cf. 1 Cor 15:40-41, 48-49). The Corinthian skeptics suffered from a severe lack of apocalyptic imagination about the magnificence of the resurrection body.

A catalytic event of recent history provoked the imaginative new configuration of biblical symbols that we find in Paul's letters. The event, of course, is God's resurrection of Jesus, the Messiah, from the dead.

Christ's resurrection is the hinge of Paul's argument in 1 Cor 15. It makes no sense for Christians to doubt that God will raise the dead, he argues, since the heart of Christian faith turns on a resurrection event. With devastating logic, he asks, "Now if Christ is proclaimed as raised from the dead, how can some of you say there is no resurrection of the dead?" (v. 12).

Christ's rising from the dead, however, does more than prove that resurrection must be taken seriously as a real phenomenon. It confirms that God is in the business of resurrection. It marks the advent of an end-time drama filled with the raising of the dead. History will culminate, according to Paul's argument, in God's general, apocalyptic resurrection of all deceased persons.

It is striking how tightly Paul links Christ's resurrection with the apocalyptic resurrection of the dead at the end of history. He goes so far as to claim that if the apocalyptic resurrection of all Christians is unreal, then Christ's resurrection itself is unreal. If so, Christian believers are "of all people most to be pitied" (v. 19). "Our proclamation has been in vain and your faith has been in vain" (v. 14).

Verses 13 and 16 establish the link in no uncertain terms: "If there is no resurrection of the dead, then Christ has not been raised."

The emphasis on Christ's resurrection in 1 Cor 15 assures us that it is Paul's point of focus in constructing an apocalyptic imagination out of the scriptures. Christ's passion and rising to life again has set the end times in motion. It is what has gathered the Corinthians together as an end-time community, about to inherit all of God's promises and dreams for God's people Israel. It is the reason Paul's readers should start separating themselves from the mundane routines of life, in anticipation of God's messianic banquet on Mount Zion where death no longer exists.

First Corinthians is not the only letter of Paul to contain a major section focused on apocalypticism. Another important apocalyptic discourse of Paul occurs in his first letter to the Thessalonians. First Thessalonians expresses an active apocalyptic imagination, which comes to full expression in 1 Thess 4:13–5:11.

With the help of his missionary companions Silas and Timothy, Paul established a Christian community at the Macedonian port city of Thessalonica in the summer of 49 C.E. before he journeyed south to Corinth. He was able to spend only about three months working with the new Thessalonian Christians. After that, the Jews of the city, jealous at Paul's success at converting the populace, forced him to flee (Acts 17:4-10). Paul hated being separated from the Thessalonians, unable to work personally at strengthening their new faith. Prevented from visiting, he wrote the young church a letter from Corinth before the end of the year 50. It was a highly apocalyptic letter.

The Bible preserves this remarkable document from 50 C.E. as the earliest New Testament writing, 1 Thessalonians.

Paul's apocalyptic "master symbolism" emerges most elaborately in the course of his letter as he turns to address pastoral issues surrounding the deaths of Thessalonian community members (1 Thess 4:13-18). The Thessalonians had learned from Paul

177

to expect Christ's climactic return at any moment, to vindicate and perfect their small, end-time community (cf. 1 Thess 1:10; 2:19; 3:13; 4:15; 5:23). With their focus trained excitedly on their imminent new communal bonding with Christ, the resurrection of the dead seemed mostly abstract. The Parousia of the Lord would surely occur, they believed, within the lifetimes of house-church members.

Since Paul's absence, however, death had been shattering their community and raising anxieties. As death ripped away their loved ones, it became vital to learn as much as possible about the resurrection of the dead. How exactly would the resurrection of loved ones figure into the community's coming association with Christ? When exactly would those who remain alive see their loved ones again?

The Thessalonians' problem is one that did not occur to the Corinthians. The Corinthians' error, as we just learned, was not taking seriously enough the death of the corporeal body. Paul had to work hard to get the Corinthians to feel anything of the cold chill of the grave so that they could appreciate the resurrection. No work was needed to get that message to the Thessalonians. They took the grave seriously. They would readily receive Paul's renewed apocalyptic teaching about the resurrection of the dead.

Paul confronts the Thessalonians' anxiety with a vibrant apocalyptic imagination. That imagination, as 1 Cor 15 has attested, was built primarily out of echoes of the Hebrew Bible. Sounding most loudly in 1 Thess 4 are scriptural echoes about God's end-time gathering of the faithful from all over the world.

Paul's skill as an apocalyptic pastor is impressive. The theme of an eschatological gathering and reuniting of all God's people directly meets the anxieties of a community fractured by death. God's apocalyptic ingathering, Paul perceives, will soon heal all painful fractures and create an ideal community of worship.

We have seen that Paul alludes to God's end-time ingathering in 1 Cor 15. Here in 1 Thess 4, at verse 14, he goes beyond allusions to foreground the theme.

Verse 14 reads, "If we believe that Jesus died and rose, so also, through Jesus, God will *gather to be with him* those who have died" (my translation, cf. AB). (Second Thessalonians 2:1 expresses the same thought: Jesus' second coming is the time of being gathered together to him.) Paul's idiom directly echoes eschatological passages in the Greek Septuagint. They include

178

Isa 11:12; 35:10; 40:11; 43:5; 52:12; 60:4; Jer 38:10; Ezek 11:17; and Zech 2:10.

All these scriptures point ahead prophetically to God's gathering of all God's people into one great community of fellowship at the end of days. Early apocalyptic texts in Isaiah, such as Isa 56:8 and 66:18, specify that Gentiles are included as well.

Paul adds a distinctive slant on the scriptural theme of ingathering. He links it tightly with the resurrection of the dead. He bases the link on Dan 12 and on the gospel's new revelation that the resurrected Jesus will be God's special instrument in the ingathering. Since God will use the resurrected Jesus, the harbinger of the general resurrection, as the instrument of gathering the faithful, this gathering, Paul reasons, must have everything to do with the raising of the dead.

Jesus' second coming means *togetherness*, Paul argues, including togetherness with believers who have died.

Paul reinforces his argument in verses 15-17, quoting an apocalyptic saying of the earthly Jesus. I argued in the preceding chapter that Matt 24:30-31 preserves the same saying (cf. Mark 13:26-27). This word of Jesus has a striking scriptural background in Isa 27:12-13, a text we saw Paul quote in 1 Cor 15:52. Both the Jesus saying and the Isaiah passage refer to a heavenly trumpet call and a gathering of the elect from the ends of the earth.

The Greek Septuagint of Isa 27:12-13 states in part, "Gather one by one the children of Israel. . . . They shall blow the great trumpet, and the lost ones in the land of the Assyrians shall come, and the lost ones in Egypt, and shall worship the Lord on the holy mountain in Jerusalem."

Again, Paul provides his own unique take on Scripture. When the apocalyptic trumpet summons together the living and dead, a rapture, or "snatching" (Lat., *raptus*), takes place, he claims. Verse 17 (AB) states, "We who are alive, who are left, will be snatched up together with them in the clouds to meet the Lord in the air; and so we shall always be with the Lord." The closest parallels to the idea occur in texts such as Gen 5:24 and 4 Ezra 14:9, where God snatches living figures off the earth to heaven.

A huge amount of modern speculation has built up around Paul's reference to rapture, much of which would probably leave Paul aghast. In a clever rhetorical ploy, Paul is simply turning some contemporary language about death on its head.

Paul's contemporaries spoke of death as snatching people from the world, now and forever. Greek epitaphs, for example, lament how Fate snatches people away from their loved ones. With the concept of rapture, Paul offers a retort. He counters that, yes, the death of believers does involve a snatching, but not the kind that people think. Christians believe in the kind of snatching that will occur at the Parousia, one whose consequence is everyone reuniting with their deceased relatives and companions.

Abraham Malherbe argues the point brilliantly. He writes, "The dead in Christ will rise, and their separation from those who were left is overcome as, ironically, they are snatched up together with them. In a neat twist, Paul uses the conventional language of grief to comfort."[6]

Paul's persistent point thus far is that his readers' radical expectations about the future should be a comfort. In particular, these expectations should give readers a sense of the goal and the end of life and history, which lends hope and meaning to the present.

Paul's apocalyptic imagination, however, does more than provide comfort. It instills a sense of urgency about diligently maintaining a moral and spiritual life in the here and now. Paul turns to emphasize these points in 1 Thess 5:1-11.

From the initial verses of this section, it appears that some Thessalonians were speculating about God's timetable in bringing about history's end. Certain local prophets felt themselves adept at timing God's blueprint for history (v. 1). They assured their companions there was nothing to get excited about at the moment; the end times were delayed (v. 3). Paul counters their claims with a declaration that God's timing of the end is mysterious. It is not subject to human calculation and prediction.

The nearness of the apocalyptic "day of the Lord" is no object of speculation, Paul argues, but a basis for moral diligence.

Since Jesus will come suddenly, like a "thief in the night," there is urgency about keeping oneself blameless and holy in preparation for meeting him. If one knows that Jesus may return at any time, one naturally wants to remain morally and spiritually fit to meet Jesus. Paul is not appealing to readers' selfish desire for an imminent reward at the Parousia. Rather, he instills an apocalyptic imagination to provide readers with orientation and inspiration for doing what is right and healthy in any case. The Parousia does not spell selfish reward anyway, but the end-time establish-ment of mutual, selfless love in community (1 Thess 3:12-13).

Paul directly exhorts his readers to live in conformity with their membership in a different sphere of existence from the pagan world. Christians should live into their divine calling as "children of light" (v. 5). The language, of course, is highly reminiscent of the apocalyptic terminology of the Qumran community. Paul jux-taposes light and darkness here as two dualistically opposed spheres, just as we have seen in the writings of the Qumran sect, such as the *Community Rule* scroll (1QS), columns III.13–IV.26.

Paul's warnings against spiritual inaction and laziness in this section are surely central in the ongoing relevance of 1 Thes-salonians as Christian scripture. The call for diligence as Christians strikes home in an age when the coming of the Son of Man often seems unreal, or at least distant, compared to the pressing concerns of a packed, accelerated lifestyle.

We may conclude this discussion of Paul and the world of his letters with a word about the social settings in which he pro-pounded an apocalyptic imagination.

From Paul's comments in his various epistles, we know he brought his early house-churches into existence as apocalyptic communities. Waiting for the coming of Jesus and the reign of God was an integral part of the community members' new orien-tation to life from the start. Their conversion, Paul states, turned them from the service of idols to "wait for his Son from heaven, whom he raised from the dead—Jesus, who rescues us from the wrath that is coming" (1 Thess 1:10). The approaching wrath is the anger of God on judgment day. Paul's Greek syntax betrays his belief that the anger is soon to come.

Paul had an apocalyptic action plan for how his new converts should live through the end times. It revolved partly around issues of internal group life, such as abounding in love for one another and comforting one another. The plan also included stay-ing involved in life within the wider society.

The early house-churches founded by Paul did not withdraw from Greco-Roman, urban culture as the Dead Sea Scroll com-munity at Qumran did. House-church members were not to escape from the world (cf. 1 Cor 5:9-10). Paul expected them to continue to interact with outsiders, and to do so in a manner becoming to them.

181

What we know about Paul's early house-churches discourages us from thinking of their members as a downtrodden underclass or as revolutionary proletarians. These categories of people are conspicuously absent from the literary evidence about Paul's converts. We should not imagine deprivation, persecution, or alienation from the world as the causes of the apocalyptic imagination of Pauline Christianity.

The churches founded by Paul generally included a cross section of Greco-Roman society, ranging from societal leaders to prosperous household heads to slaves. At Thessalonica, the household of a prominent citizen named Jason became a crucial base of operations for Paul and his first converts. It likely included a workshop and storefront, providing a perfect setting from which to reach out to a wide spectrum of the populace.

At Corinth, one elite convert was a city official named Erastus. His name has been found on a costly public pavement that he donated to the city. The diversity and social stratification of the Corinthian Christians was actually so significant that it created serious conflicts for them, impairing life and worship.

Nor can one reduce Paul's apocalyptic message to a saccharine remedy for his audience's hardships and frustrations. It would be more accurate to say the apocalyptic imagination brought frustration and anguish with it, creating conflict with common assumptions. It generally jostled one's orientation to life, demanding a radical reorientation and transformation.

Although affliction, or hardship, was not a particular quality of their preconversion way of life, it did arise with the early Christians' conversion to apocalyptic religion (see especially 1 Thess 1:6). In the Greco-Roman world in general, entrance into a philosophic or religious community frequently involved emotional and psychological confusion and disorientation. This experience no doubt applied to Paul's early Christian converts.

Abraham Malherbe has studied ancient reports about the experience of new converts to Greco-Roman philosophical schools, and found them comparable to the experience of "affliction" of the early Christians. The philosophic school of Epictetus, a Stoic philosopher contemporary with Paul, advocated a belief system and lifestyle less radical than Paul's apocalyptic theology, but joining it still meant a real break with common thinking that exposed one to ridicule.

Epictetus describes a typical encounter a convert might experience with the uninitiated populace: "Some white-haired old man with many a gold ring on his fingers will come along, and then he will shake his head and say, 'Listen to me, sonny; one ought of course to philosophize, but one ought also to keep one's head; this is all nonsense.' "[7]

Despite the associated "affliction," however, the early Christians found a tremendous positive side to the apocalyptic imagination. It offered a coherent universe of meaning that, in comparison with mundane perceptions of the human condition, was filled with joy. No wonder Paul recalls that the Thessalonians received his apocalyptic preaching with the "joy inspired by the Holy Spirit" alongside of "affliction" (1 Thess 1:6).

THE APOCALYPTIC DISCOURSE OF THE GOSPELS

The three Synoptic Gospels share a parallel testament of Jesus about the end of the ages, often called the "little apocalypse." It is found in Matt 24, Mark 13, and Luke 21. Lacking such literary features as elaborate visions, celestial archetypes, and pseudonymity, the testament is technically not an apocalypse. It obviously exhibits a vibrant apocalyptic imagination, however. It expects Daniel's end-time scenario to finally play itself out, heaven and earth to pass away, and a specific series of birth pangs to usher in God's imminent reign on earth. In detailing God's apocalyptic plans in the discourse, Jesus acts the part of the heavenly intermediary typical of Hellenistic apocalypses.

I suggested in the preceding chapter that core elements of the little apocalypse go back to the historical Jesus. Such elements would include Jesus' forecasts of both the temple's destruction (Mark 13:2) and the glorious advent of the Son of Man (Mark 13:26-27). Although such elements may be authentic to Jesus of Nazareth, the present form of the apocalyptic discourse bears telltale marks of literary growth and theological reflection. In its present form, it must be an early Christian montage, combining Hebrew Bible echoes and early Christian teachings with some of Jesus' key apocalyptic sayings. Many scholars believe Jesus' early followers compiled the discourse quite early, perhaps within a few decades after Jesus' lifetime. Thus, the Gospels, which were not written until at least the 60s C.E., received the discourse largely preassembled.

Whatever its exact date of composition, the little apocalypse must have been written before Rome's destruction of Jerusalem in 70 C.E. It closely conjoins the fall of Herod's temple with the end of the world—an untenable perspective after 70 C.E., when the world failed to end. Further, it omits details from the events of 70; for example, the Romans not only demolished but also burned the temple. Such omissions would be unlikely in a prophecy made up after the fact.

The book of Mark may date before 70 C.E. too. That would explain why Mark 13's form of the little apocalypse does not adjust for facts that became obvious in the aftermath of the Jewish War with Rome. Such adjustments do appear in Matthew and Luke, as we shall see.

As the Gospels present it, the apocalyptic discourse is prompted by some reverential remarks of the disciples about the temple. "Look, Teacher, what large stones and what large buildings!" one of them says (Mark 13:1). Such comments provoke Jesus' radical prediction of the temple's total demise (v. 2). This forecast about the temple is shocking. It disturbs the disciples and raises a whole set of questions about eschatology. These questions, in turn, lead into an extended discussion of the tribulations and birth pangs presaging the end of days.

To enter the apocalyptic world of Mark 13, it helps to recognize how incredibly suggestive Jesus' prediction of the temple's destruction was to the disciples. The symbolic significance of the temple in God's relationship with Israel prevented them from conceiving of its destruction as an isolated, mundane event. It was unthinkable that God would let life go on without the temple, which symbolized God's stabilizing presence in the world.

Specific Scriptures account for the disciples' assumption that the end of days directly follows the temple's fall. The book of Daniel associates the capture of Jerusalem and the desecration of the temple with history's end (e.g., Dan 8:11; 11:31; 12:11). So too, in Zech 14, an attack on Jerusalem by mighty nations is a key end-time event (see especially vv. 1-5). It ushers in God's appearance on earth, to reign with all "holy beings."

In his apocalyptic instruction, Jesus satisfies much of the disciples' curiosity about the end times. He reminds them of biblical descriptions of the darkening of the sun and moon (v. 24; Isa 13:10) and the fall of stars from heaven (v. 25; Isa 34:4). He describes specific signs of the end, such as the appearance of Daniel's "desolating sacrilege" in the temple (v. 14).

His tone is urgent; the end is imminent: "Truly I tell you, this generation will not pass away until all these things have taken place" (v. 30). Far from encouraging "endist" speculation and alarmism, however, his emphasis falls on discernment and patient endurance (vv. 5, 13). Readers must prepare themselves for inevitable troubles in the here and now (vv. 9, 23) and be on the alert for the coming of the Son of Man (vv. 33, 35, 37).

Imagining the world of the earliest disciples opens an illuminating entrance into the prescriptural, primitive world of the little apocalypse. It also raises complex modern reading issues. The temple-centered Judaism of Jesus' time is alien to today's readers, including modern Jews and Christians. We no longer share the disciples' expectation that Rome's sack of Jerusalem would spell doomsday.

Is the meaning of the passage permanently moored in the ordeal of Judea's ancient conflict with Rome? If so, our text becomes a worthy but abortive dream. The events of 70 C.E. have come and gone, and "all things continue as they were from the beginning of creation" (2 Pet 3:4).

Jesus' pronouncement in verse 30 is especially jarring. Did Jesus make a false or mistaken prophecy? Most historical critics, in fact, argue he did. This understandably disturbs more than a few present-day followers of Jesus.

I want to suggest a reading approach that avoids domesticating the text as a time-bound, abortive prophecy. A close look at the language of Mark 13, together with attention to its canonical shaping in Matthew and Luke, suggests an alternative interpretation of the passage differing from that of most modernist critics. Christianity preserved the little apocalypse as Scripture beyond the events of 70 C.E. The early churches must have valued the text's potential to aid readers in living through repeat experiences of apocalyptic tribulations, beyond Rome's destruction of Jerusalem.

Mark 13 showed itself to be true prophecy to early Christians in anticipating the trauma of the Jewish War with Rome. Verse 30 foretells Jerusalem's fall within a generation. Verse 2 correctly predicts the extent of the destruction, noting that the temple will literally be flattened. Describing Jerusalem's fall from a historian's vantage point, Josephus records that when Titus ordered the temple demolished, he directed it be "razed to the ground."

Simultaneously as it anticipates the events of 70, Mark 13 exhibits a rich capacity to point beyond those events. It exemplifies how biblical apocalyptic texts prove illuminating, at their best, of multiple contexts of salvation history, aiding the faithful in living appropriately in whatever time and era they find themselves. In this regard, the text possesses a vitality not unlike that of Daniel's apocalyptic visions, upon which it depends.

For example, take Daniel's prediction of a "desolating sacrilege" in the Jewish temple (Dan 9:27; 11:31; 12:11), which Mark 13:14 quotes. This prediction has found repeated fulfillments within biblical history. The "sacrilege" surfaces concretely during Maccabean times in the deeds of Antiochus, at the time of Daniel's composition. That did not exhaust its meaning. The first readers of Mark 13 experienced the "desolating sacrilege" again, in the deeds of Caligula and Titus. Revelation 13, written still later (about 95 C.E.), looked to a still future antimessiah to fulfill Daniel's predictions (cf. 2 Thess 2:3-5).

The language and rhetoric of Mark 13 gives the little apocalypse of the Gospels the same capacity for multiple fulfillments as Daniel's apocalyptic predictions. A clear tension in the language of Mark 13 allowed later (post-70) readers to see it refer not only to the tribulation of 70 C.E. but also, *simultaneously,* to climactic events yet to come.

Note the tension between the language of verses 29-30 and verses 32-33. The former verses affirm that one can recognize tribulation birth pangs. One can even observe them build to a climax. The latter verses (vv. 32-33) insist that no one, not even the Son of God, has any idea when the Parousia will occur. As a completely sealed divine secret, the Parousia cannot be timed—not even roughly. If one takes verses 32-33 seriously, Mark 13 simply cannot be moored down in 70 C.E. One must infer that doomful events such as those of 70 may turn out retrospectively to be only preliminary apocalyptic eruptions. Earth can experience such close brushes with apocalyptic chaos while "the end is still to come" (v. 7).

The tensive, dialectical language of Mark 13 allows for the tribulations of the post-Easter age to reach critical mass from time to time. When they erupt into a crisis, it prefigures dooms-day. These eruptions are necessary harbingers of the end, but there is never any guarantee about when the end actually comes. Only God knows the timing of the collapse of the cosmos and the Parousia of the Son of Man.

Commenting on Mark 13:30, William Lane writes:

> The events to be fulfilled within the generation of Jesus' contem-poraries (verse 30) should be regarded for what they are, prelimi-nary events only. The parousia cannot take place until after they have occurred. They are the necessary precursors of the parousia, yet in themselves they do not determine the time of that event, which is known only to God (verse 32). The thrust of Jesus' dis-course, as Mark has recorded it, is to warn the disciples not to be disturbed by the preliminary signs nor to confuse them with the end itself.[8]

We may now turn to Matthew's treatment of Mark 13 to test this approach to reading the little apocalypse. Matthew 24 expands and develops Mark 13, clarifying its tensive language. If we are on the right track, Matthew should clarify the inherent vitality and capacity for multiple fulfillment of the little apocalypse.

The Matthew group wrote their gospel around 85 C.E., well after the destruction of the temple in 70. Despite the nonoccur-rence of cosmic collapse (Matt 24:29) and the Parousia (Matt 24:30), the community continued to treasure Jesus' apocalyptic testament. In fact, they highlighted it as one of Jesus' five major teaching discourses in the gospel of Matthew. This only makes sense if they believed that the dynamic, expansive quality of its language transcended the recent horrors perpetrated by Titus.

At several points in Matt 24, the Matthew group makes clear that the apocalyptic discourse points to a future beyond 70. According to verse 29, they never gave up the idea of an *immedi-ate* connection between a desecration of the Jerusalem temple and the collapse and rebirth of the cosmos. Not even Mark 13 makes the link this tight. Since the events of 70 did not have an immediate apocalyptic result, the Matthew group must have believed the recent crisis to be a mere harbinger and prefigure-ment of a fuller form of the same events. The pattern of 70 would repeat itself with a rebuilt temple and a repeat desecration.

The Matthew group altered the apocalyptic discourse to reflect this expectation. They expanded verse 14 to emphasize that the end of days would be delayed until the "whole world" had a chance to receive the gospel. They modified verse 20 with the thought that their own audience would have to flee a new, restored Jerusalem. The added prayer of verse 20 that the flight from Jerusalem might not occur "on a sabbath" has Matthew's Jewish-Christian readers in mind. Some of these readers still observed the Sabbath.

As Davies and Allison write, verse 20 shows that Matt 24 "is not historical description but eschatological prophecy; for what would be the point of inserting an imperative to pray about a past event, that it not take place at a particular time?"[9]

Most notably, Matt 24 alters the wording of the little apocalypse to make clear that the events of 70 do not amount to the end-time crisis but *prefigure* it. The events surrounding Titus's destruction of Jerusalem were only a preliminary apocalyptic upsurge, separate from doomsday and the Parousia. Whereas Mark 13 blurs and foreshortens the distinction between the two apocalyptic crises, Matt 24 decompresses them and sharpens the contrast.

Matthew 24 makes a particular effort to interpret the meaning of verse 34, "this generation will not pass away until all these things have taken place." The possibility that the verse is mistaken was as much a problem for the Matthew group as it is for readers today. What exactly are "all these things" to which the verse refers? In what sense could Jesus' generation have experienced them?

Matthew's solution is straightforward. Matthew 24, through its structure and rhetoric, defines the phrase "all these things" in a specific and narrow way. For this gospel, "all these things" are the tribulation events of 70, which prefigured the full-blown birth pangs of the end times. The first generation of disciples did in fact witness "all these things," in that Herod's temple met its demise 40 years after Jesus' death.

One should not necessarily have expected this same generation to have witnessed doomsday and the Parousia. Matthew 24 clarifies that these phenomena are not included when Jesus spoke of "all these things."

Matthew spells this all out by expanding and clarifying the apocalyptic discourse's initial exchange between Jesus and the disciples about the doomed buildings of Herod's temple. Unlike

Mark 13:2, Matt 24:2 refers to these structures specifically as "all these things." "All these things," namely, the components of Herod's temple, will be torn down.

Matthew then decompresses and unpacks the disciples' question of the next verse (Matt 24:3). Over against Mark 13, the disciples in Matthew now ask Jesus, "Tell us, when will *these things* [i.e., the dismantling of the temple] be?" (NASB, my emphasis). Only then do they go on to ask, "And what will be the sign of your coming and of the end of the age [i.e., the Parousia and the apocalyptic termination of history]?" Two questions are distinguished as separate issues. Only the first concerns "these things"— Herod's temple.

For Matthew, the language about "all these things" in verses 2-3 clearly anticipates verse 34. This verse, for Matthew, presents a focused answer to the disciples' particular question about the temple. This generation will not pass away, according to verse 34, until the complete destruction of Herod's temple—"all these things." This narrowly specified claim was vindicated by history in 70 C.E.

As verse 8 states, "all these things" are just the beginning of birth pangs. They do not guarantee an immediate Parousia. The second question of verse 3, where the disciples ask about the Parousia and the eschaton, must await verse 36 for a response. The response is "God only knows." Only God is able to time the Parousia.

That Matthew intends verse 34 to double back to the disciples' specific question about Herod's temple in verses 2-3 is clear from the rhetorical structure of the verses. As noted, both verse 2 and verse 34 refer to "all these things." They also both have Jesus use the same expression: "Truly I tell you."

The Matthew group knew that the first generation of Jesus' disciples would not live to see the Parousia. They shaped the little apocalypse to clarify how verse 34 of the text need not be read to mistakenly claim otherwise.

Canonical shaping of Jesus' apocalyptic discourse in the Gospels over time increasingly emphasized Christian wakefulness. Over against the form of the discourse in Mark 13, Matt 24 adds several illustrations suggesting that the basic practical response to the apocalyptic message of the gospel is moral and spiritual diligence.

Going beyond what we find in Mark, the gospel of Matthew warns that many people will be as unprepared for Jesus' return as they were for Noah's flood (Matt 24:37-41). Then, Matthew adds a parable about a watchful householder (vv. 42-44), one about a faithful and wise servant (vv. 45-51), and further additions in chapter 25. The parables share a common warning to be on the alert, to keep oneself morally and spiritually prepared for Jesus' coming and his ushering in the reign of God.

The way that the gospel of Luke handles this little apocalypse of the Gospels gives more examples of canonical shaping. Luke edited the text in his own unique way to bring out its relevance and value for his audience years after the immediate, apocalyptic crisis of the destruction of the Jerusalem temple in 70 C.E. More so than in Matthew, clear editing and shaping in Luke shows the reader of scripture how a text composed in apocalyptic fervor may remain relevant for life in the mundane world over the long haul, as God delays the world's end.

By the time of Luke's version of the little apocalypse, it was apparent that Jesus was delaying his return to earth. In this light, Luke views his task less as explaining emergency preparations for the Parousia than as presenting the apocalyptic imagination in a way making sense to all potential disciples. In a striking shift from Mark 13:3, Jesus does not explain apocalyptic knowledge privately, but openly at the temple (Luke 21:5-7). He offers it to all who would be his followers.

Downplaying the idea of an imminent end of the world, Luke modifies the little apocalypse to better focus on helping Christians live their daily lives. The apocalypse is surely coming, according to Luke, but for now the apocalyptic imagination works best as a long-range perspective that helps Christians avoid preoccupation with daily life and its worries (Luke 21:34).

The same apocalyptic perspective shows Christians of all times that they must be prepared to face preliminary, small-scale versions (microcosms) of apocalyptic calamities and persecutions. Before the terrors and the great signs of doomsday, Luke's Jesus explains, there will be trials and persecutions to bear. Christians should use these hardships as opportunities to bear testimony to the gospel (Luke 21:13).

The way Luke phrases verse 12 suggests that bearing effective testimony under difficult conditions, not apocalyptic fervor about signs of the end, is the most apt lesson of apocalyptic teaching. Jesus' words are usually translated: "Before all this occurs, they will arrest you and persecute you." Although this translation is fine, the Greek words "before all this" can also mean "more important" (cf. Jas 5:12; 1 Pet 4:8). The wording suggests that "more important" than determining the signs of the Parousia is a focus on present witness in the face of all sorts of troubles, even from official quarters and close relatives.

CHAPTER 9

THE BOOK OF REVELATION

ISSUES IN READING

The book of Revelation is the latest of the Bible's major apocalyptic writings and the most intricate and sophisticated. Its sophistication, indeed, makes it one of the greatest literary and theological writings among the Scriptures. Most scholars date the book to about 95 C.E., during the reign of the Roman emperor Domitian (d. 96 C.E.). This places Revelation's initial composition about a decade after Matt 24's version of Jesus' apocalyptic discourse. As discussed in the final section of this chapter, its author, John of Patmos, is probably not to be identified with John the apostle. Rather, he was an itinerant Christian prophet, who cultivated an apocalyptic imagination among his colleagues and followers.

Revelation arose as a letter to early house-churches in Asia Minor, that is, the Roman province of Asia located in modern Turkey (Rev 1:4-6). We have encountered early Christian apocalyptic letters before in our probes of 1 Corinthians and

1 Thessalonians. Revelation differs, both in its full-blown apocalyptic genre, replete with astounding visions, and in being intended from the start as a circular letter, written for multiple audiences.

Seven churches receive individual prophetic messages in chapters 2 and 3 of Revelation, but the entire book is also one coherent, relevant letter for the members of each church. Each congregation is to read all the visions and revelations of chapters 4–22. Christ commands the author at Rev 1:11, "Write in a book what you see and send it to the seven churches, to Ephesus, to Smyrna, to Pergamum, to Thyatira, to Sardis, to Philadelphia, and to Laodicea."

Revelation's literary structure is treated below, but a preliminary outline of its four main sections may aid readers who are new to the book:

Revelation 1–3	Prologue; John's Vision; Messages to the Churches
Revelation 4–16	Seal, Trumpet, and Bowl Judgments
Revelation 17:1–21:8	The Defeat of Evil on Earth
Revelation 21:9–22:21	The New Jerusalem; Epilogue

Entering the world of Revelation, readers will immediately notice key differences from New Testament writings in general and even from other early Christian apocalyptic texts, such as 1 Thessalonians and the synoptic apocalypse. Jesus and Paul taught about transcendent reality and its coming impact on earth, but spoke from an earthly perspective. John of Patmos, on the other hand, is granted the privilege of heaven's vantage point. Revelation discloses heaven's perspective on this world.

Revelation 4:1-2 reads, "After this I looked, and there in heaven a door stood open! And the first voice, which I had heard speaking to me like a trumpet, said, 'Come up here, and I will show you what must take place after this.' At once I was in the spirit, and there in heaven." From this point on, John sees events transpire just as the courtiers in God's heavenly throne room do.

John's heavenly perspective in Revelation allows him to communicate to readers what is really going on in their world and what its ultimate outcome must be. This invigorates their imaginations with a completely new perspective. Richard Bauckham expresses the point well:

The effect of John's visions, one might say, is to expand his readers' world, both spatially (into heaven) and temporally (into the eschatological future), or, to put it another way, to open their world to divine transcendence. The bounds which Roman power and ideology set to the readers' world are broken open and that world is seen as open to the greater purpose of its transcendent Creator and Lord. It is not that the here-and-now are left behind in an escape into heaven or the eschatological future, but that the here-and-now look quite different when they are opened to transcendence.[1]

God's sovereignty and cosmic prerogative often appeared distant or unreal to Revelation's original audience, facing the Roman Empire's arrogation to itself of divine rule over the world. Today's readers as well may often see heaven's rule as distant or ethereal. Many alternative political, economic, and military spheres of concern claim priority. Revelation aims to unmask these claims as false. It unveils, instead, the world's true Lord and argues that the conflicting claims of earth and heaven arise from a spiritual battle raging behind the scenes of daily life.

Because Revelation aims to contest earthly, imperial claims of prerogative, interpreters frequently are tempted to reduce the book to a political tract, one aimed against Roman ideology. This is a flat-footed move, which hardly does justice either to Revelation's literary complexity or to the vitality and vigor of its images.

Reifying the text leaves too much of Revelation's splendor, surplus of meaning, and digressive traits out of the picture. It would be like reducing the popular *Lord of the Rings* trilogy by J. R. R. Tolkien to an allegory of the events and personalities of World War II—something Tolkien vehemently denied was appropriate.

Readers of Revelation should prepare themselves to enter a new symbolic universe. What they see is neither coded descriptions of ordinary, banal reality nor abstract, ethereal truths. In this imaginative new worldview, earth and heaven appear from God's perspective. Earth's pretensions look increasingly bloated and ephemeral. Simultaneously, the celestial realm develops before the reader's eyes into something sharply visible and fundamentally solid. Above all, heaven appears relentlessly aggressive.

Revelation's perspective is no mystical flight without earthly relevance. According to the new meaning structure offered by the book, God's new creation is irrupting into the world and increasingly demanding that human lifestyle accord with it. The book calls readers to embrace this surging new creation and its associated values, which effectively counter those of current, God-ignoring existence.

G. K. Beale describes the pressing relevance of Revelation's new universe of symbols:

> The symbols describing the new world spell out the eternal significance and consequences of Christ's life, death, and resurrection and of the present choices and behavior of the readers. Part of the main point is to motivate the readers not to compromise with the world but align their thoughts and behavior with the God-centered standards of the new creation. They are to see their own situation in this world in the light of the eternal perspective of the new world, which is now their true home.[2]

The radical new imagination of Revelation confronts human brokenness and reorients human experience. It promotes hard, critical thinking, helping readers discern the elemental struggles at stake in life. It energizes readers to leave passivity and timidity behind and to engage these struggles wholeheartedly. Such engagement confronts all spheres of life, including the political, the economic, and the cultural.

Revelation claims, however, that unconventional methods are key to readers' successful engagement with the world. The key player in Revelation is an immolated lamb, who conquers the forces of evil and death through humility, selflessness, and sacrifice (Rev 5:5-6, 9-10). Following the example of this lamb (Christ), readers are to effect tangible social change through faith, endurance, and willed suffering (Rev 12:11). What a paradox, that such means constitute effective, aggressive forces that upend the whole world.

The symbolic universe of Revelation is incomprehensible apart from knowledge of the Hebrew Bible. Scriptural symbols and images form the very fabric of its visions. As with Daniel, a concerted effort at puzzling over the Scriptures must have been instrumental in the book's formation, providing the building blocks of its new imagination. The term *allusive language* is appropriate. Instead of formal quotations, biblical echoes and diction saturate the book.

Revelation's many scriptural allusions are key to unlocking its mysteries. Knowing the original historical milieu of John of Patmos helps in understanding the text, but interpreters will gain a more immediate grasp of its literal sense by reading it in the context of the Bible's own inner world. Innerbiblical cross-referencing gives the interpreter a vital framework for understanding this complex apocalypse.

TRACING SCRIPTURAL ALLUSIONS IN REVELATION

Revelation alludes to many types of Hebrew Bible texts, including the Bible's creation accounts and its narratives of the exodus. References to prophetic and apocalyptic texts are especially numerous. Revelation brims with the language and images of Hebrew prophecy, including the words and visual symbols of Isaiah, Jeremiah, Ezekiel, Joel, and Zechariah.

As with the apostle Paul, the events of Christ's life, death, and resurrection shook the traditional, Hebraic worldview of John of Patmos. Functioning as a catalytic event, Christ's victorious work on earth provoked an imaginative new conception of reality. Christ, the conquering lamb, had recently fulfilled the messianic expectations of the prophets and inaugurated the coming reign of God. Given this fact, John's group gathered and reinterpreted foundational symbols and hopes of the biblical and prophetic tradition in a new symbolic universe emphasizing summation and climax. Some selected examples help demonstrate this.

The vision of demon locusts in Rev 9:1-12 draws directly on Joel and its devastating locust plague, presaging doomsday. As the locusts are released from the cosmic Abyss (Rev 9:2), the sun in heaven darkens just as in Joel (2:10, 31; 3:15). Both Revelation and Joel experience the invading locust armies as stampeding horses, arrayed in battle armor (Rev 9:7; Joel 2:4), possessing the teeth of lions (Rev 9:8; Joel 1:6), and sounding like chariots rushing to battle (Rev 9:9; Joel 2:5).

As in Joel, Revelation's locusts reveal humanity's state of crisis and need of God. Whereas Joel experienced the crisis in microcosm, in Revelation's visionary landscape it comes to its ultimate head.

Revelation does not echo Joel slavishly. It differs in envisioning no human lamentation or repentance in response to the locust invasion. The book gives no hint of a change of heart on the part of the godless, even when faced with a paradigmatic doomsday plague (cf. Rev 9:20-21).

Revelation 11:3-6 is another text reverberating with the Hebrew Scriptures. Here, two witnesses of God, representing the community of faith, appear on earth during the end-time tribulation period. The text presents them using the symbolism of Zech 4, where two olive trees in the Jerusalem temple supply oil to the temple lampstand—an archetype of God's fiery presence and power. The olive trees are ideal human leaders, whom Zechariah envisions sharing in God's witness and outreach to humankind.

Revelation uses Zechariah's images to depict the true import and power of the church's prophetic witness on earth (cf. Rev 1:12, 20). It proclaims that during the end times, this witness will grow brilliant enough to fulfill Zechariah's apocalyptic hopes. Though fully opposed by the deceit and coercion of wickedness, Revelation's two witnesses make clear to the entire world that God deserves all possible glory (Rev 11:13). Their work promulgates God's light to all humanity.

Revelation's image of an apocalyptic Antichrist figure also derives from Hebrew Bible symbolism, particularly from Daniel. The "beast" of Rev 13:1-10 resoundingly echoes Dan 7's description of the arrogant "little horn" of the end times. Both figures arise out of the sea, the waters of cosmic chaos (Rev 13:1; Dan 7:2-3). Like Daniel's little horn, Revelation's beast makes blasphemous boasts (Rev 13:1, 5, 6; Dan 7:8, 11, 20, 25; cf. 11:36) and has a reign so tyrannous that God limits it to a symbolic three and a half years (Rev 13:5; Dan 7:25; cf. 12:7). Like Daniel's horn, Revelation's beast wars with the faithful and begins to overpower them (Rev 13:7; Dan 7:21), but God steps in to bring him down (Rev 19:20; Dan 7:22). Clearly, Revelation presents what it envisions to be the ultimate fulfillment of Dan 7 and its picture of the world's ultimate tyrant.

The oracle against the prostitute Babylon in Rev 18:1–19:8 pronounces the grim fate of all human systems that arrogate to themselves the place of God, that seduce humans to offer them loyalty and worship. The passage is a patchwork of Hebrew prophetic texts, not arbitrarily chosen but consisting of the major prophecies against Babylon in the Hebrew Bible. The biblical echoes drive home how the pride, idolatry, and persecution of the world's power structures are transient and destined for exposure and judgment. Just as ancient Babylon fell as prophesied, modern "Babylon" will surely meet the selfsame fate.

The Hebrew prophecies represented in this section include Isa 13:1–14:23; 21:1-10; 47; Jer 25:12-38; 50–51. Images from these texts counter prostitute Babylon's powerful seduction, exposing it as elaborate fantasy, hollow parody, and spiritual sacrilege. The potent language of Ezek 27's dirge against Tyre also makes a strong showing. It illustrates the shock of Babylon's supporters and dependents at its downfall.

The passage's opening words in Rev 18:2 come from Isa 21:9, "Fallen, fallen is Babylon." An appeal to "Come out of her, my people" follows in verse 4, stemming from Jer 51:45 (cf. Jer 50:8; 51:6, 9). Verse 7 illustrates Babylon's deluded hubris with an allusion to Isa 47:8:

> "I am, and there is no one besides me;
> I shall not sit as a widow
> or know the loss of children."

Verses 9-19 colorfully depict the weeping and lamenting of those who witness Babylon's downfall. As in Ezek 27:29-32, the seafarers and merchants who trafficked in her cargoes survey the disaster in astonishment. Their idolatrous confidence in Babylon's economic security stands incontrovertibly discredited.

As a final example of Revelation's allusive and anthological style, note the direct relationship between Rev 20:7-9 and Ezekiel's apocalypse in Ezek 38–39 (cf. also Rev 19:17-21). These chapters of Ezekiel depict the end-time attack and destruction of Gog of Magog, a "mythic-realistic" encapsulation of all enemy forces opposed to God and God's people. Revelation affirms the reality of this pivotal apocalyptic battle and situates it immediately before the final judgment of all humankind (Rev 20:11-15). After these events comes the descent of the New Jerusalem from heaven (Rev 21:1-8).

Verse 8 of Rev 20 explicitly depicts the gathering of Gog and Magog from earth's four corners. As in Ezekiel, the enemy forms a monstrous horde (Ezek 38:9, 16; Rev 20:8) converging on Jerusalem, God's beloved city (Ezek 38:8, 12; Rev 20:9). Then, at the critical juncture, heaven intervenes. Fire from heaven destroys the horde and rescues God's people (Ezek 38:22; 39:6; Rev 20:9).

CONTENTS AND THEOLOGICAL HIGHLIGHTS

Revelation exhibits the features of several genres of biblical literature simultaneously, requiring great agility from readers. The first verse of the book describes it as an *apokalypsis,* a "revelation," about "what must soon take place." The third verse of chapter 1 identifies the work as a written prophecy, a divine message relevant for the course of history (cf. 22:7, 18-19). Then, verses 4-6 form the conventional opening of an ancient letter.

We have barely begun reading the book, and already we are encountering an apocalypse, a prophecy, and an epistle. Beyond these three genres, readers soon discover other forms of language. In particular, the book is full of hymns and liturgy from the realm of Christian worship.

Some key features of Revelation are closer to Christian prophecy than to the genre apocalypse. John of Patmos often comes across as a traditional prophetic messenger, acting as a mouthpiece or channel of divine communication. Like the prophets, he speaks in his own name, not that of an ancient worthy, such as Daniel or Enoch. Further, in the manner of a Hebrew prophet, he reports his own commissioning by God (Rev 1:10-11, 19; 10:8-11). John doubtless considered himself similar to John the Baptizer, a figure standing at the culmination of the whole tradition of biblical prophecy.

Revelation is not traditional prophecy, however, but a full-blown apocalypse. It is biblical prophecy's summation and finale, not merely an additional exemplar. The visions of the book whisk John to heaven and disclose transcendent reality. This reality, John quickly learns, is about to invade earth supernaturally and thunderously, establishing the reign of God. An eschatological salvation is envisaged at history's coming end. Traits such as the form of a sealed scroll and an interpreting angel confirm the book's apocalyptic genre.

The messages to the seven churches at the start of Revelation are no mere epistolary preface to a separate apocalypse. They are an integral part of the book's apocalyptic argument and imagination. Both the messages to the churches and the apocalyptic visions of Revelation aim to reframe readers' understandings of their day-to-day experience. Both parts of the book aim to evoke earthly lifestyles oriented on the irruption of God's brand new creation into human experience.

Already in the messages to the churches, John begins to reveal the deeper dimensions behind his readers' experience in the world, showing the transcendent importance of their communal life and witness. According to Rev 1:12, 20, the seven churches are lampstands of God in the world. Revelation 11:4-6 will specify that these lampstands are God's force of light and truth on earth, countering the lies and trickery of "the beast."

The messages of Rev 2–3 do not yet mention "the beast," but they do begin to reframe readers' understandings of their local struggles in terms of a larger, spiritual battle. The messages repeatedly call readers to "overcome," to "conquer" (Rev 2:7, 17, 26; 3:5, 12, 21). Revelation 21:7 will later spell out the apocalyptic meaning of this "conquering." It leads to a place in the New Jerusalem, which is about to descend to earth from heaven. Revelation 3:12 already mentions this New Jerusalem.

Other allusions within the messages of chapters 2–4 corroborate the apocalyptic goal of Christian perseverance in the here and now. Perseverance leads directly to the right to eat of the "tree of life" in the coming paradise of God (Rev 2:7; 22:2, 14, 19). It means never having to worry about the "second death"—permanent separation from God (Rev 2:11; 20:6, 14; 21:8).

Revelation's visions are complex and multifaceted, but a close reading discerns a basic apocalyptic schema behind many of the book's scenes. The schema arises out of traditional biblical sources, especially Daniel, the synoptic apocalypse, and the sequence of Egyptian plagues in the book of Exodus.

The sequence of events prophesied in the synoptic apocalypse—itself closely dependent on Daniel—is particularly evident in Revelation's series of seal judgments in chapter 6.[3] The trumpet and bowl judgments that come later in the book present a comparable sequence, reworked based on the plagues of the exodus.

Revelation falls into major divisions, based on literary indicators and patterns of content. There are either seven or eight sections of the book, depending on whether 17:1–19:10 and 19:11–21:8 constitute a single section or two separate ones. A sevenfold scheme for sectioning the book would accord with Revelation's heavy emphasis on that number (e.g., its messages to seven churches, its sets of seven judgments: seven seals, seven trumpets, seven bowls). An eightfold scheme, however, could symbolize God's new creation, a radical new push beyond the first creation's seven stages. The book may intentionally allow for both possible schemes.

Revelation 1–3	Prologue; John's Vision; Messages to the Seven Churches
Revelation 4–7	The Worthy Lamb; The Seal Judgments; An Interlude
Revelation 8:1–11:14	The Seventh Seal; The Trumpet Judgments; An Interlude: The Little Scroll and the Two Witnesses
Revelation 11:15–14:20	The Seventh Trumpet; The War of the Ages: The Woman, the Child, and the Dragon; Unnumbered Visions Concerning the Beast and His Prophet and the Harvesting of the Earth
Revelation 15–16	The Seven Bowl Judgments
Revelation 17:1–19:10	The Ungodly Prostitute: "Babylon" and Its Destruction
Revelation 19:11–21:8	The Final Defeat of God's Foes: The Conquering Messiah; The Millennium; The Lamb's Bride Adorned
Revelation 21:9–22:21	The New Jerusalem; Epilogue

Revelation's outline appears challenging and confusing, not only to beginning readers but also to professionals. Distinguished scholars have sometimes declared it a jumble, the result of incompetent editing. If one does not throw up one's hands too quickly, however, careful study discerns an intricate artistry to the book's literary structure. Let us survey some of this.

A major factor contributing to the complexity of Revelation's overall schema is its literary pattern of "interlocking."[4] "Interlocking" in a text involves an overlap of sections created by having key transitional passages refer both backward and forward. Such an overlap occurs, for example, when Revelation's seventh seal of judgment (Rev 8:1-6) is opened within the book's section containing the trumpet judgments. The seventh, final trumpet (Rev 11:15-18), in turn, is positioned to create another overlap. It sounds within the book's subsequent, central section describing the war of the ages. Revelation 15:2-4 forms a similar transition, rounding off the book's central core after the start of the following section, which presents the seven bowl judgments.

Displacing concluding fragments from their own sections to lie within successive narratives binds the book's parts together. It also conveys a sense of depth and mystery to God's end-time plans, by "nesting" later sections within the scope of earlier ones. All hopes of precisely timing God's apocalyptic plans are abandoned as readers move progressively deeper into nested layers of the book. A literary journey through Revelation reveals levels of complexity within apocalyptic time and the futility of human attempts to "calendarize" end-time phenomena, such as the rapture, the tribulation years, and the battle of Armageddon.

A few observations about Revelation's literary arrangement quickly reveal key themes and theological highlights of the book.

First, the book's outline has a central core in Rev 11:15–14:20. The section begins with God's final trumpet of judgment, the climax of God's seven-part blueprint for ushering in the new creation. As the trumpet blows, loud voices in heaven cry out:

> "The kingdom of the world has become the kingdom of our Lord
>   and of his Messiah,
> and he will reign forever and ever." (Rev 11:15)

They announce the goal and central truth of Revelation. The ancient biblical hope for God's reign on earth is now reaching a final, consummated fulfillment.

The central place of Christ reigning alongside the Lord God in Rev 11:15 is most striking. The pronouncement links "our Lord" and "his Messiah" so closely that the reader is left wondering precisely which of the two "will reign forever and ever." The ambiguous Greek syntax probably implies an inseparable unity between God and Christ. If so, this is a remarkable biblical affirmation of Christ's deity.

Revelation 12, the next part of the book's core, presents the celestial warrants that allow God and the Messiah to assume their apocalyptic reign. The chapter goes beyond earlier visions in the book by revealing the transcendent conflict lying behind the struggles of the faithful on earth. The conflict builds to open combat in heaven at the time of Christ's crucifixion, resulting in heaven's definitive victory over all opposing forces. Because of its key significance, chapter 12 will be treated more fully below.

The next point to make about Revelation's overall structure is that its sections align themselves with each other in a balanced way around the book's core. Leading up to the core, chapters 1–11 outline the tribulations of the end times. They presuppose a conflict between God and the world, requiring heaven to unleash forces of transcendent evil on the earth. The core chapters of the book then reveal Satan—the chaos serpent of old—as the ultimate combatant of heaven and the true source of all transcendent evil. Through his instruments—the beast, the false prophet, and the prostitute Babylon—the devil cements the world's antagonism against God. Following the core section, the book's second half returns to depict the tribulations of the end times with increased intensity. It echoes earlier depictions of God's apocalyptic triumph, and it traces the demise of Satan and his instruments in the reverse order that the core presented them.

The presence of interludes is another notable feature of Revelation's organization. The outline above notes the two interludes that scholars most often identify: Rev 7:1-17 and 10:1–11:14. The first of these creates a pause in chapter 7 before the breaking of the seventh, final seal. The second occurs before the sounding of the seventh, final trumpet. Rather than introducing new events, both interludes function parenthetically to reveal background for understanding the divine wrath of their contexts.

The presence of interludes in Revelation interrupts the relentless pace of God's purifying and punishing judgments, revealing God's restraint and complete control of end-time events. Their contents show God at work to purify the faithful and witness to humanity as a whole even in the midst of climactic judgment. Tragically, this witness goes largely unheeded.

Revelation 7 reveals God's protective sealing of the faithful and presents a glorious vision of God's ultimate saving purpose in judging the earth. Just as God seals faithful servants in chapter 7, so also Rev 10–11 reveals God sealing Christians for a ministry of witness during the church age. The world's negative reaction and intractable impenitence in the face of this witness help explain God's apocalyptic wrath.

The outline of Revelation's structure involves several sequences of divine, end-time judgments. The sequences of seven seal judgments, seven trumpet judgments, and seven bowl judgments are the most obvious examples. Other sections within the book, however, also survey the progress of the end times. Revelation 11:15–14:20 is one good illustration of this.

In several of these cases, John's visions of the end times seem to cover the same ground: the doomful scenario of history's last years. This cautions us against reading the events of the book as one linear, chronological progression. Rather, readers should expect Revelation to periodically double back and repeat its base apocalyptic scenario, perhaps in a more profound or intense form. Scholars speak of this literary phenomenon as a pattern of recapitulation in Revelation.

One sure sign of literary recapitulation in the book is that apocalyptic tribulations build up to a radical climax on more than one occasion. Already at the end of the book's initial series of seal judgments, for example, cosmic disturbances shatter the created order. The sun blackens, the stars fall, and earth's mountains and islands move out of place (Rev 6:12-17). Far from some preliminary judgment, this can only represent history's end.

The language of the book, unfortunately, sometimes obscures the fact that recapitulation is taking place. Revelation 4:1; 7:1; and 15:1, for example, all contain chronological language. In many cases, such language probably serves merely to organize John's visionary experiences. It provides an order for presenting John's visions to the reader, not an overall sequence of the events of the visions.

Also obscuring recapitulation in the book, Revelation's language is often especially ambiguous and elastic. An angel provides interpretations of the book's symbols and archetypes at points (Rev 7:13-14; 17:7-18), but more often, these visual images must simply speak for themselves. This leaves the book's visionary sequences open to diverse interpretations, so that they do not necessarily appear to cover the exact same ground.

In point of fact, Revelation's literary ambiguity means interpreters should not doggedly insist on no other possibility than the book's repeated rehearsal of one short eschatological stretch of time. Rather, multiple interpretive readings of the book's recapitulated sequences appear legitimate. These sequences confront the reader with a surplus of meaning, not any fixed signification.

This richness allows them to speak to the interpretation of a variety of historical eras.

In one reading, for example, Revelation's middle series of trumpets corresponds to Christ's incarnation, which overturned the order of the world. Another reading interprets the series of four celestial horses at the start of Rev 6 as the great empires that succeeded each other in biblical history: Assyria, Babylon, Persia, and Greece. The last portion of chapter 6 would then describe Revelation's own Roman era.

READING REVELATION AS CANONICAL SCRIPTURE

Revelation stands out from other apocalyptic writings of the Bible for its beautiful hymns and liturgies. These compositions appear in great scenes of worship of God in heaven. Such major scenes occur at Rev 4–5; 8:1-6; 11:15-19; 15:1–16:1; and 19:1-10. But beyond these scenes, liturgical language appears throughout the book. Note, for example, the seven liturgical acclamations of Christ appearing in Rev 1:4-7; 5:9-10; 5:12; 5:13; 7:10; 11:15; and 19:6-7.[5]

This liturgical content of Revelation has had enormous influence through the centuries, strongly contributing to the shape of Christian worship. Episcopalians, for example, are intimately familiar with the worship lyrics of Revelation through much of the service music in the Episcopal hymnal. Much contemporary Christian music, moreover, draws heavily from Revelation.

This is one keystone for a canonical appreciation of the book. We are seeing evidence about a way Revelation has functioned for those who have treasured and preserved it. Beyond being a book about the future, Revelation's meaning has revolved around the church's worship in the here and now. Readers' thinking and experience of worship cannot remain commonplace and lackadaisical in the face of the book's revelation of the beautiful, impassioned worship of God in the transcendent sphere.

Revelation's vision of ideal human life is a community of persons—fully individual, yet convergent in purpose—gathered comprehensively, but not indiscriminately, for worship of God. Revelation centers its readers' imaginations on the living God as the center of earthly life. Worship of this God gives life coherence, sustaining purpose, and steady direction.

The book of Revelation speaks to the here and now in a second major way. As in other apocalyptic texts of the Bible, Revelation teaches readers that doomful, apocalyptic events are not confined to earth's final days at time's end. The climactic patterns and paradigms that play themselves out at the end of days find preliminary prefigurements throughout history.

As with other apocalyptic texts of the Bible, this makes Revelation relevant and applicable on a repeating basis. The book possesses immeasurable value for the faithful in its ability to help them discern the nature of their times and the full dimensions of the baneful events they may encounter. This inherent quality of Revelation is a key reason the faithful have treasured and preserved the book as Scripture. Attention to this dynamic is crucial to reading Revelation as canonical literature of the church.

A fascinating text at the center of the book, Rev 11:19–12:17, makes particularly clear that the heavenly patterns and archetypes of the Apocalypse manifest themselves on earth periodically. Although they have their concluding, climactic finale at history's end, they surface in various guises long before then. Not coincidently, significant surfacings occur at key junctures of salvation history.

Good and evil portents are destined to materialize—and clash vehemently—at those times when God moves decisively to advance the divine agenda for creation. As Scripture, Revelation unveils the celestial backdrop and significance of salvation-historical events.

As Rev 11:19–12:17 begins, readers realize they are about to discover a mystery at God's very heart. The doors of God's heavenly temple open, accompanied by "flashes of lightning, rumblings, peals of thunder, an earthquake, and heavy hail." The point of focus is the ark of the covenant, symbol of God's plan to reign among the faithful. Readers are about to receive insight into the apocalyptic dimensions of that plan and how its details must unfold on earth.

Chapter 12 consists of celestial images of salvation history arrayed about a core in verses 7-12. These verses describe a supernatural conflict in the heavenly sphere, in which troops of the archangel Michael defeat and expel a great serpentine dragon and his minions. The section is noteworthy for its celestial locale, ambiguous time frame, and lack of human participation. An inserted hymn alerts us that whatever is at stake is profoundly significant.

"Now have come the salvation and the power
and the kingdom of our God
and the authority of his Messiah." (v. 10)

Many cultures of the globe possess mythic poems that parallel the basic underlying plot of verses 7-12. In these myths, the deity defeats a serpent or other sea monster in a primordial struggle, bringing order and blessing to creation. The mythic repertoires of the major ancient Near Eastern cultures all know such a tale. The celebrated combat myth appears across the Fertile Crescent, from Ugarit, where Baal defeats Yam (the roaring sea), to Babylon, where Marduk defeats Tiamat (chaotic seawater). Related, specialized myths describe the expulsion from heaven of a presumptuous, anarchic rebel who covets the deity's throne.

Well before the composition of Rev 12, biblical writers clearly perceived the paradigmatic character of the ancient myths of divine combat with a watery dragon.[6] It was left to the apocalyptic imagination to conceive of mythic symbols not only as celestial molds or patterns but also as realistic entities that could invade history.

Scholars universally recognize the archetypal, paradigmatic character of the core of Rev 12. The war in heaven it depicts stands behind earthly, human experience, explaining and accounting for it. Players from concrete history are conspicuously absent—even Jesus Christ, Revelation's central figure. Just as the combat myth in general has a paradigmatic character, the imaginative, celestial episode of Rev 12:7-12 is polyvalent—finding repeating application (valence) within salvation history.

First, the episode explains the origin and primeval fall of the "great dragon," the "ancient serpent." This was the application of the story most familiar to its first hearers. The combat myth described a primordial event in the ancient Near Eastern and Mediterranean world, understood to have taken place at creation's beginning (cf. Gen 6:1-4; Isa 14:12-15; Ezek 28:11-19; 2 Enoch 29:4-5). Verse 4 of Rev 12 accords with this valence. It depicts the dragon in celestial combat long before the Messiah is born on earth.

Second, the combat paradigm fits the time of history's last days. In various apocalyptic texts, the birth pangs of God's new creation involve a resurgence of primeval chaos, including the return of the cosmos's ancient mythological foes. Hermann Gunkel's revolutionary work on Rev 12 (1895) established the connection between end time and creation time. Ever since Gunkel, interpreters expect apocalyptic texts to recapitulate the primordial drama of God's mythic combat with the chaos dragon.

According to Isa 27:1, for example, in the apocalyptic day, "The LORD with his cruel and great and strong sword will punish Leviathan the fleeing serpent, Leviathan the twisting serpent, and he will kill the dragon that is in the sea." (Compare *Sibylline Oracles* 5.512-13; the *Melchizedek* text from Qumran Cave 11, 11QMelch 9–15; the Qumran *War Scroll*, 1QM 15–19.)

Revelation 13:1 accords with this second valence. It depicts the dragon cast to earth and standing on the seashore, about to give the end-time Antichrist and false prophet supernatural powers. The context is explicitly the last half of the tribulation period at the world's end (Rev 13:5; cf. 11:2). This places the serpent's ouster from heaven in earth's last days.

A third valence of the combat paradigm is perhaps most significant in the present context. Within chapter 12, the scene of heavenly combat with the dragon closely connects to the time of Christ's crucifixion.

Verses 7-12 interrupt a narrative sequence about the progress of salvation history on earth. Their depiction of celestial war breaks into the sequence precisely where the messianic child is born and caught up to God. This narrative juncture (v. 5) likely refers to Calvary. John 16:21-22 speaks of the crucifixion using similar birthing imagery.

Verse 11 confirms that the war in heaven correlates closely with the crucifixion. According to the verse, the power of Christians to overcome the dragon comes from "the blood of the Lamb." The faithful can take courage, since Christ, the Lamb, has gained a cosmic victory over the dragon through his death on the cross.

By correlating the crucifixion with the mythological combat paradigm, Rev 12 makes Christ's death and resurrection the pivotal moment in the cosmos' destiny. Heaven conquers evil and death—it declares—at that moment. From then on, at least proleptically, God reigns in the cosmos.

As the child is born and exalted, Michael and the troops of heaven establish God's sovereignty over all chaotic forces furiously opposing the world's apocalyptic renewal. With Christ's work on earth accomplished, the devil burns with wrath. He knows that "his time is short" (v. 12); now nothing can stop God's planned transformation of humanity and the cosmos.

Turning to verses 1-6 and 13-17, which describe the unfolding of salvation history on earth, we see details of just how polyvalent Revelation's transcendent archetypes are. We see that celestial portents surface in history in many forms, confirming the repeating relevance of Revelation's insights into heavenly reality. The text functions scripturally to alert readers that the celestial drama is unassailably present in humanity's midst, obliging humans to take sides.

Verse 4 indirectly identifies King Herod the Great as one major instantiation of the serpentine dragon. It is hard to miss a reference to Herod's menace at the time of Jesus' birth in verse 4, where the dragon crouches before the woman in labor (cf. Matt 2:16). Yet, the dragon is not simply a cipher for a single historical figure. Verse 4 alludes equally to the dragon's presence behind the crucifixion, where all was at stake. Along with the nativity, the crucifixion involved a painful experience of "birth pangs" (v. 2, cf. John 16:21).

The archetypal woman of chapter 12 goes unnamed, since like the dragon she is instantiated multiple times within salvation history. She is Eve, whose progeny is destined for conflict with the serpent of Eden (Gen 3:15). She is Israel, whom the prophets foretold would give birth to the Messiah and to God's new creation (Mic 5:3; Isa 26:17; 66:7-9). She is Mary (called "woman" in John 2:4; 19:26); and she is all God's faithful people of both the old and new covenants. Her children include faithful Christians, who persevere in the end times (Rev 12:17).

The male child of the chapter is the ideal Davidic king. Thus, verse 5 echoes Ps 2, where God's king, enthroned on Zion, subdues the serpentine forces of chaos that rage against the cosmos's axis *(axis mundi)*. He is equally the Messiah of Israel, destined to make his advent "when she who is in labor has brought forth" (Mic 5:3). And he is the eschatological rebirth of God's faithful people. In delivering a son, Isa 66:7-9 prophesies, Zion in labor delivers a whole nation of children in one moment.

If instances of the heavenly signs and portents of apocalyptic literature can surface multiple times throughout history, the apocalyptic imagination has immediate practical relevance for all its subsequent readers. The forces of Armageddon are active here and now, even if the end times have not yet arrived. The possible immediate presence of such celestial portents on earth call for the reader's keen discernment in identifying and exposing them wherever they may be surfacing. The apocalyptic texts call for alert endurance in the face of those portents and for active engagement with them.

Among the characteristics of Revelation gleaned from chapter 12 is an essential feature of the book, one necessary for understanding its unique contribution to the apocalyptic imagination of the Scriptures. According to chapter 12, heaven has already fought and won the critical, climactic battle of salvation history. John observes the definitive apocalyptic contest of verses 7-12, and attests to its accomplished outcome.

This notion profoundly alters the traditional apocalyptic perspective. Normally, as we have observed in preceding chapters, apocalypses look primarily to the future for God's decisive combat with evil and its defeat and judgment.

Revelation maintains, conversely, the paradoxical perspective that heaven's ultimate battle with evil is over—fought and won. For all intents and purposes, the end time is an accomplished event. The faithful no longer wait expectantly for evil's demise, but merely for God's vanquished enemies to play out subordinate roles in what are essentially anticlimactic, mop-up operations within salvation history.

Front and center, it is the crucifixion and resurrection of Jesus Messiah that has accomplished God's violent defeat of evil and death. Christ's cross and empty tomb have become the ultimate apocalyptic weapons, according to Revelation. According to Rev 12:12, the dragon is now cast to earth, defeated by these weapons. He has lost the cosmic war in heaven. He knows "his time is short!"

Revelation's altered apocalyptic imagination did not arise from nowhere, but entails brilliant new insight into inherited traditions.

The notion of "proleptic eschatology"—a substantial delay between Christ's inaugurating work and the full advent of God's reign—is not new. Jesus' apocalyptic discourse in Matthew and Luke presuppose such a delay.

Neither is the idea new of a messiah destined for rejection and suffering. We saw this attested in the messianic hymns of Qumran's Thanksgiving Scroll. Later, it formed a key teaching of Paul. The idea was probably a part of Jesus' own self-understanding, at least in the view of several reputable New Testament historians.

Where Revelation offers a new departure is in its unique, cosmological understanding of Christ's catastrophic passion. In Revelation, John is invited to "come up here," and see things heaven's way. His new celestial vantage point gives him a unique, altered perspective for comprehending the cross. Now privy to the cosmos's two separate ontological dimensions, John discovers the full truth about what Christ accomplished on earth decades earlier, at his first advent.

Translated to heaven, John sees the truth and celestial reality behind the events of Christ's work of love, nonpower, and sacrifice. Christ's humble, sacrificial messiahship on earth was mirrored by aggressive, supernatural combat in heaven (Rev 12:7-12). As Christ died and rose on earth, open combat in heaven decisively defeated Satan, ending his tyranny and reconciling humanity with God.

Christ's earthly messiahship entailed only love and frailty. In transcendent perspective, however, these means reveal their concrete, aggressive power to win cosmic victory. From heaven's vantage point, Jesus, on the cross, accomplished the atonement of humanity as an apocalyptic warrior—*Christus Victor*.

Revelation's insight into Jesus' transcendent identity as *Christus Victor* explains the book's altered apocalyptic imagination. If the cross and resurrection were apocalyptic weapons that have already won God's definitive victory over sin and death, then the true end times are now behind us. As Brevard S. Childs writes:

> The effect of [Revelation's new] christological understanding is that the whole apocalyptic scenario, inherited from Daniel, when viewed from the perspective of the heavenly reality has been reinterpreted as completed action. It does not lie in the future because Christ has encompassed the past, present and future into one redemptive purpose. . . .

... The major point being made is that in the cross, which is God's decisive moment within history, human history receives its meaning.[7]

A final significant observation should be made. Commentators frequently note Christ's absence from the heavenly war of Rev 12:7-12 but rarely grasp its import. They often attribute the enigma, regrettably, to John's use of a pre-Christian myth, which lacked mention of Jesus the Messiah.

John of Patmos undoubtedly used sources in composing his book, but readers should still take the final, scriptural form of Revelation seriously. Revelation 12 presents a central paradox of Christianity in absenting Christ from Michael's heavenly field combat.

As noted, the present form of Rev 12 emphasizes God's mysterious use of the most unlikely means to win indisputable cosmic victory: an earthly lifestyle of nonpower, humility, and sacrifice. It could not make this point if Christ was present fighting alongside Michael in heaven.

But this is not the only way the chapter's canonical shape inverts readers' expectations. The heart of chapter 12 turns the normal pattern of the apocalyptic imagination on its head. At the core of the chapter, as the male child appears on earth, historical reality ceases to mirror transcendent paradigms as it does in most apocalyptic thinking. Rather, the apocalyptic equation reverses itself. Power dynamics in transcendent reality radically and unalterably shift in consequence of earthly events.

The terrestrial events in question, of course, are Christ's crucifixion and resurrection. According to Revelation, Christ's dying and rising on earth provoke a fundamental transformation of the structure of transcendent reality.

The fact that Christ's accomplishment is based on earth and within history is key. It shows how seriously God takes human history and physical, material reality. It proves the lengths to which Christ goes to free humanity from Satan's tyranny, abandoning his presence and prerogative in heaven to die on earth.[8]

Revelation's witness to Christ's apocalyptic victory on the cross has obvious relevance for the here and now. Readers privy to this mystery receive both warning and assurance from their new knowledge.

They must take warning, since they live at a critical juncture. They face a mortally wounded dragon—still alive and in a state of rage. Profound caution is clearly the order of the day. As earth's history marches forward, readers can expect political, economic, and religious systems on earth increasingly to mirror the face of the dragon.

At the same time, readers can take courage that cosmic victory is already won through the power of the slain Lamb of Revelation. Even when politics and culture clash head-on with faith, readers have grounds for profound hope and endurance. They have grounds even for endurance unto death.

In the words of Rev 2:10-11: "Do not fear what you are about to suffer. Beware, the devil is about to throw some of you into prison so that you may be tested, and for ten days you will have affliction. Be faithful until death, and I will give you the crown of life. Let anyone who has an ear listen to what the Spirit is saying to the churches. Whoever conquers will not be harmed by the second death."

GROUP ORIGINS AND SOCIAL BACKGROUND

The book of Revelation gives almost no direct biographical information about John, its author. There is little independent, external information about him either, since he is probably distinct from John the apostle, the son of Zebedee. (Revelation 21:14 refers to the apostles as people other than the author.) John of Patmos may be connected with the circle behind the gospel of John, but this informs us mostly about the general theological stream of tradition within which he operated. To infer something of John's place in society, we must work mostly from indirect evidence in his book.

The contents of Revelation make obvious that John of Patmos was a Christian apocalyptic visionary, but we have seen that visionaries may have a variety of social backgrounds, including that of bureaucrat, priest, and apostle. The textual evidence of Revelation shows that in John's case, an apocalyptic imagination has arisen in one holding the social role of Christian prophet.

The role of prophet was not a fixed institution within the organization of Christianity's early house-churches, but an unofficial channel of inspired revelation to the faithful community.

Revelation 22:6 classes John as such a channel, affirming that it is "prophets" to whom God reveals what the future holds, "what must soon take place." John specifically calls his message "prophecy" in Rev 1:3; 22:7, 10, 18, 19. Furthermore, Rev 10:8-11 presents a prophetic commissioning of John modeled on the commissioning of the prophet Ezekiel in Ezek 2:9–3:3.

John of Patmos did not perform his prophetic role in isolation.[9] The angel addressing him at Rev 22:9 refers to "your comrades the prophets," implying his membership in a larger prophetic circle or guild. The message of Revelation came not to John alone, but to his whole circle. Jesus states in Rev 22:16 that his angel has testified about Revelation's message for the churches to "you all"—a plural "you" in the Greek. Given his deep familiarity with the Hebrew Scriptures, John and his prophetic colleagues were likely Jewish converts to Christianity—Jewish Christian prophets.

As might be expected, John's prophetic and apocalyptic circle operated in the face of competing groups. The book names at least one prophetic rival, classing her as a false prophet. In Rev 2:20, John refers to a certain "Jezebel," a prophetess from Thyatira. The reference is an epithet, a derogatory allusion to the ancient Israelite queen notorious for her idolatry (see 1 Kgs 16:29-31; 19:2; 21). This clash of early Christian prophetic groups comes as no surprise. In discussing 1 Thess 5:3, we saw that Paul also faced a group of prophetic rivals in at least one of his house-churches.

At least three or four types of prophets operated within the social matrix of primitive Christianity at John's time. Most prophets by far were constituent members of local Christian communities (cf. 1 Cor 14:29-33). Other prophets, however, pursued special missions outside of their home bases (cf. Acts 11:27-28; 21:10-11). An early manual of church order (*Didache* 6–15) suggests still other figures pursued an ideal of prophetic homelessness, refusing to settle in any one community. Related to this last type would be itinerant Christian prophets, who formed relationships with specific churches along a definite prophetic circuit. Which type of Christian prophet was John?

John's messages to individual church audiences in chapters 2–3 presuppose he had developed close relationships with a series of churches, including at least seven congregations. His detailed knowledge of these house-churches suggests he had visited each of them repeatedly. He is familiar with the local issues each congregation faces (e.g., Rev 2:14-15; 3:4) and alludes to prior personal interactions with church members (e.g., Rev 2:21). The church locales in question all lie on an established Roman highway circuit in Asia Minor.

All this evidence points in the same direction. Before going to the island of Patmos, John must have traveled a circuit between at least seven Christian communities in Asia Minor as an itinerant prophet.

John did not write Revelation amid his seven Asian house-churches but from the small island of Patmos in the Aegean Sea southwest of Ephesus (Rev 1:9). Popular wisdom holds that Roman persecution landed him there as an exile, but the text never explicitly says that. It is equally possible that John traveled to Patmos willingly, in obedience to a divine command or on his own, seeking a special revelation.

Christian prophets did not always deliver spontaneous messages received in the immediate context of Christian worship. They sometimes received revelations in private, which they later passed on to the faithful (cf. Acts 10:9–11:18). The literary intricacy of Revelation requires that we think of it as the latter type of prophetic communication. Whether or not John went to the island of Patmos in order to cultivate the visions behind his book, he directly claims to have received them in a state of spiritual ecstasy there (Rev 1:10).

The claim that the Romans forcibly exiled John to Patmos relates to a common assumption that the apocalyptic imagination of his book arose amid persecution and martyrdom. Apparently supporting this assumption are references to tensions with society in the messages to the churches (Rev 2–3). Further, martyrs appear in the visions of the book (e.g., Rev 6:9-11; 7:14-17).

There is no doubt that some early Christians experienced sporadic persecution and martyrdom. For example, a man named Antipas seems to have died for the faith at Pergamum (Rev 2:13). Further, Revelation anticipated a tribulation to usher in God's reign. Its ordeals, the book foretells, will surely involve the martyrdom of Christians. Several considerations, however, challenge the common theory that Revelation's apocalypticism presupposes an extant situation of extreme crisis and deprivation. Revelation is no tormented book, provoked by contemporary horrors.

The radically transcendent imagination conveyed by John of Patmos far outstrips most commentators' sociological and psychological etiologies. It belies their idea of a visionary reaction against current miserable experience.

Jacques Ellul puts it well, "Human hope is what most commentators inflict upon the Apocalypse. . . . In this case there has been exactly superposition of a rather simplistic hope upon the most intense formulation of hope."[10]

The era of the Roman emperor Domitian, from which Revelation comes, did not involve any large-scale, systematic persecution of Christians. Domitian was not particularly blasphemous or despotic, at least as Roman emperors go.[11] What Revelation confronts and opposes is not a program of persecution perpetrated by one perverse emperor, but the general hubristic ideology of Roman rule and the imperial cult associated with it.

The imperial cultic system, including emperor worship, provided the backbone of Roman social order in Asia Minor in Domitian's era. Massive building projects in Ephesus at the time illustrate the fact.[12]

At the period of Revelation, Ephesus saw the construction of the temple of the Sebastoi, dedicated to the worship of the emperors Vespasian, Titus, and Domitian. Contemporaneously, the Ephesians constructed a bath-gymnasium complex in their harbor area. This immense sports complex, where local Olympic games could be held, most likely honored Domitian as Zeus Olympios. Together, the two building projects reoriented the entire urban plan of the city of Ephesus on reverence for Roman authority.

John's messages to the churches in chapters 2–3 imply only sporadic and local persecution at the time he composed his book. There is little mention of open conflict with Rome. This accords with what we know of the times. Under Domitian's reign, Christians and Jews generally lived peaceably amid their neighbors in Asia Minor. If the visions of Revelation were true, however, that situation would have to change. Christians would have to awaken and confront Rome's claims to divine honors. That would surely destine them to come under the violent censure of their society.

Revelation offers the hope that a new world is coming to both the "small and great" (Rev 11:18; 19:5), thus including those from various social stations in Greco-Roman society, including the upper strata. From hints in chapters 2–3 of Revelation, this wide range of social standing fit the membership of the house-church communities along John's prophetic circuit. As we have observed in studying the audiences of Paul's apocalyptic letters, some early Christians in the New Testament world owned large houses and acted as benefactors of civil and religious groups.

Like rich Christians among Paul's followers, some of the addressees of Revelation were affluent. At Laodicea, Christians were saying, "I am rich, I have prospered, and I need nothing" (Rev 3:17). At Pergamum, similarly, Christians were neither poor nor alienated. Rather, they were living lifestyles of compromise with the dominant social order (Rev 2:14). These original readers, at least, did not count themselves as huddled wretches. The common idea that John of Patmos wrote Revelation to a persecuted, deprived audience is without foundation.

NOTES

1. ENCOUNTERING APOCALYPTIC WORLDS

1. John J. Collins, *The Apocalyptic Imagination: An Introduction to the Jewish Matrix of Christianity* (New York: Crossroad, 1984), 138.
2. Dale C. Allison, *Jesus of Nazareth: Millenarian Prophet* (Minneapolis: Fortress, 1998), 219.
3. Daniel J. Harrington regards the text as "the best (almost philosophical) analysis of Jewish apocalyptic thinking that I know." See his "Jesus and the Dead Sea Scrolls," in *Jesus: A Colloquium in the Holy Land* (ed. D. Donnelly; New York: Continuum, 2001), 33-34. For an excellent annotated translation of the text, see Michael A. Knibb, *The Qumran Community* (Cambridge Commentaries on Writings of the Jewish and Christian World, 200 B.C. to A.D. 200, vol. 2; New York: Cambridge University Press, 1987), 93-103.
4. John J. Collins, "Introduction: Towards the Morphology of a Genre," in *Apocalypse: The Morphology of a Genre* (ed. J. Collins; *Semeia* 14; Atlanta: Society of Biblical Literature, 1979), 9.
5. English translations (with good introductions) of the apocalyptic texts among the Old Testament Pseudepigrapha are conveniently collected in James H. Charlesworth, ed., *Apocalyptic Literature and Testaments* (vol. 1 of *The Old Testament Pseudepigrapha;* ed. James H. Charlesworth; New York: Doubleday, 1983). An English translation of 4 Ezra, along with exegetical annotations, can be found in a good study Bible that includes the Apocrypha, such as *The New Oxford Annotated Bible* (third edition) or *The HarperCollins Study Bible*. Beginning commentary on 4 Ezra is found in Michael E. Stone and Theodore A. Bergren, "2 Esdras," in *The HarperCollins Bible Commentary* (ed. J. L. Mays; revised edition; San Francisco: HarperSanFrancisco, 2000), 705-17. A good introduction to the intertestamental literature in general is George W. E. Nickelsburg, *Jewish Literature Between the Bible and the Mishnah: An Historical and Literary Introduction* (Philadelphia: Fortress, 1981).
6. Stephen L. Cook, "Apocalypticism and the Psalter," *ZAW* 104 (1992): 82-99.

7. Sidnie White Crawford, "Apocalyptic," in *Eerdmans Dictionary of the Bible* (ed. D. N. Freedman; Grand Rapids: Eerdmans, 2000), 72-73.
8. Paul D. Hanson, "Apocalypses and Apocalypticism," *ABD* 1:280.
9. Eugene H. Peterson, *Reversed Thunder: The Revelation of John and the Praying Imagination* (San Francisco: HarperSanFrancisco, 1988), 70.
10. Norman Cohn, *Cosmos, Chaos and the World to Come: The Ancient Roots of Apocalyptic Faith* (New Haven, Conn.: Yale University Press, 1993), 223, 221.
11. Eibert J. C. Tigchelaar, *Prophets of Old and the Day of the End: Zechariah, the Book of Watchers and Apocalyptic* (OtSt 35; Leiden, Netherlands: Brill, 1996), 247.
12. Trudy Carter Thomas, "Crisis and Creativity: Visual Symbolism of the Ghost Dance Tradition" (Ph.D. diss., Columbia University, 1988), 3; cf. pp. 191, 201-2.
13. Claude Lévi-Strauss, *Structural Anthropology* (trans. C. Jacobson and B. G. Schoepf; New York: Basic Books, 1963), 229.

2. THE DANGER OF DOMESTICATING THE APOCALYPTIC TEXTS

1. N. T. Wright, *The New Testament and the People of God* (vol. 1 of *Christian Origins and the Question of God;* Minneapolis: Fortress, 1992), chapter 10, esp. pp. 331-34. See also N. T. Wright, *Jesus and the Victory of God* (vol. 2 of *Christian Origins and the Question of God;* Minneapolis: Fortress, 1996), 320-68.
2. G. Vermes, *The Dead Sea Scrolls in English,* 2d ed (London: Penguin Books, 1975), pp. 159-60.
3. See James Mooney, *The Ghost-Dance Religion and Wounded Knee* (1896; repr., Mineola, N.Y.: Dover, 1973), 788-89.
4. Ibid., 788-89.
5. Ibid., 789.
6. Tim F. LaHaye and Jerry B. Jenkins, *Left Behind: A Novel of the Earth's Last Days* (Wheaton, Ill.: Tyndale House, 1995), 214.
7. Jean-Pierre Prévost, *How to Read the Apocalypse* (New York: Crossroad, 1993), 61.
8. Ibid., 23.
9. See Tina Pippin, *Death and Desire: The Rhetoric of Gender in the Apocalypse of John* (Literary Currents in Biblical Interpretation; Louisville: Westminster John Knox, 1992), 81.
10. Sacvan Bercovitch, *The Puritan Origins of the American Self* (New Haven, Conn.: Yale University Press, 1975), 65.
11. Catherine Keller, *Apocalypse Now and Then: A Feminist Guide to the End of the World* (Boston: Beacon, 1996), 45, 46, 76-77.
12. Pippin, *Death and Desire,* 77.
13. Ibid., 81.
14. Keller, *Apocalypse Now and Then,* 82.
15. Ibid., 172.
16. Ronald L. Farmer, *Beyond the Impasse: The Promise of a Process*

Hermeneutic (StABH 13; Macon, Ga.: Mercer University Press, 1997), 157.

17. Farmer, *Beyond the Impasse,* 144 n. 20.
18. Jacques Ellul, *Apocalypse: The Book of Revelation* (trans. George W. Schreiner; New York: Seabury, 1977), 61-62.

3. A NEW SEARCH FOR THE LITERAL SENSE OF APOCALYPTIC TEXTS

1. Jacques Ellul, *Apocalypse: The Book of Revelation* (trans. George W. Schreiner; New York: Seabury, 1977), 24.
2. Helge S. Kvanvig, "The Relevance of the Biblical Visions of the End Time: Hermeneutical Guidelines to the Apocalyptical Literature," *HBT* 11 (1989): 47-48.
3. Ellul, *Apocalypse,* 10.
4. Eugene H. Peterson, *Reversed Thunder: The Revelation of John and the Praying Imagination* (San Francisco: HarperSanFrancisco, 1988), 71.
5. J. R. R. Tolkien, *The Two Towers: Being the Second Part of the Lord of the Rings* (New York: Ballantine, 1965), 186-87.
6. See the comments of Pablo Richard, *Apocalypse: A People's Commentary on the Book of Revelation* (The Bible & Liberation Series; Maryknoll, N.Y.: Orbis, 1995), 173.
7. Ward Ewing, *The Power of the Lamb: Revelation's Theology of Liberation for You* (Cambridge, Mass.: Cowley, 1990), 46.
8. See Elisabeth Schüssler Fiorenza, *The Book of Revelation: Justice and Judgment* (Philadelphia: Fortress, 1985), 192.

4. THE SOCIAL WORLDS BEHIND THE APOCALYPTIC LITERATURE

1. See Lester L. Grabbe, "Introduction and Overview," in *Knowing the End from the Beginning: The Prophetic, The Apocalyptic, and Their Relationships* (ed. L. L. Grabbe and R. D. Haak; JSPSup; Sheffield, England: Sheffield Academic Press, forthcoming).
2. Helge S. Kvanvig, *Roots of Apocalyptic: The Mesopotamian Background of the Enoch Figure and of the Son of Man* (WMANT 61; Neukirchen-Vluyn, Germany: Neukirchener Verlag, 1988), 610.
3. See the helpful summary of the social-scientific evidence in Lester L. Grabbe, "The Social Setting of Early Jewish Apocalypticism," *JSP* 4 (1989): 27-47.
4. Robert R. Wilson, "From Prophecy to Apocalyptic: Reflections on the Shape of Israelite Religion," *Semeia* 21 (1981): 86.
5. For arguments and bibliography related to this discussion, see Stephen L. Cook, *Prophecy and Apocalypticism: The Postexilic Social Setting* (Minneapolis: Fortress, 1995), 55-84.

5. EARLY APOCALYPTIC TEXTS AMONG THE PROPHETIC BOOKS

1. For a list of texts in the Holiness Source, see Israel Knohl, *The Sanctuary of Silence: The Priestly Torah and the Holiness School* (Minneapolis: Fortress, 1995), 104-6. The Holiness, or H, source of

the Pentateuch is concerned with holiness and ceremonial and ethical purity.

2. See Moshe Greenberg, *Ezekiel 21–37* (AB 22A; Garden City, N.Y.: Doubleday, 1997), 569.

3. See Richard J. Clifford, "The Roots of Apocalypticism in Near Eastern Myth," in *Encyclopedia of Apocalypticism* (ed. J. J. Collins, B. McGinn, and S. J. Stein; New York: Continuum, 1998), 1:3-5.

4. David E. Aune, "Eschatology (Early Christian)," *ABD* 2:594.

5. For examples, see Stephen L. Cook, *Prophecy and Apocalypticism: The Postexilic Social Setting* (Minneapolis: Fortress, 1995), 68-74. Thomas W. Overholt, *Prophecy in Cross-Cultural Perspective: A Sourcebook for Biblical Researchers* (Atlanta: Scholars Press, 1986), 215-30.

6. Recently, there have been several significant studies of Yehud in the Persian Period. See especially Charles E. Carter, *The Emergence of Yehud in the Persian Period: A Social and Demographic Study* (JSOTSup 294; Sheffield, England: Sheffield Academic Press, 1999) and Jon L. Berquist, *Judaism in Persia's Shadow: A Social and Historical Approach* (Minneapolis: Fortress, 1995).

7. Eibert J. C. Tigchelaar, *Prophets of Old and the Day of the End: Zechariah, the Book of Watchers and Apocalyptic* (*OtSt* 35; Leiden, Netherlands: Brill, 1996), 32-39.

8. Stephen L. Cook, "The Metamorphosis of a Shepherd: The Tradition History of Zechariah 11:17 + 13:7-9," *CBQ* 55 (1993): 453-66.

9. See Cook, *Prophecy and Apocalypticism*, 154-56.

10. Joseph Blenkinsopp, *Isaiah 1–39* (AB 19; New York: Doubleday, 2000), 347.

11. See Robert R. Wilson, "The Community of the Second Isaiah," in *Reading and Preaching the Book of Isaiah* (ed. C. Seitz; Philadelphia: Fortress, 1988), 53-70.

12. See Norman Cohn, *The Pursuit of the Millennium* (New York: Oxford University Press, 1970), 55, 58.

13. Paul D. Hanson, *The Dawn of Apocalyptic: The Historical and Sociological Roots of Jewish Apocalyptic Eschatology* (Philadelphia: Fortress, 1979).

14. Brooks Schramm, *The Opponents of Third Isaiah: Reconstructing the Cultic History the Restoration* (JSOTSup 193; Sheffield, England: Sheffield Academic Press, 1995), 179.

15. Carol Bechtel Reynolds, "Malachi and the Priesthood" (Ph.D. diss., Yale University, 1993), 162-63.

16. Michael Adas, *Prophets of Rebellion: Millenarian Protest Movements against the European Colonial Order* (Chapel Hill: University of North Carolina Press, 1979), 3-11, 94-99.

6. THE BOOK OF DANIEL

1. John J. Collins, *Daniel: With an Introduction to Apocalyptic Literature* (FOTL 20; Grand Rapids: Eerdmans, 1984), 63.

2. John J. Collins, *Daniel: A Commentary on the Book of Daniel* (Hermeneia: A Critical and Historical Commentary on the Bible; Minneapolis: Fortress, 1993), 227.
3. Gerhard von Rad noted the role of apocalyptic visionaries as learned interpreters of the cosmology of ancient myth. See his *Old Testament Theology, Volume II* (New York: Harper & Row, 1965), 308. For a thorough survey of scholarly research into Daniel 7's background in the mythology of the ancient Near East, see Collins, *Book of Daniel*, 280-94.
4. Michael Fishbane, *Biblical Interpretation in Ancient Israel* (Oxford, England: Clarendon Press, 1985), 493-94.
5. John G. Gammie, "On the Intention and Sources of Daniel I-VI," *VT* 3 (1981): 286.
6. See Katrina J. A. Larkin, *The Eschatology of Second Zechariah: A Study of the Formation of a Mantological Wisdom Anthology* (Kampen, Netherlands: Kok Pharos, 1994), 239.
7. Hector I. Avalos, "The Comedic Function of the Enumerations of Officials and Instruments in Daniel 3," *CBQ* 53 (1991): 580-88.
8. Daniel Berrigan, *Daniel: Under the Siege of the Divine* (Farmington, Pa.: Plough, 1998), 38.
9. Helge S. Kvanvig, "The Relevance of the Biblical Visions of the End Time: Hermeneutical Guidelines to the Apocalyptical Literature," *HBT* 11 (1989): 50.
10. S. R. Driver, *The Book of Daniel* (Cambridge Bible for Schools and Colleges; 1900; repr., Cambridge, England: Cambridge University Press, 1912), lxix.
11. Paul L. Redditt, *Daniel* (New Century Bible Commentary; Sheffield, England: Sheffield Academic Press, 1999), vii.
12. See Robert R. Wilson, "From Prophecy to Apocalyptic: Reflections on the Shape of Israelite Religion," *Semeia* 21 (1981): 81-83, 88.

7. APOCALYPTICISM AND THE JESUS GROUP

1. See the arguments and responses collected in *The Apocalyptic Jesus: A Debate*, ed. Robert J. Miller (Santa Rosa, Calif.: Polebridge, 2001).
2. Israel Knohl, *The Messiah before Jesus: The Suffering Servant of the Dead Sea Scrolls* (trans. David Maisel; Berkeley: University of California Press, 2000), 75-80.
3. Dale C. Allison, *Jesus of Nazareth: Millenarian Prophet* (Minneapolis: Fortress, 1998), 166.
4. Rudolf Bultmann, *Theology of the New Testament* (trans. Kendrick Grobel; New York: Charles Scribner's Sons, 1951), 1:31.
5. See Brevard S. Childs, *Isaiah* (OTL; Louisville: Westminster John Knox, 2001), 507.
6. Michael O. Wise, *The First Messiah: Investigating the Savior before Jesus* (New York: HarperCollins, 1999), 222-26.
7. Knohl, *Messiah before Jesus*, 24; cf. Wise, *First Messiah*, 224.
8. See Wise, *First Messiah*, 216-19.

9. N. T. Wright, *Jesus and the Victory of God* (vol. 2 of *Christian Origins and the Question of God;* Minneapolis: Fortress, 1996), 599-600.
10. See Allison, *Jesus of Nazareth,* 53-54.
11. Wright, *Jesus and the Victory of God,* 559-60.
12. Knohl, *Messiah before Jesus,* 25; cf. p. 111 nn. 64, 65; cf. also Wise, *First Messiah,* 224.
13. Knohl, *Messiah before Jesus,* 17.
14. William L. Lane, *The Gospel According to Mark* (NICNT 2; Grand Rapids: Eerdmans, 1974), 508.

8. Apocalyptic Worlds and the Early Christian Churches

1. See Alexandra R. Brown, "Paul's Apocalyptic Word of the Cross: Perception and Transformation in 1 Corinthians 1–2" (Ph.D. diss., Columbia University, 1990), 33-34; compare her *Cross and Human Transformation: Paul's Apocalyptic Word in 1 Corinthians* (Minneapolis: Fortress, 1995), 8-10.
2. J. Christiaan Becker, "Recasting Pauline Theology: The Coherence-Contingency Scheme as Interpretive Model," in *Thessalonians, Philippians, Galatians, Philemon* (vol. 1 of *Pauline Theology,* ed. J. Bassler; Minneapolis: Fortress, 1991), 17.
3. Richard B. Hays, *Echoes of Scripture in the Letters of Paul* (New Haven, Conn.: Yale University Press, 1989).
4. Dale C. Allison, "A Response," in *The Apocalyptic Jesus: A Debate* (ed. Robert J. Miller; Santa Rosa, Calif.: Polebridge, 2001), 86.
5. Richard B. Hays, *First Corinthians* (*Interpretation: A Bible Commentary for Teaching and Preaching;* Louisville: John Knox, 1997), 253.
6. Abraham J. Malherbe, *The Letters to the Thessalonians: A New Translation with Introduction and Commentary* (AB 32B; New York: Doubleday, 2000), 276.
7. Epictetus, *Discourse,* 1.22.18-19; quoted in Abraham J. Malherbe, *Paul and the Thessalonians: The Philosophical Tradition of Pastoral Care* (Philadelphia: Fortress, 1987), 38.
8. William L. Lane, *The Gospel According to Mark* (NICNT 2; Grand Rapids: Eerdmans, 1974), 448.
9. W. D. Davies and Dale C. Allison, *The Gospel According to Saint Matthew, Volume III* (ICC; Edinburgh, Scotland: T & T Clark, 1997), 349.

9. The Book of Revelation

1. Richard Bauckham, *The Theology of the Book of Revelation* (New Testament Theology; Cambridge, England: Cambridge University Press, 1993), 7-8.
2. G. K. Beale, *The Book of Revelation: A Commentary on the Greek Text* (NIGTC; Grand Rapids: Eerdmans; Carlisle, U.K.: Paternoster, 1999), 175.

3. See Mathias Rissi, "The Rider on the White Horse: A Study of Revelation 6:1-8," *Interpretation* 18 (1964): 413-14, and the helpful chart in Louis A. Vos, *The Synoptic Traditions in the Apocalypse* (Kampen, Netherlands: Kok, 1965), 186.
4. Adela Yarbro Collins, *The Combat Myth in the Book of Revelation* (HDR 9; Missoula, Mont.: Scholars Press, 1976), 16-19.
5. Jean-Pierre Prévost, *How to Read the Apocalypse* (New York: Crossroad, 1993), 4-8.
6. David E. Aune, *Revelation 6–16* (WBC 52B; Nashville: Thomas Nelson, 1998), 668.
7. Brevard S. Childs, *The New Testament as Canon: An Introduction* (Philadelphia: Fortress, 1984), 512-13.
8. For further discussion see Jacques Ellul, *Apocalypse: The Book of Revelation* (trans. George W. Schreiner; New York: Seabury, 1977), 68.
9. David E. Aune, "The Social Matrix of the Apocalypse of John," *Papers of the Chicago Society of Biblical Research* 26 (1981):18-19.
10. Ellul, *Apocalypse*, 56.
11. See Leonard L. Thompson, *The Book of Revelation: Apocalypse and Empire* (New York: Oxford University Press, 1990), 171.
12. For an accessible presentation of the evidence from Ephesus, see Steven Friesen, "Ephesus: Key to a Vision in Revelation," *BAR* 19/3 (1993): 24-37.

SELECTED BIBLIOGRAPHY

Allison, Dale C. *Jesus of Nazareth: Millenarian Prophet.* Minneapolis: Fortress, 1998.

Aune, David E. *Revelation 1–5.* Word Biblical Commentary 52A. Dallas: Word, 1997.

———. *Revelation 6–16.* Word Biblical Commentary 52B. Nashville: Thomas Nelson, 1998.

———. *Revelation 17–22.* Word Biblical Commentary 52C. Nashville: Thomas Nelson, 1998.

Bauckham, Richard. *The Theology of the Book of Revelation.* New Testament Theology. Cambridge, England: Cambridge University Press, 1993.

Beale, G. K. *The Book of Revelation: A Commentary on the Greek Text.* The New International Greek Testament Commentary. Grand Rapids: Eerdmans; Carlisle, U.K.: Paternoster, 1999.

Berquist, Jon L. *Judaism in Persia's Shadow: A Social and Historical Approach.* Minneapolis: Fortress, 1995.

Berrigan, Daniel. *Daniel: Under the Siege of the Divine.* Farmington, Pa.: Plough, 1998.

Brown, Alexandra R. *The Cross and Human Transformation: Paul's Apocalyptic Word in 1 Corinthians.* Minneapolis: Fortress, 1995.

Carter, Charles E. *The Emergence of Yehud in the Persian Period: A Social and Demographic Study.* Journal for the Study of the Old Testament: Supplement Series 294. Sheffield, England: Sheffield Academic Press, 1999.

Childs, Brevard S. *The New Testament as Canon: An Introduction.* Philadelphia: Fortress, 1984.

Cohn, Norman. *Cosmos, Chaos and the World to Come: The Ancient Roots of Apocalyptic Faith.* New Haven, Conn.: Yale University Press, 1993.

Collins, Adela Yarbro. *The Combat Myth in the Book of Revelation.* Harvard Dissertations in Religion 9. Missoula, Mont.: Scholars Press, 1976.

Collins, John J. *The Apocalyptic Imagination: An Introduction to the Jewish Matrix of Christianity.* New York: Crossroad, 1984.

————. *Daniel: A Commentary on the Book of Daniel.* Hermeneia: A Critical and Historical Commentary on the Bible. Minneapolis: Fortress, 1993.

————. *Daniel: With an Introduction to Apocalyptic Literature.* The Forms of the Old Testament Literature 20. Grand Rapids: Eerdmans, 1984.

Collins, John J., B. McGinn, and S. J. Stein, eds. *Encyclopedia of Apocalypticism.* 3 vols. New York: Continuum, 1998.

Cook, Stephen L. *Prophecy and Apocalypticism: The Postexilic Social Setting.* Minneapolis: Fortress, 1995.

Ellul, Jacques. *Apocalypse: The Book of Revelation.* Translated by George W. Schreiner. New York: Seabury, 1977.

Ewing, Ward. *The Power of the Lamb: Revelation's Theology of Liberation for You.* Cambridge, Mass.: Cowley, 1990.

Fishbane, Michael. *Biblical Interpretation in Ancient Israel.* Oxford, England: Clarendon Press, 1985.

Hanson, Paul D. *The Dawn of Apocalyptic: The Historical and Sociological Roots of Jewish Apocalyptic Eschatology.* Philadelphia: Fortress, 1979.

Hays, Richard B. *First Corinthians.* Interpretation: A Bible Commentary for Teaching and Preaching. Louisville: John Knox, 1997.

Keller, Catherine. *Apocalypse Now and Then: A Feminist Guide to the End of the World.* Boston: Beacon, 1996.

Knohl, Israel. *The Messiah before Jesus: The Suffering Servant of the Dead Sea Scrolls.* Translated by David Maisel. Berkeley: University of California Press, 2000.

Kvanvig, Helge S. *Roots of Apocalyptic: The Mesopotamian Background of the Enoch Figure and of the Son of Man.* Wissenschaftliche Monographien zum Alten und Neuen Testament 61. Neukirchen-Vluyn, Germany: Neukirchener Verlag, 1988.

Malherbe, Abraham J. *The Letters to the Thessalonians: A New Translation with Introduction and Commentary.* The Anchor Bible 32B. New York: Doubleday, 2000.

Miller, Robert J., ed. *The Apocalyptic Jesus: A Debate.* Santa Rosa, Calif.: Polebridge, 2001.

Peterson, Eugene H. *Reversed Thunder: The Revelation of John and the Praying Imagination.* San Francisco: HarperSanFrancisco, 1988.

Pippin, Tina. *Death and Desire: The Rhetoric of Gender in the Apocalypse of John.* Literary Currents in Biblical Interpretation. Louisville: Westminster John Knox, 1992.

Prévost, Jean-Pierre. *How to Read the Apocalypse.* New York: Crossroad, 1993.

Redditt, Paul L. *Daniel.* New Century Bible Commentary. Sheffield, England: Sheffield Academic Press, 1999.

Richard, Pablo. *Apocalypse: A People's Commentary on the Book of Revelation.* The Bible & Liberation Series. Maryknoll, N.Y.: Orbis, 1995.

Schramm, Brooks. *The Opponents of Third Isaiah: Reconstructing the Cultic History of the Restoration.* Journal for the Study of the Old

Testament: Supplement Series 193. Sheffield, England: Sheffield Academic Press, 1995.

Schüssler Fiorenza, Elisabeth. *The Book of Revelation: Justice and Judgment.* Philadelphia: Fortress, 1985.

Thompson, Leonard L. *The Book of Revelation: Apocalypse and Empire.* New York: Oxford University Press, 1990.

Tigchelaar, Eibert J. C. *Prophets of Old and the Day of the End: Zechariah, the Book of Watchers and Apocalyptic. Oudtestamentische Studiën* 35. Leiden, Netherlands: Brill, 1996.

Wise, Michael O. *The First Messiah: Investigating the Savior before Jesus.* New York: HarperCollins, 1999.

Wright, N. T. *The New Testament and the People of God.* Vol. 1 of *Christian Origins and the Question of God.* Minneapolis: Fortress, 1992.

———. *Jesus and the Victory of God.* Vol. 2 of *Christian Origins and the Question of God.* Minneapolis: Fortress, 1996.

INDEX

Aaronides, 93, 117, 121-22
abomination of desolation. See desolating sacrilege
Abyss (sea of chaos), 41, 42, 59, 69, 129, 144, 196, 197, 207, 208. See also chaos
Adam, 25, 125, 175
Adas, Michael, 221
Alexander the Great, 51, 134, 143, 145, 146
Allison, Dale C., 22, 155, 173, 188, 218, 222, 223
angels, 24, 29, 75, 104, 127, 135, 162, 165, 166, 206. See also interpreting angel
Antichrist (antimessiah), 51, 63, 68, 72, 126, 133, 138, 143, 144, 186, 197, 203, 208
Antiochus IV, 45, 47, 49, 51, 68-69, 125, 132, 138, 139, 140, 142, 143-44, 147, 186
archetypes, 24, 36, 42, 52, 65, 67, 96-98, 117, 129, 142, 143, 169, 175, 183, 206, 212. See also inbreaking; visions
Armageddon, 74, 77, 86, 95, 202, 210
Assyria, 97, 112, 179, 205
Aune, David E., 96-97, 221, 224
Avalos, Hector I., 222

Babylon, 66, 72, 94, 98, 99, 111, 112, 125, 145, 146, 197-98, 205, 207. See also Babylonian exile
"great whore" of (prostitute), 27, 53-54, 197-98, 201, 203

Babylonian exile, 91, 93, 106, 107, 125. See also Babylon
Bauckham, Richard, 193-94, 223
Beale, G. K., 195, 223
beast, the, 27, 72, 76, 197, 200, 201, 203
Becker, J. Christiaan, 170, 223
Belshazzar, 126, 127, 130, 136
Bercovitch, Sacvan, 219
Bergren, Theodore A., 218
Berquist, Jon L., 221
Berrigan, Daniel, 135-36, 222
binary pairs. See dualism
birth pangs, 31, 73, 147, 183, 184, 186, 188, 189, 207, 209
Blenkinsopp, Joseph, 221
Borg, Marcus, 31, 149
Branch, the, 46, 103-4
Brown, Alexandra R., 223
Bultmann, Rudolf, 156, 158, 222

canonical approach, 27, 39, 50-53, 57-59, 62, 64-70, 98-99, 101, 111, 112, 119, 138-45, 169, 171, 175, 185-91, 205-13
Carter, Charles E., 221
catastrophe, sense of, 20, 21-22, 64, 70-71, 82, 105, 107, 110, 196
chaos, 28, 36, 60, 64, 68-69, 72, 73-74, 79, 96, 98, 101, 102, 114, 115, 116, 147, 186, 209. See also Abyss
Charlesworth, James H., 218
Childs, Brevard S., 211-12, 222, 224
Clifford, Richard J., 221
Cohn, Norman, 33, 219, 221

229

DATE DUE

JUL 0 3 2015		
JUL 2 3 2015		
JAN 0 4 2017		